A NATION GONE BLIND

Also by Eric Larsen

An American Memory

I Am Zoë Handke

ERIC LARSEN

A NATION GONE BLIND

AMERICA IN AN AGE OF SIMPLIFICATION AND DECEIT

Shoemaker  Hoard

Library of Congress Cataloging-in-Publication Data
Larsen, Eric.
A nation gone blind : America in an age of simplification
and deceit / Eric Larsen.
p. cm.
ISBN 13: 978-1-59376-098-4
ISBN 10: 1-59376-098-1
1. Political culture—United States. 2. Social change—
United States. 3. National characteristics, American.
4. United States—Civilization—1970- I. Title.
JA75.7.L633 2005
973.92—dc22   2005033895

Text design by David Bullen
Printed in the United States of America

Shoemaker & Hoard
An Imprint of Avalon Publishing Group, Inc.

AVALON
publishing group incorporated

1400 65th Street, Suite 250
Emeryville, CA 94608
Distributed by Publishers Group West

10 9 8 7 6 5 4 3 2 1

A Nation Gone Blind
is
Dedicated to

Nafeez Mosaddeq Ahmed,
Michel Chossudovsky,
Thomas de Zengotita
David Ray Griffin,
Lewis H. Lapham,
Michael C. Ruppert,
Gore Vidal,
Gary Webb,
and to
All the Children of the World

TABLE OF CONTENTS

I

Watching America Go Blind

II

The Death of Literary Thinking in America:
How It Happened and What It Means

III

Consumerism, Victimology,
and the Disappearance of the Meaningful Self

NOTES

If we should perish, the ruthlessness of the foe would be only the secondary cause of the disaster. The primary cause would be that the strength of a giant nation was directed by eyes too blind to see all the hazards of the struggle; and the blindness would be induced not by some accident of nature or history but by hatred and vainglory.

Reinhold Niebuhr, *The Irony of American History*

I

WATCHING AMERICA GO BLIND

*All writing is communication; creative writing is communication through revelation
—it is the Self escaping into the open. No writer long remains incognito.*
William Strunk Jr. and E. B. White, *The Elements of Style*

one

It's impossible not to be dismayed by how extraordinarily and dangerously soft we've become in our national culture. Or, in any case, by how soft (that's the word I'll use, for the moment) we've become in those aspects of the culture I happen to know best, the literary aspect and the political, or sociopolitical, aspect.

The prospect for the national well-being is grim. For reasons I hope to show, there seems little cause for optimism, for example, that the literary arts in America will ever rebound from their present state of passivity and anemia—that America will ever again produce a literature beyond the sort it does now: a depleted, imitative, unimpassioned, unoriginal, essentially un*thinking* literature.

For the same reasons, the social-political future is equally or more unpromising. The odds in favor of the United States remaining a free country are insufficient to encourage a bet on the prospect. Worse, the question as to whether we're *now* a free country may be a mere technicality.

What has happened? My short answer is that we have at last entered fully into what I call the Age of Simplification. My long answer is the book that follows.

❖   ❖   ❖

I have become grateful for the fact that I was born in 1941, since if I had come onto the scene even, say, five or six years later, I would have missed one of the most important experiences of my life, which was being privileged to get a meaningful impression, at first hand, of what I and many others now think of, rightly, as the "old" America.

That is, I was born just early enough that I was able to see, hear, smell, feel, taste, and walk around in the "first" America, the real one, as opposed to the one we're left with now: the mass media America, the corporation America, the television America—the empty America.

It can be a bad sign, it seems to me, when certain highly important topics, having been talked and written about widely for a time, seem one day just to disappear quietly and from then on go unmentioned. An example is the "dumbing down" of America, a topic that a decade ago was on the lips of all[1] but today is seldom heard of, if ever—a bad sign indeed if the reason it goes unmentioned is that it goes unnoticed. Dumbing down, in other words, may have succeeded so well that people, having themselves been dumbed down, no longer see the dumbing-down around—or within—them.

Or television. For how many years was it widely feared and hypothesized that television was a damaging and ruinous force, that just the act of watching it, content aside, was detrimental, and that the medium possessed the certainty of doing civilization-sized harm socially, emotionally, and intellectually?[2] My own view is that television *has* done a major share of such damage, but the point of concern for the moment is how little the risks and dangers of television seem to be talked about any longer. Both subjects, dumbing down and television, did, it's true, make a blip-sized reappearance with the publication in the summer of 2004 by the National Endowment for the Arts of its research results about American reading habits, *Reading at Risk: A Survey of Literary Reading in America*.[3] Already as much as forgotten, the report nevertheless did present itself with appropriate seriousness. "For the first time in modern history," wrote NEA chairman Dana Gioia in a preface, "less than half of the adult population now reads literature, and these trends reflect a larger decline in other sorts of reading." Gioia doesn't take the decline lightly, saying that

> anyone who loves literature or values the cultural, intellectual, and political importance of active and engaged literacy in American society will respond to this report with grave concern. (p. vii)

Concern, indeed, and it must all be television's doing—or so one might have heard said back in, well, 1960, perhaps. And of course it *is* television's doing, although television with a lot of help from its friends, as we'll see. For now, though, the interesting point is that, in the report, television not only isn't perceived as centrally influential in bringing about the cultural decline but is actually presented as being *helpful* in staunching the literary blood-loss. "If the 2002 data represent a declining trend," we read, "it is tempting to suggest that fewer people are reading literature and now prefer visual and audio entertainment." But that tempting thought isn't permissible, since "the data" don't bear it out, and "television does not seem to be the culprit." The report explains that in 2002, "those who do read and those who do not read literature watched about the same amount of TV per day—three hours' worth" (p. 30). (Possibly, though, the report does add, "the Internet . . . could have played a role.")

Not only, then, is television not the *cause* of our cultural hemorrhaging, but "in some cases," we're amazed to learn, "TV watching may have a positive impact on literary reading." *What?* How can this be?

Thus:

> Authors regularly appear on TV to promote their books, and some TV book clubs have been extremely popular. In fact, in the spring of 2002, most book publishers were very disappointed when Oprah Winfrey cancelled the book club related to her talk show. (p. 15)

And there rests the case, minimizing the deleterious effects of television and maximizing the meliorative—though the report does add, suggesting at least a touch of uncertainty, that "the effects of mass media, particularly television, movies, and the Internet, merit further scrutiny and research" (p. 15).

And indeed they do. If dumbing down goes unmentioned because the nation is too dumbed down to *perceive* the dread phenomenon anymore, it seems only logical that television—for the moment, a.k.a. the mass media—might be seen (by the *NEA*, no less) as a guide and aid to the improvement of literary culture. What conceivable literary culture, though, can the NEA possibly have in mind if it's one that can be bolstered and enriched by *television?* I ask this question not to be querulous but only because it seems to me so obvious, as I have long assumed it must seem to every thinking person in the land, that television as we know it is essentially, if not absolutely, without content. If a contentless medium becomes guide to the enrichment of a dying literary culture, is this not as clear an example of the blind leading the blind as might ever have been dreamed of?

Unfortunately, from much that I've been reading lately, the case seems so.

two

Actually, my statement that television as we know it is essentially without content is both true and not true.

First, let me talk about the true part. After all, we've known for a very, very long time now—certainly from as far back as *Omnibus* in 1952—that television programming, essentially, is created in order that *ads* can be run, rather than, in spite of what many may still think, ads being created in order that *programming* can be run. From television's infancy, corporate and business sponsorship clearly played an essential role in making broadcasting possible *and* in shaping what was—and what wasn't—put on the air. Government, of course, also played a role in these matters, and it was a role, like the corporate role, that grew enormously and rapidly as the economy itself grew. And, as the economy grew, both the corporate and governmental *stake* in television grew also, in a kind of mutual reinforcement that increased exponentially.

These relationships came into place in the years immediately following 1947—birth year of the National Security Council, one can't help also noting—and haven't changed since, except to become ever more intimate and complete. These, in other words, were the years when the "new" America was defined—when the Cold War began its four-decade life; when, for the first time in the nation's history, the commitment was made to a militarized economy during peacetime; and when, as it were, the corporate fox was invited in through the door of the governmental henhouse. In the case of the mass media—also born into its, or their, "new" form in these years—the event parallel to the entry of the fox was the entry of the corporate sponsor into the broadcast studio and in through the door of the programmer's office.

The knitting together of government and corporation, with the military as catalyst, was—and remains to this day—preponderantly secretive and devious. On the other hand, the knitting together of equivalent forces in the broadcast industry was never, from its inception, anything if not blatantly, intrusively, *obviously* visible to everyone. After all, the presence of ads on television, by their very nature, couldn't be hidden, and, from the start, televised ads were considered to be—because they *were*—the tail that wagged the dog: the little short snippets at beginning, middle, and end of shows that had more to do than any other power or force with determining what the *content* of the show would or wouldn't, could or couldn't, be.

As the Cold War went on, and as the economy continued its unprecedented expansion, so, too, did television grow enormously —but only in certain kinds of influence and power; or, more accurately, it grew *only* in influence and power while it never did grow in *content*. Another way of saying the same thing is that television failed to grow as a medium that undertook, or that continued, or that encouraged, or that could even *allow* the expression of anything whatsoever that really mattered. Television *could not* be serious, since nothing could or would be allowed to appear on it that mattered *significantly* in regard to anything other than the single thing it depended upon for its very existence: advancing the profit interests of the corporate, or government-corporate, sponsors.

Thus, it became both natural and inevitable, due to this

"commercial" arrangement for supporting national television broadcasting, that television would come to excel in the only way left open for it to excel *in:* as an around-the-clock filler of airtime with material of little or no content or significance or importance whatsoever.

✤ ✤ ✤

Clearly, in order for programming to be acceptable to television's corporate sponsors, it had to be neutral in any way that mattered significantly. At the most basic level, for example, programming couldn't be allowed blatantly, or even not so blatantly, to advocate the sponsor's interests. After all, our society is a free one, and such a transparent intrusion into freedom of expression over FCC-regulated airwaves couldn't be tolerated. Inside the ads themselves, however, since that's what the ads are designed and intended for, such advocacy and pitching were perfectly acceptable.

On the other hand, television programming's attitude toward its corporate sponsor could, just as obviously, not be permitted to be negative, for the simple reason that negativity would be intolerable to the sponsor. The result? There must be nothing whatsoever said, seen, or implied, either positive or *negative*, good or bad, that might express artists' or producers' attitudes, beliefs, or feelings in regard to the merits or faults of their corporate sponsors.

Now, what about other, wider, more important values, beliefs, or interests that might be dear to the corporate sponsors—or that the corporate sponsors might *claim* are dear to them? Suppose that the sponsoring corporations are growing nicely as a result of the expanding national economy, a growth that's resulting in large part from an expanding defense budget. If this is the case, the sponsor is clearly not going to tolerate any criticism whatsoever—direct, veiled, or remotely implied—of government itself, say, or of government policy, or of the institution of the military, or of current applications of military policy.

On television, therefore, the subjects of politics, economics, and the current uses and applications of military force—these, *on any meaningful level,* must be cut out, go unmentioned, be made as if not to exist. The military-corporate-governmental boat must not be rocked, and using lies of omission—the omitting of nothing less than most of life itself and *all* of inward or intellectual life from the heads of those on television and from the heads of those watching television—becomes one of the central ways to keep these otherwise troubled waters calm.

And the result is that television as we know it, and as we have known it all along, is kept empty, toothless, neutral, and "safe," in greatest part simply by means of the omission of significant content from it. Not all may agree that such a practice constitutes lying, although in an important sense it does. Lies of omission, after all— the *not* telling of things that are true—are guarded against in the very oath of honesty itself, by which one swears not only to tell the truth and nothing but the truth, but also "the whole truth."

The applying of such an oath to television could make of this now wretched and pernicious medium something significant and mighty indeed, but such a thing can't and won't happen. The actuality is that in addition to the programmatic omission of entire realms of material, television also routinely prevaricates even when it *does* take up a subject. It does so by revealing *some* of the truth but not all of it, just as the oath prohibits. The result is the infamous half-truth.

Consider the half-truth. It's easy today to find people who are passionately convinced that the typical American corporation is evil through and through, satanic from first inception to final buyout. Whatever elements of truth there are in such a view, or however *many* elements of truth, they still don't make up a *whole* truth any more than the statement "Girls are no good at math" does. The repugnance of this form of lying—called bigotry in the ignorant, propaganda in the purposeful—is evident to all, and I would skip the entire subject if I could. But the fact is that the subject of television *is* the subject of lying, and, further, that the subject of our media-drenched culture *is* the subject of lying. The sixty years that have brought us the new America have brought us also a virtually perfected sociopolitical culture of lies and lying, a culture built on a foundation of lying, framed by walls of lying, covered by a roof of lying.

So big is this subject, even in regard to television alone, that one isn't certain where to start. But let me take a central example of basic and standard prevarication, then follow where it leads.

The lie—assertion, slant, party line, half-truth—I'll choose is very simple and goes like this: All sponsoring corporations are *good;* all such corporations are *nice;* the management and employees of all these corporations are *also* nice; corporations all exist for the *purpose of doing good;* corporations all support and maintain the well-being of the nation; corporations exist in order to serve the needs and interests of the people; corporations succeed in this purpose.

Now, there are those who will argue that this isn't a falsehood or half-truth at all, but just an expression of plain truth—possibly minus the part about management and employees all being *nice.* But to hold the view that corporations are good, let alone endemically or innately good, is obviously every bit as untrue, by merit of being a half-truth, as holding the view that every corporation is wholly satanic from start to end. It's perfectly true that national and international affairs, combined with the extraordinarily dangerous and discreditable state of our nation just now, might sway even certain normally thoughtful people toward the "evil through and through" view. But even when corporations *are* evil—as, by and large, they do too often seem to be just now—one can argue that it's the regulation, the nonregulation, or the fraudulent regulation of them that's really at fault, and that there's no necessary reason why corporate-capitalism *must* be or become corrupted and corrupting of the good. But this isn't the direction of argument I want to go in. My subject in this book isn't political in the sense, say, of comparing left and right, or taking up the merits of social- ist economies versus capitalist, controlled markets versus free, or pondering whether the heart of man is, by instinct and nature, a thing of darkness or a thing of light.

Instead, the subject I want to explore is this: the state of our nation, and the state of daily life in our nation, and the state of people's *minds* after sixty years of the omnipresence and infiltration of the mass media and, concomitantly, of a culture that has become essentially a culture of lies. The questions that arise are not only whether such a nation can remain a free nation, but whether the individual minds of those within it can remain free minds.

On, then, to the subject of lies. It may be that the greatest enemy of us all, from radical left to radical right, is the lie, as I've said, that consists of the half-truth. The half-truth I cited above, about the nature and purpose of corporations, is a classic example and, like any half-truth, is by definition also a classic example of the lie of omission. As we'll see, this kind of half-truth has become a scourge, an omnipresent and corrosive sickness, in our daily and national life, intellectual life, artistic life, and in our culture at large.

The half-truth is capable of becoming tyrannic and crippling, of course, only when it is actually accepted as a *whole* truth. And many more ways than one serve to bring about such acceptance. Ignorance, for example, inexperience, lack of information—these, clearly, can lead to acceptance of half-truths as whole truth. Imag- ine, for example, a person so sheltered and naive as to have had *no* experience or to have gained *no* knowledge of corporate malignity, rapaciousness, hypocrisy, or greed. Such a person, a kind of Can- dide, would happily accept as a whole truth my paragraph-long half-truth assertion about corporations.

But that example is simple, maybe even simple-minded. No one could be *that* naive. Yet just stop for a moment and consider:

Since 1947 (not even to include its long life in American social and economic history *before* 1947), this particular half-truth has done possibly more than any other to define, color, prescribe, dictate, determine, and fine-tune not only the content, pitch, tone, and approach of virtually all major advertising seen on television but also the content, pitch, tone, and approach of most, if not all, major national *programming* on television, and it has done so, without cessation, remission, hesitation, qualification, or any *effectively* significant or retardant criticism, challenge, or control, *for an unbroken span of almost sixty years.*

Now, if the example of a person naive and inexperienced enough *actually* to accept as whole the half-truth that corporations are dedicated solely to the interests of the people—if the example of that person appears simple-minded, then it seems to me only logical to conclude that we as a nation must be, by logical extension, also and equally simple-minded, since we have *in effect* accepted it *for almost sixty years,* allowing it into our heads, onto our screens, into our magazines, onto our billboards and buses, into our subways, onto our airplanes and radios, allowing ourselves to be so thoroughly drenched in it, so thoroughly contaminated by it, so thoroughly exposed to it and to the look and feel and texture and atmosphere of it and of its countless progeny—not only ads, but programming itself—that it has come not only to seem perfectly natural and quite real indeed but all too often a thing desirable in and of itself.

The word *it* in that paragraph admittedly carries a heavy burden and may even make a few quick costume changes before the end. But *it* has to be used in at least the double sense of referring to the half-truth itself *and* to the varied and many *expressions of* that half-truth, not to mention also the need for reference to the varied and many results, omissions, implications, and colorings (in programming, imagery, assumption, approach) that result both from the half-truth's existence *and* from the exercise of the authority that backs, supports, and promotes it.

It is, after all, through our acceptance of these myriad results and effects, all of them manifest in audible and viewable forms, that we in effect do indeed accept the originating half-truth itself. *We let it go on being said. We don't oppose it. Therefore, we effectively accept it.* This fact is extraordinarily important, acutely interesting, and deeply depressing. I don't for a second imagine that very many readers of these pages—perhaps not any—would, if asked, respond that, yes, they do believe that all corporations are nice, that the only purpose of their existence is to do good, and that their sole interests are the interests of the people. Yet at the same time, it's highly unlikely that any of those same readers, or any but a very tiny percentage, would in actual fact and in the mundane carrying on of their own lives, consciously disapprove of, repudiate, eschew, oppose, or reject any but a near-infinitesimal part—if even that much—of the implicit and explicit manifestations, and images, and assertive presentations of that very same half-truth's presumed validity that exist with almost incalculable frequency and in almost unlimited numbers all around every single one of us as we do nothing more than go through the mundane living of our daily lives.

Take only *niceness* for a moment, leaving aside the other parts of the half-truth, and consider to what an extraordinary extent the presumption of *niceness* or the insistence upon *niceness* or the intentional omitting of other elements of life in order to have *niceness* be the distillation that's left behind—consider to what an extraordinary extent manifestations of such kinds surround us all the time, in print ads, radio ads, television ads, in television programming. Sure, there are "gritty" shows, formulaic in their own ways, but the true hallmark of prime-time programming is the *nice* and cute family, the *nice* and cute couple, the *nice* and cute group of friends, etc., etc.—not to mention the accumulated kinds of rose-tinted "lore" or "legend" or "myth," like the myth of the *nice* small town, the *nice* crossroads village, the *nice* bucolic farm—

things whose actual existence has been eliminated from real life by the bulldozers of "progress" while simultaneously those same things—in the form of nostalgic ideas, half-memories, and feeling-thoughts—fuel easily half of the corporate-backed mass media programming and advertising budget.

The point isn't whether it's actually *half* the budget, or whether there *are* other kinds of things on television, or whether there really *is* still sufficient variety of programming so as to provide choice. These questions all come to nothing more than the splitting of hairs and contain little or no significance in light of the far greater fact of the near-monolithic *aesthetic* of the mass media: the sound of it, the feel of it, the atmosphere of it, the assumptions behind it that circumscribe, direct, and control the final product so that it has finally the unremitting quality of *sameness* about it, the quality I am now calling the mass media's *aesthetic*.

This "aesthetic," after all, is itself the real, true, actual *content* of the mass media. And so we are brought back to my earlier point, when I said the assertion that television as we know it is essentially without content was both true and not true. So far, we've seen some of what's *not* on television. It's a lot. Now we can look at what *is* on television.

three

And the truth is that what's on the air isn't what *seems* to be on the air—soaps, news, sports, games, cops, sitcoms, ads, etc., etc. Instead, the true content on television and in all the mass media is something else: It's the *aesthetic*, the *quality,* the *flavor,* the *experience of the medium itself*—or, indeed, of the media themselves.

For, in actuality, nothing else of importance or significance *can be* on television; in actuality, nothing else of importance or significance can be *allowed* on television. To the extent that corporate ownership and corporate-government interest take control of other dimensions and areas of the mass media—publishing, for example, or pop music—the same becomes true there as well, with the result that, increasingly, just as with television, nothing of its own importance or significance *can be* published. No books of their own kind of importance or significance can be *allowed* to be published. The only publishable books are those that are predictable in all of the ways necessary to ensure that their true content is in fact not the story they tell or the theme or subject they appear to take up; but that their true content, instead, is the familiar *aesthetic,* the *tone, quality, stance, feel, sense, aura*—in short, the *experience* of the mass media itself. Or, again, of the mass media themselves.

Over six decades, the situation has developed whereby corporate interest—as far as the mass media are concerned—lies *solely* in presenting one or another major half-truth as if it were a whole truth. The implications of this simple fact are enormous, and those implications, in turn, have vast relevance, as we will see, to a certain bedrock question about freedom—namely, whether, in such a situation, it can conceivably be preserved.

Some will argue that, whatever I may claim, there *is* "content" on television. And, indeed, I will agree with them, but only in the most excruciatingly literal sense. There's content, yes, but that's a far, far different thing from agreeing that there's also, therefore, either importance or significance.

Corporate sponsorship, with its desire to pass off half-truth as whole truth, will naturally want to do *nothing* that might cause an audience to think or that might lead an audience even *toward* thinking. Thought, after all, is the corporate interest's great enemy and is corrosive of that interest's purposes and values. In all the universe, after all, there is only one tool that can defend against the half-truth's successfully being put into general currency as a whole truth. And that tool is *thought.* That one tool is *thinking.*

And so what has come about is something I would call genuinely and truly diabolic if I knew it to have been planned as such. The greater likelihood, though, is that, in spite of some undeniable presence of the mean, willful, self-serving, and malicious, it has more generally just evolved, has simply happened, albeit with plentiful shapings and adjustments over the years, adjustments themselves sufficiently diabolic by merit of being based on the fine-tunings made possible through success, experience, and observation—all of this over *six decades,* and all of it toward the perfecting of a means by which the corporate (and conjoined governmental) interests could to the greatest conceivable extent and with the best conceivable effect continue to present the half-truth as a whole truth.

What came about was indeed a way to put *nothing* on television and yet still keep the airwaves filled day and night, addressing ever more viewers, so that ads could go on being aired with ever more influence and effect. That the thing used for filling the airwaves was indeed *nothing* should come as no surprise. Anything *other* than nothing, after all—anything, that is, possessing significance or importance—might trigger emotion[4] or inspire thinking, thereby harming or endangering the sponsor's interest by jeopardizing the continued acceptance of the half-truth as whole.

This is by no means a new idea. It has been said routinely and for a very, very long time indeed that television is empty, that there's "nothing on," and all the way back in 1961 came Newton Minow's famous comment that television was "a vast wasteland."

What interests me, however, isn't exactly this question. After all, the essential dreariness, emptiness, triviality, and insignificance of the huge majority of television airtime simply isn't *interesting*—by definition can't be, since it's trivial, *interesting.* Two other questions very closely related to programming's inanity, poverty, and emptiness, however, are very, very interesting indeed.

The first of these is simply the question of why programming on commercial television has never gotten any better over all these decades—in the sense, that is, of gaining *content,* of achieving *consequence,* of taking the significant risk necessary for thought or meaningful response to occur from the experience of the programming. Television probably has in fact improved, if only in a purely technical sense—noncomic dramas, which always looked tacky and home-made in comparison with those, say, from England, sometimes now look skillful and professional—like *The Sopranos,* for example. But that show itself is a good example of what might be called an "unimproved improvement" in programming. For, however "real" it may purport to be, the show remains endemically and devotedly trivial—it fails, that is, and most likely never even tries (or knows or even wonders how to try), to achieve *consequence.* What risks does it take? Sure, it puts in lots of swear words and vulgarity. Big risk—what could be more trivial? And, sure, it's about the mob. So? What risk does it take that a thousand cheap or popular or elite novels (or movies) about the mob haven't taken and continue to take? *The Sopranos,* in fact, doesn't just show its characters to be exactly like everybody else, but it shows them to be exactly like everybody else in all other inconsequential noncomic television drama. Sure, they rub people out, sometimes even cut off heads. In effect, though (more on this later), it's all in good fun—something passing, a little scary, somewhat creepy, not unlike the same kind of thrill one might get from, say, Hitchcock or Joyce Carol Oates. Would HBO, on the other hand, run a noncomic and nonfictional dramatic series about U.S. government figures or agencies assassinating foreign statesmen and American citizens, laundering money for corporate interests, importing drugs into the United States, or "allowing" catastrophes like 9/11 to occur, if only by not preventing them, for the purpose of reaping political benefit therefrom?

Perhaps I'm getting ahead of myself, but the point I'm making is real, true, and valid. And it's this: Essentially, nothing can appear on television, nothing *can be allowed* to appear on television, that's in fact bona-fide, true, and real. This means, of course, that it must be fiction.[5] And "fiction" means, in this case, yet again, anything that can't have and won't have content, and can't have and won't pose risk or doubt of any kind sufficient to achieve *consequence* in the mind (or heart) of the watcher, viewer, auditor—or, even, reader.[6]

As to why this is so, why programming in its essence hasn't improved, changed, become in any significant way meaningful or consequential: The sole, only, and central reason for this not having happened is, of course, that it would not have served the interests of those figures, entities, sponsors, and authorities that and who alone hold the power to allow (or cause) it *to* happen.

The corporate/government sponsor wanted it not to happen. It didn't happen. Case closed.

This alone may be more than bad enough as a national failure observable over the period of one's own lifetime, but I think there's more to it than just the absence of change. In his column of January 30, 2004, in the *New York Times,* Paul Krugman took up the subject of the Bush administration's failure ever to apologize, let alone change policy or personnel, after making mistakes, whether those mistakes were accidental or not. Krugman cites the false threat of weapons of mass destruction used as an excuse for the "preemptive" Iraq war. Then he cites the Bushists' "stonewalling" of the panel whose task was to investigate what happened, or failed to happen, before the 9/11 attacks. After doing *those* things, Krugman cites the inadequate monitoring of how American money is now spent—and made—inside Iraq.

I'm not going to discuss any of those matters, at least not here. As interesting—and disconcerting—as they are, there's something else that's of equal or even greater interest and importance. Let Krugman introduce it:

> Still, the story isn't about Mr. Bush; it's about what's happening to America. Other presidents would have liked to bully the CIA, stonewall investigations and give huge contracts to their friends without oversight. They knew, however, that they couldn't. What has gone wrong with our country that allows this president to get away with such things?

And thus we're led to see that over the last six decades there *has* been important and essential change. This change has not been in television, or in the mass media itself, or in the content, programming, or purpose of the mass media. The change has been, instead, in the *audience*.

✦ ✦ ✦

Here, I enter into a part of my argument that some may find subjective and unprovable. It's "just opinion," such people might say. Perhaps. But I don't think so.

Sixty years is a long time. But it's an *especially* long time if it happens to be the length of time that a central, vitally important, unprecedentedly widespread element of an entire modern national culture—that is, television—has remained, for all intents and purposes, absolutely inert and without change.

And you can double or triple the significance of those years when you add that the cultural element you're talking about is both an explicitly and profoundly exploitative one; is relentlessly regulated and controlled by the same interests and forces that are doing the exploiting; and has as its central means of cultural expression a medium—the moving image—without any precedent in all of human history; a medium that over the past six decades of its own ten-decade (at most) history has shown itself unique in its ability to enter unsought into every nook and cranny, into the very weft and woof, the very fiber itself of private and personal life, and to do so on a scale, and with such ease, with such simultaneity, and with such huge audiences, as to make it a thing never before seen, known, or imagined in the whole long sweep of human history.

Sixty years of unchanged and unchanging exposure to *that* could change a guy. Or a people.

And it has.

At this point, it's necessary to go back to the question of television's *content*. I think the argument is now sufficiently clear—

though not finished—that most of television doesn't *have* any content, at least not in the sense that other forms of cultural expression have traditionally had content. Television's sixty-year period of inertia is itself a way of showing the truth of the assertion. As I've said, sixty years is a long time, and I know of no real form of cultural expression in the modern era—by "real" I mean living, and by "modern" I mean up to 1947—that isn't on record as having changed dramatically, even radically, over an equivalent span of time. Take a look at a few examples of, say, American short fiction written in the 1860s and 1870s, and then look at the stories of Hamlin Garland (*Main-Traveled Roads*, 1891), Sherwood Anderson (*Winesburg, Ohio*, 1919), and Ernest Hemingway: What you'll see is an enormous revolution in the short story, a genre altered, changed, refocused, and adapted (though still built on the bones of its forebears) in order that it be equipped to see, identify, and express the truths of its own newer and changed world. Dramatic examples of the same kind of change, refocus, and evolution in art, over approximately the same span of time, can be seen readily in jazz, opera, poetry, the novel—until, that is, 1947 or so, when these forms, too, began rapidly to atrophy.

But television as we know it differs from the others, because its first purpose is to control, not express. Television exists hardly at all as an artistic medium but almost entirely, instead, as a tool of economic-social control.

If those two statements were true only of television, I might be considerably less alarmed than I am at the state of the culture in general. To put it most simply, television stopped developing at exactly the time it stopped existing as a form of art. Or, perhaps more accurately, television, never having been given a *chance* as a form of art, never did develop.

But television was then only beginning, and if the *end* of its life as a changeable and adaptable art form came sometime between, say, 1947 and 1950 or 1952, then it can be said to have lived only for a very short time indeed. And its death—or its birth into death— marked the beginning of the huge, uniformly empty, exploitative, and powerful entity that I'm calling the mass media. As everyone knows, this entity is both omnivorous and voracious, and its growth over sixty years has been so successful and so unremitting that not only has it come to be a part also of what is *inside* people, but it has successfully cannibalized other art forms, devouring *them* so that they, not originally parts of the mass media at all, now have been made so. Like television, those other art forms became unchanging, empty, and inert at exactly the time they stopped being art forms. This can be seen, for example, not just in television, but in the literary arts (fiction in particular), in the publishing industry itself, in popular music, and in the plastic and pictorial arts. The telltale signs are sameness and emptiness. I'll take these up later in regard to literary studies and publishing, but first I must finish what needs saying about the "content" of the mass media.

Two things need to be mentioned—the first relatively simple, the other much more difficult and complex. I'll return to both later, but they should at least be mentioned now, since they have to do with the emptiness of television, and with what television *really* says.

As bad money is said to drive out good, it seems perfectly clear that in the mass media, and in the mass culture that it controls and oversees, bad ideas and things drive out good ideas and things. I'm aware that in these righteous and hypersensitive times, the words "bad" and "good" as applied to anything touching even remotely on the subject of "culture" or "cultures" are likely to draw swift and vehement condemnation upon their user as "elitist," "hegemonic," and perhaps worse. Therefore, in the rephrasing that follows, I ask readers to pay close attention to exactly what I mean by "bad" and "good."

Thus: It seems perfectly clear that in the mass media, and in the mass culture that it controls and oversees, *simpler* ideas and things drive out more *complex* ideas and things.

Thirty-five or forty years is a good span of time to observe social or intellectual change, and, that being the time I've spent inside classrooms—as instructor, not student—I've seen enough change, and enough of certain *kinds* of change, to conclude that our age could accurately be dubbed "The Age of Simplification." Later, I will take up the notion of simplification again, but I mention it now because of its relevance to one of the two things that need to be observed about television's, and the mass media's, emptiness: namely, the extent to which the notion of "entertainment" has driven out and taken dominance over other or competing notions of content or purpose.

In my own undergraduate days, I remember there being little concern, if any, with the "entertainment" values in, really, *any* of the arts. Novel, poem, play, book, opera, movie, concert—the first thing sought or expected in none of them was "entertainment." The subject didn't come up. It was something seldom or perhaps never mentioned, at least not as such, for the reason that it was *assumed* to be there already. The entertainment was a part of the *entirety* of the thing, something of interest built into the very nature of the project. Specific discussion of the element of entertainment had no reason for being: A little bit like one's own inner organs, or the inner organs, say, of one's lover, it went unnoticed, was taken for granted, was an assumed part of the complete entity, while that complete entity itself was the thing being loved. In novel, poem, or lover, "entertainment value" never *had* any kind of separate or distinguishable existence.

But things have changed enormously. A little more than forty years have passed since I left college, and on this particular point, the world has turned upside down. From my own editors and colleagues, and throughout virtually all book reviewing and advertising, I hear near-endless talk about what once were *last* things but now are *first*—the "hook," "hooking the reader," "getting hooked," "plot," "story line," "suspense," "narrative drive," "muscularity," "sinew," etc., etc.

Nothing new in any of this, some will say; the idea has been around since the beginning of time. But I don't agree. It's new, first, in its omnipresence. And it's new in another, more significant way: The hook, drive, speed, obvious forward movement—these were once matters saliently requisite mainly to the lower of the literary arts, even the trashier; now, though, they have made their way as concepts of the first importance to *all* the literary arts, from gutter to empyrean.

Attitudes and assumptions have changed so much that even to *mention*—as I'm doing now—that plot, rapidity, and ease of entry are overrated as virtues relevant to much of anything innately important to literature or the life of the mind is to risk, once again, quick vilification on charges of pretension and elitism. Something quite fascinating and more than a little dispiriting has happened: Namely, the idea has been firmly established that it's *wrong* for something to be difficult. That this is a demonstrably false notion doesn't keep it from being used as support for its even more damaging sibling idea, the mirror twin of itself: that is, that it's *right* that things be easy.

Sixty years without exercise will lead to flaccid muscles, all will agree, but few are as likely to follow the corollary thought, that sixty years without intellectual exercise will lead to laziness and diminishment of mind. But it does. And, as we'll see, it has.

The past six decades, after all, reveal themselves now to have been powerful indeed, lending themselves to the massive un-educating, de-educating, the *conditioning* of a whole people in order that they'll fail to perceive that a half-truth is not a whole truth. Bringing about change of this magnitude is a project capable of destroying a people, a culture, and a nation.

The results are indeed profound, innocuous as they may seem at first. Often, these results reveal themselves through the substituting of one thing for another in ways deleterious to the intellectual *and* the artistic life: for example, the substitution of feeling for thinking that has swept like an infection through the academic humanities and elsewhere over the past thirty years.

Or an even simpler example—the substitution of *entertainment* for either *content* or *meaning*. The critic who dares speak disparagingly about "entertainment" will quickly find angry people attacking him with charges of elitism, hegemony, the works. "Entertainment" has been raised high, and disrespect for it is an offense to be paid for. The reason for such protectiveness isn't just that the "entertainment-for-content" substitution is easier to see and understand (and thus take up as a cause) than the feeling-versus-thinking one. But it's also that the idea of entertainment as not just equaling but outweighing and outranking content or meaning has grown now into an insistence upon the availability of entertainment as having the status of a *right*.

There's much to be said about the *rights* movement, certainly so for someone who has spent three decades in college classrooms, becoming year by year more familiar with student *rights*—the right not to read assignments, for example, not to attend classes, not to stay awake, and not to be given low grades.[7] Still, all of the varied new "rights" in fact have a common origin, one that's relevant to any discussion of television.

The *right* to be entertained produces its own corollary right, the right not to *think*, and both such convictions are built on the bedrock foundation of the belief, itself reinforced by the media for the past sixty years, that easy things are *good* and that hard things are *bad*—and, yes, that people have the *right* for things to be easy.

That is, above all, the right that *intellectual* things—all things having in any way whatsoever to do with intellect, thinking, or the mind—be easy. Just that. And in so pathetic a debasement as this, in such a repugnant narrowing of the view or the expectation of how much life *can* hold, in the manifestation of such a *simplification* of attitude and thought and assumption, we witness some of the intellectual fruits of six decades of the massive, incessant, intrusive, and unremitting telling of lies to an entire people. As we've seen, what might be called the Big Lie—the Umbrella Lie—is that any half-truth the media gives is in fact a whole truth. And the half-truth in this particular case is simply this: There's nothing wrong with entertainment.

The statement—innocuous on the face of it, and seemingly true—is nevertheless a half-truth as it's used, presented, and promoted by the mass media. As part of normal thinking, the statement would be followed by a second statement that would draw the first into the partnership of a whole truth—"But entertainment without content quickly becomes shallow," for example, or, "But there's nothing wrong with *seriousness*, either." As parlayed in the world of television and the mass media, however, any such qualifying assertion is purposely silenced or omitted, leaving the original statement, alone, to rest on the wrong and deceitful foundation of a false dichotomy, another form of chopped logic endemic to the Age of Simplification.

This particular implied or underlying false dichotomy opens out like a hand of playing cards from its first false premise on through its various and pernicious corollaries. First is the anti-intellectual and untrue notion that "entertainment" and "thinking" are opposites of one another and thus mutually exclusive. Second, there's the parallel implication that "entertainment," on the one hand, and "meaning" or "content," on the other, are also opposites and therefore also mutually exclusive. Third is the implied assertion that "entertainment" can neither produce nor include either "thinking" *or* "content," along with the reverse and equally false implication that neither can "thinking" or "content" produce or include "entertainment." And, finally—most important of all—there's the underlying or implied assertion that "entertainment" is and must be *easy* while "thinking" is and must be *hard*.

I began this chapter by remarking how *soft* we have become in our national culture, and here I return to that idea. Thinking may in fact be hard (though it isn't always), but please allow me to ask just one thing: Since when in American history before now has the fact of something's being *hard* proved a deterrent to Americans *doing* it? Where, exactly, in the great tapestry of this storied nation did *difficulty* stand in the way of achievement, accomplishment, or the fulfilling of aims? Was there ever a time, one asks, when laziness trumped diligence? When sloth was revered over hard effort? When the life of unearned ease was lauded or valued over the life of ambition, strength of will, and hard work?

And, indeed, the answers are no, no, and no—that is, not until 1947 or so, when the nation began its long, unparalleled, insidious, demeaning, and spectacularly successful program of the media-conditioning of its people so as to transform them from citizens into consumers—the more passive the better, so long as they *consumed*—whose life-purpose was no longer to continue the historically ancient work of making a better nation of better people with better lives, but simply and merely to keep the economy—the Cold War economy—expanding ever more rapidly, thus serving the interests not of we the people and not of we the republic *of* the people, but the interests, instead, of the government-corporate, or corporate-government, complex that had emerged—and had been warned of by a departing President Eisenhower—as the effective engine and leader of the state.

My own childhood, from the time I reached age ten or so, was an era not just of the Cold War, growing defense budget, and atmospheric testing of nuclear weapons, but also of brand-new and unsettling expansionist ideas like "planned obsolescence," the "waste economy," and "conspicuous consumption," this last resurrected from Thorstein Veblen and metamorphosed from a pejorative idea into something like a guide for good living in the new splendor of the 1950s, the nation's first decade of a genuine mass culture that was both media-governed *and* waste-consumption-driven.

In order for the entire plan to succeed, it was essential that the idea and meaning of materialism be changed. "Consumerism" and "materialism," after all, were really the same thing. "Materialism," however, was traditionally thought of as being a "bad" thing, since materialists, everyone knew, were decadent, unholy, and cynical. It was necessary, therefore, that materialism be stripped of its pejorative associations, then that the words "consumer" and "consumerism" be used in its place, and, finally, that "consumerism" as a way of life be strenuously encouraged by any means available. The means that was most clearly available for such encouragement, of course—and most effective—was advertising, which was delivered mainly but not only through television and which was presented in such ways as to make the practice of materialism not only good and endlessly desirable but as closely associated with a *right* as it could possibly be.

And therein, it hardly need be pointed out, lay another great lie, one akin to the great lie by omission that corporate interests are the same as the people's interests. Few will deny that the rewards of materialism, of having lots of nice things, may well be *desirable*, but to do as we have done and purposely associate it with a *right*, is to debase politics, economics, and human beings all at once.

❖ ❖ ❖

And so, the seeds having been planted long ago, we can hardly be surprised, six decades later, at the harvest we have reaped: a nation of people who have been falsified, simplified, demeaned—and who are *proud of it*, all but bursting with a smug self-contentedness at knowing that theirs is the *right* to consume, the *right* to be entertained, and the *right* not to think.

To put it another way: So many Americans, for so many decades, have been so widely and so consistently manipulated, demeaned, exploited, and lied to; have been hourly, daily, weekly, and monthly so teased, lured, flattered, and misled; have been so ill educated, un-educated, de-educated, and anti-educated; have been shown so incessantly that they, as human beings, are indistinguishable in value, significance, or meaning from the objects, goods, and merchandise that they've been encouraged to buy, use, waste, consume, and buy again; so many Americans, in short, have had these and innumerable parallel things done to them so consistently and so programmatically and for so long that it now appears quite literally a possibility that they *have become a people no longer able to understand what they are;* a people intellectually, emotionally, and aesthetically so starved, debased, deluded, and misled that they may no longer be able *to* think clearly, *to* think well, possibly even *to* think at all.

But it's time now to take a look at some actual writing—some actual writers—from the Age of Simplification.

four

On Pearl Harbor Day of 2002, the *New York Times* ran a news item by Michael Z. Wise under the headline "U.S. Writers Do Cultural Battle Around the Globe." Wise reported that "the Bush administration has recruited prominent American writers to contribute to a State Department anthology and give readings around the globe in a campaign started after 9/11 to use culture to further American diplomatic interests."

The participants include four Pulitzer Prize winners, Michael Chabon, Robert Olen Butler, David Herbert Donald and Richard Ford; the American poet laureate, Billy Collins; two Arab-Americans, Naomi Shihab Nye and Elmaz Abinader; and Robert

Pinsky, Charles Johnson, Bharati Mukherjee and Sven Birkerts. They were all asked to write about what it means to be an American writer.

George Clack, the State Department official who edited the volume, explained that because of an archaic law (the Smith-Mundt Act of 1948), the fifteen essays in the anthology were barred from publication in the United States, though the news item explained that "the essays can . . . be read on a government Web site intended for foreigners (www.usinfo.state.gov/products/pubs/writers)." It went on:

> Despite the domestic blackout, the participants are focused on the potential abroad. "There is the perception abroad that Americans feel culturally superior and are intellectually indifferent," said Mr. Ford, who won the Pulitzer in 1996 for his novel *Independence Day*. "Those stereotypes need to be burst." He added that he was eager to go to Islamic nations to help "humanize America" and present a more diverse picture of public opinion than is conveyed by the Bush administration.

And, finally, another State Department official, Stuart Holliday, was quoted as saying: "We're shining a spotlight on those aspects of our culture that tell the American story. The volume of material is there. The question is how can it be augmented to give a clearer picture of who we are."

❖ ❖ ❖

And there we are. Especially since I had myself been involved for some time in trying to define and describe the Age of Simplification, I was eager indeed to read a group of essays that had been written in order to address a number of the same questions that I had also been wrestling with. So I downloaded,[8] printed, and stapled the essays, and then, over the next couple of evenings, I read them through. They were, by and large, just awful. I decided that I should reread them, more carefully this time, and, just as I might do with any writing that comes under my review, *grade* them.

Here are the grades:

Clack, George: *Introduction*	F	(0.0)
Abinader, Elmaz: *Just off Main Street*	D	(0.5)
Alvarez, Julia: *I, Too, Sing América*	F	(0.0)
Birkerts, Sven: *The Compulsory Power of American Dreams*	D+	(1.4)
Butler, Robert Olen: *A Postcard from America*	D	(0.5)
Chabon, Michael: *Maps and Legends*	D	(1.6)
Collins, Billy: *What's American About American Poetry?*	A+	(4.5)
Creeley, Robert: *America's American*	A	(4.0)
Donald, David Herbert: *On Being an American Historian*	B+	(3.4)
Ford, Richard: *How Does Being an American Inform What I Write?*	D−	(0.5)
Hogan, Linda: *For Life's Sake*	D+	(1.4)
Jacob, Mark: *Both Sides of the Border*	B	(3.0)
Johnson, Charles: *An American Milk Bottle*	D−	(0.5)
Mukherjee, Bharati: *On Being an American Writer*	D−	(1.6)
Nye, Naomi Shihab: *This Crutch That I Love*	F	(0.0)
Pinsky, Robert: *A Provincial Sense of Time*	B−	(2.6)

The numerical values, when added together and divided by fifteen, give an average grade of 1.7, or C−. If Billy Collins were awarded an A rather than an imaginary A+ (for being best in the book), the average would fall to 1.6666, remaining C−. If, on the other hand, the top two grades were left out, the average of the remaining thirteen would fall to 1.307692307, technically a D, although soft-heartedness might lead an instructor, in spite of the numbers not allowing it, to round up to 1.4, or D+. I myself would not round up, since doing so would detract from emphasizing how desolate the showing is when lacking that small bit of strength at the top. It is, I would say, an almost unbelievably *soft* batch of work.

❖ ❖ ❖

To get an idea of what the anthology is like and what it reveals, we need a plan, so I'll propose arranging the fifteen essays into three groups.

1. *First,* what I'll call the "very worst"—Abinader, Alvarez, Chabon, Hogan, Johnson, Mukherjee, and Nye.

2. *Second,* what I'll call the "very best"—Collins, Creeley, Donald, Jacob, and Pinsky.

3. And *third,* what I'll call the "*true* worst"—Birkerts, Butler, and Ford.

Definitions of these labels and the rationale for them will emerge as we go along.

The most notable characteristics of the first group—the essays that, by and large, make up what could be called the "ethnicity" group—are, first, their smallness and simplicity of theme, and, second, the near-omnipresence in them either of nonthinking or fallacious thinking.

We can begin with Elmaz Abinader, not because her piece happens to come first (the pieces are arranged alphabetically by authors' last names), but because it so excellently shows the typical pattern. A great many of the pieces—most—use autobiography as their means into the subject, that subject, once more, having to do with the question "In what sense do you see yourself as an American writer?"

I find nothing wrong with autobiography, and I'm opposed to the schools of criticism that automatically or for the wrong reasons denigrate it. It occupies a central and vitally important place in all literature, and *certainly* in American literature, and I will never, as it were, take points off in the evaluation of a piece merely because it uses the first person singular. The only significant question about autobiography as method or subject, after all, is the question of what the author *does* with it. Putting it another way, the significant question is what or how much the writer is *aware of* in his or her writing.

And by that measure, none of the essays in the first group, really, offers anything at all. In her own case, Abinader recalls her 1960s childhood in "the small Pennsylvania town where I grew up" and where her family were shopkeepers and restaurateurs. She was happy at home, we learn, but, as she puts it, "my house had a magic door," and things were different on the outside of the door from what they were on the inside:

> My family scenes filled me with joy and belonging, but I knew none of it could be shared on the other side of that door. The chant of schoolyard slurs would intensify. Looking different was enough; having a father with a heavy accent already marked me, dancing in circles would bury me as a social outcast.

In 1964, when I was a teaching assistant at the University of Wisconsin, the illustrious Helen C. White, chair of the English department, gave me and my colleagues some advice about evaluating student papers. When you receive a paper, she said, you must have no prejudice toward it at all, positive or negative, but should assume it—logically—to be average. In reading it, then, you should look for positive aspects that might raise the grade from the hypothetical C it started with *and* look for negative aspects that might lower it from the average. If equal numbers of positive and negative characteristics were present, and if the positive and negative characteristics were themselves of equal weight or significance, the paper would end up remaining at C. And so on. The method is solid, fair, and useful—and it also works, of course, on writing that's not *student* writing.

In the Abinader piece, nothing so far has either raised or lowered the effort above or below its presumptive C. Nothing is unusual about it. Nothing unexpected has been offered. The writing is capable but not distinguished, and thus not a merit in itself. At the same time, nothing has yet been a demerit, including the choice of simple, chronological, autobiographical structure.

But then we come upon the softness, the signs that, indeed, we're dealing with an Age of Simplification writer. Not surprisingly, the first signs come precisely at that point where the essay's intellectual content deepens, or attempts to. Abinader tells us that at a certain point she'd begun to write but that she still wrote only about her own family's history ("A poem about my mother leaving Lebanon . . . a story about my grandfather living like a refugee during World War I, my father's adventures as a rubber trader in Brazil"), and she remarks that "I intuitively released these stories and poems as if the whole history was bottled up inside me."

Now, a prior point needs to be mentioned before we continue, namely, that just before this moment in the essay, Abinader has said more about her cultural isolation. In that passage, we see the author's thought beginning to grow rigid and simplistic and her prose beginning to weaken. From here on, the essay will earn a surplus of demerits over merits, resulting in its final grade of D.

"It wasn't long," writes Abinader,

> before I understood that my display of my Arab-ness served to exoticize me. In the curriculum, nothing of Arab writing was represented; on television, the only person associated with Lebanon was Danny Thomas; and *Lawrence of Arabia* became the footnote to my culture. Concurrently, the events in the Middle East clarified the sympathies in the United States as not pro-Arab; and as I grew, feelings toward Arabs became more negative and sometimes bordered on distrust, even from my own colleagues.

Notice the increasing imprecision in Abinader's phrasings, the sudden stock quality of the unthought, the unobserved, unnamed, undemonstrated, unshown—"the events in the Middle East," "clarified the sympathies in the United States," "as not pro-Arab."

Abinader, presumably, is a teacher, perhaps even a writing teacher, but she herself needs instruction in the basics.[9] *What* events in the Middle East? this writing teacher would ask her, adding that the good writer should say something exactly or say nothing at all. *Whose* sympathies in the United States? asks the teacher. The State Department's? Your in-laws'? Your mechanic's? *What* have you seen, heard, experienced that supports what you say? Good writers know that the broad generalization is a statement of nothing, often worse than nothing.

And, most revealing, most typical, most important, what do you *mean*, "not pro-Arab"? The good writer never hides behind a negative as a way to imply a positive. What *are* your in-laws, what *is* your mechanic, if *not* "pro-Arab"? A test for the unwritten, for the hinted-at generalization as opposed to the concrete assertion or statement is that the former leaves itself open to ridicule while the latter doesn't. In this case, I can make light of the phrase "not pro-Arab" by suggesting that if they're not pro-Arab, then they must be pro–Santa Claus, or perhaps the writer means—yes, she *must* mean—that they're pro–dental hygiene.

The writer, solely the writer, and no one other than the writer is responsible for every single thing the writer writes. The morality of writing is the same as the morality of thought or action: If it isn't honest, it isn't moral. Now, this trick in a writer, of hiding behind a negative in order to imply a positive—without having to *say* the positive—is, in that sense, dishonest. Worse, it's evasive, enabling the writer to adopt a position free of responsibility. Worse still, it's *code,* and *secret.* In a word, it's *propaganda.*

✤ ✤ ✤

And there we are, right at the rancid heart of the Age of Simplification and Deceit. All the time, people accuse rightists of dishonesty for using code, but less often is this charge brought against the liberal intellectuals, who, after all, have read 1984 and "Politics and the English Language" and know all there is to know about euphemism, propaganda, lies of omission, and so on.

But either they *don't* know or, if they *do* know—if they preach but don't practice—then they're not just deceivers but hypocrites too.

I can imagine the objections that might arise at this point, just as they do when matters like these come up in the classroom: You're making a big thing out of nothing. You can't justify accusing and excoriating a poor writer for so small a thing as this. And, besides, you *know* what she meant.

But not so. The thing I *couldn't* justify would be remaining silent. My professional ethics and the standards of my training are both being debased here by one of my peers, and it's my professional— that is, ethical—responsibility to make judgment accordingly. (What if one heart surgeon saw another taking a dangerous short-cut on a patient or making a dangerous omission and said nothing?) Further, in this particular case there's the additional matter of a prominent showcase being involved: Abinader, along with Alvarez, Chabon, Hogan, Johnson, Mukherjee, and Nye, have been made cultural emissaries by the Department of State, their words going out to the entire world in a putative exploration not only of "what it means to be an American" but of "what it means to be an American *writer*." The contributors to the anthology, then, are not "poor writers" who should be treated gently and allowed to remain unexamined; rather, they are figures who have been elevated, *as writers,* to be representatives, in important cultural ways, of an entire nation.

Now, if from this visible and important elevation, what's demonstrated is that American writers deceive, twist, omit, evade responsibility for their own assertions, and propagandize, then the matter is very important indeed.

As for the anthology's degeneration into code, no defense can be mounted by arguing that "anyway, we know what the writer *means*." If we know what she means anyway, that is, there's no reason for criticism, since, in effect, there's been no lapse, offense, or error.

But again, not so. Writing in code, when done intentionally for mean or depraved ends, is deceit and abomination. "But," I hear, "none of *us* is doing that, no one in *this* anthology would do such a thing."

I pray and trust not, though I don't see why or how there could ever be a guarantee. Someone might have poison in their medicine chest—will they use it? That aside, writing by shortcut, by stock phrase, by shorthand code aimed at those who don't need anything named or explained because they're known to agree with the writer already—this kind of writing is pernicious and harmful in another and deeply important way: It allows, even encourages, the *disappearance* of thinking, the substitution of words *for* thinking, and, finally, the absence of thinking entirely.

In other words, writing of this kind—as we see it here and throughout the anthology—fools even the writers themselves, who in fact don't *know* what they're saying and don't *know* what they mean.

They *feel* that they mean something. And what they *feel* is that they mean something *good*.

And, having fooled themselves that they knew what they meant when they *didn't* know, they end up producing writing that's just like television for the very reason that *there's nothing in it*.

This emptiness grows more clear in Abinader's essay, even though, in this respect, as we'll see, she's not the anthology's worst offender.

Her essay reaches its intellectual turning point when she suggests —through the oblique negative that we've looked at—that politics has *some* kind of relation to her apparent isolation and victimization. Again, these are concepts that she only asserts but doesn't show: She is, in short, writing in code again, since those who know the truth don't need to hear it said. And what is that truth? All we hear is that she "did not feel welcome outside the door."

As for why *not,* we must take the matter on faith. Well, it's obvious, it's because she's *Arab,* someone might cry out in disbelief. But her being Arab is not a *reason,* certainly not to me and certainly not to myriad others I know. Any *true* reason why she may feel—or *be*—unwelcome remains unsaid, unspoken, and, to us, unknown.

A perfectly fair question for the reader to ask is this one: Does *she* know the reasons? After all, to repeat, every writer alone is responsible for what's said—just as every writer alone is responsible for what's not said—in a piece of writing. Both of these bedrock truths of English 101, however, are facts little known, tolerated, or understood by those dwelling in the Age of Simplification.

More unstating, unquestioning, unshowing, unexamining carries Abinader through her next flurry of familiar and at times contradictory assertions. Typical of the Age of Simplification's "soft" denizens—accustomed to the "rights" of easiness, of being "entertained," of instant gratification—Abinader tells us that she didn't like the homework her professors assigned:

> [In] my classroom, in my bachelor's and master's program, some years later, the literature we read was as foreign to my natural sensibility as Barbie was to my childhood milieu.

I'm going to ask a question. The reader will perhaps be so good as to think for a moment and then come up with two reasons why my asking it would be considered outrageous, illogical, and unacceptable by Abinader, her fellow anthologized writers, and, very possibly if not probably, by the State Department.

The writer has said she didn't like the assigned literature and that it was as "foreign" to her "natural sensibility" as a Barbie doll.

My question is: So?

If this were a classroom, we could pause for a moment while people pondered first my question itself, then my questions *about* the question. But there can be little doubt that Abinader and the other group one writers would indeed be outraged at the fact of my asking "So?" But the important question is the second one: *Why would they be outraged?*

A parallel example might help.

Suppose that Abinader had said, "I don't like spinach," and I'd answered with the question, "So?"

Would there be outrage? Of course not. Why is there outrage, then, when all she said was, "I didn't like the literature we read"?

Here are the two answers:

1. It's different in the second case because there the author is speaking in *code*. In the corollary example, "spinach" means "spinach," and that's all. But "the literature we read" is code, *and unless we're on the inside, we don't know what it stands for* (and, very possibly, neither does the writer, though that's an additional and more complicated matter, for later).

2. And the second case is different from the spinach case because, in the Age of Simplification, speaking in code *is a right.* And not only can you not *attack* someone or *criticize* them for exercising their *rights,* but neither can you so much as show *any disrespect toward them whatsoever* when or as they are exercising those *rights.*

I said earlier that the gathered "ethnicity" essays were characterized by their smallness and simplicity of theme, then by their fallacious thinking. Both characteristics are intertwined as Abinader brings her own to a close.

Let us return to the matter of the assigned literature that Abinader said was "foreign to [her] natural sensibility," whatever that may have been, since, again, we aren't told. The author *does* say the following, which I cite in a single quote even though it raises more than one question:

The models for writers included a substantial number of European-identified male authors who wrote eloquently about mainstream American culture. In my writing corner of the world, I penned stories of children dying during the Ottoman siege of our village in Lebanon. I felt music in my poetry that was strange to American ears; my images gathered in a shiny brocade of detail, more lush than other writing of the 1970s.

As you can see, most of the passage is, again, in code, one thing after another nonwritten, nonsaid, nondetailed—because the author assumes her readers to have prior understanding of what she means *and* to be in prior agreement with it. In this sense, the passage and indeed most of the essay are *unwritten*. Almost everything in it is vague. *Male* writers—oh, now I understand *exactly* what you mean. *Mainstream* American culture—would that be fast food? Foreign policy? Jazz music? Streets and roads? These males did, in any case, write "eloquently," whatever that means, and whatever Abinader means *by* it (hint to reader: it's code for something mainly bad). Now, we know already, from the essayist, that these males' writing was "foreign" to her "natural sensibility." Earlier, when I asked my "So?" question on this point, I did it in order to point out Abinader's heavy reliance on code. But two other points need to be clarified in regard to the same passage: one about the applicability of the word "soft" and one about the applicability of the word "simple."

When people used to read Emerson, for example, or Melville, or when people used to be serious about writers like, say, Camus, Sartre, Simone de Beauvoir—in those times, the idea of *self-reliance* was still very much alive, widely understood to play a vitally important part in much of the greatest American and European literature. Self-reliance was centrally important in the art of figures as different from one another as, say, Emily Dickinson and Mark Twain, or as both of those are different from Fyodor Dostoevsky.

Now, though, self-reliance has disappeared almost entirely from the worlds of academia, literature, and the arts: the concept—in the French writers I've mentioned, in Beckett, in countless others—that each and every human being is a free agent and accordingly is responsible not only for everything he or she does, but also for everything that he or she *doesn't* do. This grand, high, austere, profoundly serious, intense, and demanding idea, however, has, in the Age of Simplification, been taken over and replaced by the simple, in fact the puerile, concept of *rights*.

There was a time when, if a person, particularly in academia, felt that their natural sensibilities weren't in tune with, say, a certain literature, music, artistic period, or genre, it was up to that out-of-tune person to discover what merit, if any, resided in the genre or period sufficient to make it part—perhaps a required part—of an education. In other words, it was once understood that the world did not turn around any one individual or exist to please one person, but that, instead, the world held treasures that were greater than any one person and that it was up to each to become familiar with the world, not for the *world* to bend to the pleasure of each.

As time passed, though, buzzwords like "relevance" came along, flattering the individual that the world should bend to it, not it to the world, and the curricular changes of the late 1960s and early 1970s built further on that same foundation of the self-involved. By then, too, the *aesthetic* of the mass media had grown sufficiently omnipresent, powerful, and transformative as to cause people—largely by making them increasingly self-centered and passive—to begin judging reality and the nature of existence by the *mass media's* portrayal of reality and the nature of existence rather than by the real world's.

The result is the powerful shortsightedness of the full-blown "me-ism" whose effects are evident everywhere in the Abinader essay and in the other essays of the ethnicity group. What began as an assumption has by now rigidified into a bedrock foundation with the unexamined authority of an article of religious faith: not the old-fashioned "I must examine and explain the world," but the new "the world must understand me." The unanalyzed *self* as the center of things, and as the point at which all vision originates, also makes the lapse into code all the more understandable: The important thing—the only thing—is what the writer *is* and what the writer *knows;* and it's the writer's job to know what she knows, to be what she is, but no longer her job, first, to analyze and examine what she is and what she knows, and then, second, to set about explaining those things *to* the world. A paradigm change, in short, has taken place: The world is now to be judged in reference to the individual, the individual no longer in reference to the world.

❖   ❖   ❖

What kind of clarity, strength, and power are achievable through a literary art born and nurtured in an age like this one, an age of the puerile, an Age of Simplification? I mentioned the buzzword "relevance" a moment ago. A new buzzword has arisen lately and is used just as commonly in discussions of writing and the literary arts as it is everywhere else. The word is the noun "issue," or "issues," and, revealingly, it seems to have replaced the words "subject" and "theme," as they would be used in asking, "What are the central subjects or themes in *Hamlet?*" Now, you're as likely to hear, "What are the issues raised by *Hamlet?*"

The change is seemingly picayune, but its implications for the arts are enormous. Consider the concluding sections of Abinader's essay, where she tells about coming upon Maxine Hong Kingston's *The Woman Warrior* and finding it an inspiration:

> This book not only led me to the body of literature available in the Chinese-American canon, but I found African-American, Latino, Native American writers, whose voices resounded about some of the same issues: belonging, identity, cultural loneliness, community, and exoticization.

The end of a literary essay is where we expect its clarity, strength, power, and insight to be hinted at or gathered in some kind of revelation or at least in some kind of emphatic close. As we near the close of Abinader's essay, though, the end of things seems to be a non-end; the achievement to be a non-achievement; the result a non-result. Literary works, it seems, aren't even any longer literary works, but they are "voices" that are "about" things, and these things are called "issues." And what *are* these "issues"? Well, at the very least we can say that they have to do not with writing, but with the writer. In the passage above, the phrase could just as well be recast to read "whose voices resounded about some of the same issues: me, me, me, me, and me."

Now I'll have to defend myself. I can imagine that what I just said will seem even more insensitive and rude than my hypothetical question, earlier, of "So?"

So let me explain.

The subject of the State Department anthology, presumably, is literature, which is to say *writing*. The subject within *that* subject is the meaning of being an *American* literary writer ("The assignment: In what sense do you see yourself as an American writer?"). But the essayists aren't doing their assignment. We'll find that in the first group none of the essays are about writing, none are about literature, none are about writing *in* America, and *none are even about being a writer.*

The plain truth is that nothing of literary import is said in any of the seven "ethnicity" essays that couldn't rightly and justly be said by *anyone*. In truth, the only thing about the essayists being writers that matters in the least conceivable way is this: *If they hadn't been writers in the first place, they wouldn't have been asked to contribute.*

But they haven't *told* us anything about writing or *said* anything that even identifies them as writers—aside, that is, from *saying* that they write, citing their own titles, and so on.

Why on earth do you suppose not?

Let's look and see. Abinader comments that "the chant of school-yard slurs would intensify." And when her family came to the United States from the Dominican Republic, Julia Alvarez tells us, "for the first time in my life I experienced prejudice and playground cruelty." I ask: Of whom, of how many others throughout the history of the world might the substance of these remarks not *also* be true? *When* have groups *not* molested, oppressed, maligned, or held back *other* groups? When in the history of the world has the malignancy of such oppression *not* been a part of the human story? When has there been a time when kids did *not* experience "playground cruelty"?

The answer, as everyone knows, is never. That doesn't mean it isn't all hateful, ignorant, and bigoted that groups behave this way. But there's another point, one more relevant to the subject at hand. And that point is that nowhere, ever, in all the histories of all the peoples in all the civilizations and nations on all the continents, has anyone ever had to be a *writer* in order to know these things, experience these things, or even to commit these things.

Says Alvarez, "My sisters and I were caught between worlds, value systems, languages, customs," and adds later: "Under pressure from its own marginalized populations and from its growing number of immigrants, the nation was being forced to acknowledge its own diversity and become more inclusive." This is an anyperson, not a writer, talking, a person who, although without a sure grip on the history of immigration, is clearly interested not in writing but in an "issue," however important she or others may consider that issue. We do know that Alvarez addresses the matter with shaky grammar and enormous cliché ("We are becoming a planet of racial and cultural hybrids. We need an open mind and a big heart and a compassionate imagination to allow for all the combinations we are becoming as a nation and as a human family"), though in this particular failing she runs a distant second to Naomi Shihab Nye, whose essay is positively vibrant with banality and cliché ("Have people lived up to their best dreams of what human beings could be? Have we helped one another enough? How often do we really listen to others? . . . Does greed guide too many decisions?").

One more point, then on to the next group of essays. We won't learn anything further by remaining longer with the first group, but, even so, the intellectual penury and the slightness that inform that group are revealed in one last way that deserves notice. It also, this time around, *does* make me feel sorry for this batch of writers, just as it makes me feel sorry for us all who live in a starved, mal-treated, and endangered nation.

As she brings her shower of platitudes to a close, Nye describes a multiethnic gathering and remarks of it that "this festival feels like a reunion, since we have all met before and read one another's work and value the power of communication above everything else." But communication of *what?* Here yet again, in Nye, we have a writer who isn't a writer but instead is a person concerned with something other than writing, an "issue." In Nye's case this issue appears to be multiculturalism, whatever that might really mean. "How various we are," the author enthuses, "in our eccentric, multi-colored land, our trails dotting so many landscapes, cultures and histories up till now," with the fairly clear result that, in Nye's case, multicultural-ism seems to mean nothing more than a *feeling*, not unlike Elmaz Abinader's when she declares that, "in addition, I found a commu-nity" made up of "American writers and artists of color."

And so the great question—communication of *what?*—finds its answer: of feeling. Once again we find ourselves in the very deeps of the Age of Simplification, where feeling really has successfully replaced thinking, and, worse, has done so within groups of a kind that most clearly seem to *believe* themselves to be powerfully and purposefully adversarial against the corporate-consumerist state. The truth is, however, that they themselves have not only been created *by* that very state but have been formed and manipulated by it into a condition of near-perfect impotence as regards any hope of raising fruitful opposition against it.

The pathos is intensified by some of Nye's subsequent words:

> To this day, no one has ever said to me, *You cannot say that thing.* They may have said, *Thank you, but we do not wish to publish this thing,* or, *This thing could certainly be improved upon,* but they have not said, *You cannot say it.* [emphasis in original]

Immersed in, surrounded by, inhaling, even *wearing* the omnipresent aesthetic of the corporate mass media; being urged by it monthly, weekly, daily, hourly to revel in self-consideration; to put feeling in the place of thinking without knowing or seeing what one has done; to be equally and similarly disoriented and misled by a failed and corrupted academia; to have all this happen to you; to undergo the metamorphosis, as if by some diabolic equivalent of lobotomy, of your intellect itself into a happy little chamber of airy nothingness; to undergo all of this and *then* to show your gratitude by raising childish hymns of thanksgiving for the guarantees of the First Amendment—such a thing evokes not just pathos but hints at the true extent of the danger facing us:

> Freedom of speech is the greatest gift America has given us all and I will treasure it forever and continue to remind people about it because sometimes if you have had it forever, you don't realize you have it.

five

Of the five writers in the "very best" group, Robert Creeley and Billy Collins demonstrate virtues similar to those of all five, but the two poets are the most interesting *and* entertaining. In the interests of space and time, I will focus on them.

It's not really surprising that in turning to this group one finds oneself suddenly back among actual *literary* people and no longer stifled by the Age of Simplification. The reason for this is—age. Billy Collins was born in my own birth-year of 1941, Robert Pinsky in 1940, and Robert Creeley, who died shortly after the writing of this book, fourteen years earlier even than that. These are writers who not only lived in the world *before* 1947 but also watched the process of simplification as it took place, impossibilities for any young poet, artist, or academician born in, say, 1974. The Age of Simplification comes closer and closer to a diabolic perfection as there become fewer and fewer people with any living memory from before 1947.

And the difference is stunning, extraordinary, amazing: Both Collins and Creeley write on the subject as assigned. Both demonstrate the ability to talk about themselves *with* objectivity, *without* solipsism or a sense of righteousness, *without* code, and *without* drifting from, dropping, or losing the subject of literary art. Both are poets, both know that what poets do is write poetry, and so, in talking about the self, each talks about the *poetry-producing* self. Both, too, show themselves able to talk capably about ethnicity, identity, and origins, and to do so in ways that are *germane to the questions* their essays are seeking to address.

Both know what they're talking about (what it means to be an American writer), and both talk about it well. And, perhaps above all, unlike *any other writer* in the first (or, as we'll see, in the last) group, *both Collins and Creeley not only have senses of humor but excellent ones!*

The significance of this last point is immeasurable: The rigidity, the partitioned quality, of the minds of those in group one, the characteristics of intellect and attitude that make them unable to think about things broadly without falling into code or cliché, or, equally important, that make them unable to think about *more than one thing at a time*—these characteristics not only wipe out every last possibility of humor, but, more dreadful still, eliminate all possibility of these thinkers being able to function as literary artists who in any way really *are* literary.

What distinguishes art from argument, and has done so ever since time began, is the fact or presence of aesthetic complexity.[10]

Here may not be the place to talk about this idea at length, but it's the presence of exactly this complexity in the essays of Collins and Creeley that floods them with meaning, life, resiliency, color, energy. They're *literary*. And, in consequence, they're like the fresh breezes of the open sea in contrast with the small, windowless, airless, puritanical rooms that are the minds of the writers in the other groups.

The "complexity" that makes art what it is—this complexity doesn't have to be (though at times it is) hard, difficult, or onerous. Sophocles' *Oedipus Rex* is a classic example: Never was there an *easier* play to read, yet never was there a play more alive with ambiguity, irony, misprision, and the *production of content through aesthetic means*.

Without the presence of complexity of this kind, art goes dead. That presence doesn't have to occur in great amounts, but it must be there, at the heart and inception of the thing. If it's at the heart, it will inform the whole.

The very *nature*, then, of the Age of Simplification works against the essence, the soul, the very nature of art.

Collins calls his own essay "What's American About American Poetry?," and that, indeed, is what he writes about: American poetry.

He starts with Walt Whitman, saying that, "Surely, Whitman was the first poet to try to get his arms around the continent so as to hold the lumberjack and the secretary and the Eskimo in one loving cosmic embrace." Here are "ethnicity," "class," and "origins," the claptrap of the Age of Simplification, yet all treated not as "issues" but as and for what they are, part of the land and of its life, and part of the *poetry* of that land.

Listen to Collins for a moment as he continues:

> If a writer is the sum of his or her influences, then my own poems are unavoidably the result of my exposure to the sounds and styles of both British and American poetry. I even find myself playing one diction off against another, usually for ironic effect. But more specifically, in thinking about myself as an "American poet," and thus committing the dangerous act of auto-literary criticism, I find that a number of my poems seem determined to establish an American rootedness distinct from European influence.

The focus, the exactness, the staying on the subject, the direct and clear statement *of* the subject—none of these are incompatible with the poet's lightness or humor. This compatibility is the result of the *complexity* I spoke of, the ability to hold more than a single thing in the mind at once. Here, this mental facility even permits the humor to be *self-deprecating,* a form of complexity no longer conceivable or possible in the Age of Simplification, where people, unable to experience two or more divergent and simultaneous responses to the same thing, have lost their ability to perceive irony, so that self-deprecation is taken, all amiss, all wrong, and all flatly, as self-*criticism.*

Before turning to Creeley, look for a moment at the same presence of complexity—and humor—as Collins talks, not about "ethnicity" or "national origin" (though he does), not about "class" or "rank" or "elitism" (though he does), but as he talks about the *bricks* of poetry—the words—American style as opposed to British:

> I had never really considered myself a particularly American poet until I went to England some years ago to give a series of readings. I had put the tour together myself, and it looked

it. The odd range of venues included a sixth form class, a jazz club in Brighton, a college of Sheffield University, and a community center in a small Yorkshire village. It was at this last site, by the way, that an elderly, agrarian-looking man rose from the audience during a question-and-answer session to ask: "Mr. Collins, are *all* your poems written in prose?" But regardless of the audience or the venue, each reading left me with the same small but nagging realization: that my poems were written not in English but in American. At every reading I could sense dead spots occurring when I would utter a phrase such as "eggs over easy" or "sweat the final." I became convinced that the mention of "a state flower" in one of my poems must sound to the British ear like "estate flower." I was discovering that idiomatic American is difficult to translate not only into French or German, but into English. Just as one cannot understand what it is to be an American until one leaves the country, I was not aware of my own American voice—my written accent, so to speak—until I had faced several audiences of British listeners.

✤ ✤ ✤

Creeley, too, fulfills the given assignment with focus, wit, sensitivity, humor, and seriousness. He moves to the subject of the poetry *of* America after saying a word or two about poetry *in* America: "If the sad events of September 11, 2001, provoked a remarkable use of poems as a means wherewith to find a common and heartfelt ground for sorrow, it passed quickly as the country regained its equilibrium, turned to the conduct of an aggressive war, and, one has to recognize, went back to making money."

These words then follow, unintentionally apropos to a discussion of the Age of Simplification:

Is poetry of such little consequence in this country because it does not "make money," can be hardly called a "profession" or even a sensible "vocation," seems most aptly undertaken by adolescents and older, emotional women? Does poetry "tell" us anything of any relevance? What does it *mean?* All those questions have clear and very simple answers—but they will not be found here. Rather, one wants it recognized that, in America, poetry prompts a response much as Marianne Moore's ironic first line, "Poetry? I too dislike it." Another artist once said, "Poets are like harmonica players. Terrific, but not much use for them."

So that's a sad condition to work in, like bad air, poor light, long hours. Who would ever think to be a poet in this country if he did not feel literally that he had to be?

Creeley's wit of omission is as unlikely to succeed in the Age of Simplification as was Collins's humor of self-deprecation: "All those questions have clear and very simple answers—but they will not be found here." Rather than feeling drawn in by the mystery of the unsaid—which makes one want the *more,* not the *less,* to know what those answers might be—readers today are likely to resent Creeley as arch and elitist, a hoarder, a keeper of secrets, and thus resent and ignore him. After all, to enjoy—or under*stand*—this kind of wit, a reader must be not only willing but easily able to keep at least three things in mind simultaneously: one being the significance of what Creeley *is* saying, another being the significance of what he is *not* saying, while yet another is the significance of the irony created by the tension between the two.

In good literary writing by gifted, well-trained, and capable literary people, easiness and simplicity (albeit, admittedly, sometimes without directness) in giving answers to a question can be the point. But the point, though never the *only* one, can also be *complexity* of the kind we're talking about here—at once handmaiden to and producer of nuance, subtlety, tone, mood, and, yes, irony, *all* of these missing entirely or being gravely endangered in the writers, writing, and thought of the Age of Simplification.

Again, since the word I'm using is "complexity," and because, as we've seen, the very notion of complexity is anathema to the Age of Simplification—for these reasons, let me repeat that the aim is *not* difficulty, obscurantism, exclusion, or elitism: The aim is the production of meaning through aesthetic structures.

And possibly most important of all—though tragically lost on those of the Age of Simplification—is that the meaning produced or expressed in this way—the art-meaning—*can't be expressed or produced in any other way.* This fact itself—that art means what art means—is part of what has driven whole generations of writers *away* from literature, the writers in the State Department anthology's first group being prime examples. They write, yes, but they aren't writers, certainly not literary ones. The logic of what happened to them is cruel, dismal, and plain. As the process of intellectual simplification went forward, the ability to *respond to the complex* was also lessened, grew weak, and died. With the loss of that ability went necessarily also the loss of a love for literature and for the art of literature. The cause of *that* loss was that people, their intellects having been simplified, were no longer able to *respond to* the art-meaning, were no longer able to *receive* the art-meaning, and thus remained blindly unaware of just how full and whole and rich and human and felt and engaging that meaning is. To them, capable of hearing amid such great wealth only a tiny part, the equivalent, say, of a single instrument's voice out of all the glories of a Beethoven symphony: Being capable of only that much, they turned their backs on literature, thinking of it as being *insufficiently related to life.*

Their writing stopped being art and became message. Elmaz Abinader, unwittingly, speaks directly to this point, praising it as a good thing: "Now I began to understand," she says. "As a writer, I was also an activist." The truth, though, would have to be phrased differently. The *joining* of writing and activism that Abinader believes in is in actuality the abandoning of one thing for another. At the very least, she would have to say that as an activist she was no longer a *literary* writer. Or that, in joining activism with writing, she had become a *message* writer. Neither she nor Creeley, it's true, is writing poetry or fiction in the State Department anthology, but the essays themselves speak in ways that are literary or not, full and rich, on the one hand, or thin and flat, on the other, harmonic and historied and humane, on the one hand, or toneless and shallow and issue-driven, on the other. Look, for example, at this passage from Creeley, at the way he starts *from* poets and poetry and then, widening and widening, ends with an embrace of the nation, perhaps of the world:

> My generation was for years divided between those who followed T. S. Eliot's instance and so looked to a classically developed poetry in the English tradition and those as myself who doggedly followed Dr. [William Carlos] Williams. When he was asked where it was he had got his "diction," he answered curtly, "Out of the mouths of Polish mothers." We wanted, much as Charles Olson puts it, "to leave the roots on." We wanted our writing to be fact of our own social body, evidence of our own collective family person, our Polish, Irish, Italian, German, Chinese, African, French, Russian mothers and fathers, uncles, cousins, and neighbors.

How beautifully, naturally, humanely, democratically, feelingly, uncondescendingly said: "Out of the mouths of Polish mothers." And how wonderfully natural, Olson's metaphor of wanting "to leave the roots on." Oh, sorrow, sorrow, oh, sorrow. For all the incessant talk, everywhere around us, of roots, origins, ethnicities, and identities, the truth is that in the Age of Simplification the roots of us all, of the nation itself, are thin, unseen, diseased, hardly left on at all.

six

In ending this chapter, I turn to two of the three well-known literary writers whose essays in the State Department anthology fail so badly, so abysmally, as to be almost spectacular. I have scrutinized, pondered, studied, and restudied these three pieces (because of space, time, and duplication of effect, I'll discuss only two of them here) in an effort to identify exactly what it is that goes so wrong in them—wrong in very nearly the same way—and *why*. The conclusion I've come to is simply that none of these writers have any idea *what* to say about the assigned question, since none are able to answer it, strain and wrestle as they may.

This is the group that I've called the "true worst," since the writers are more eminent and a reader may thus expect more of them. From the start, though, the essays here reveal certain of the characteristics of the essays back in the first, or "ethnicity," group. Like those, these are devoid of humor. Also like those, these are stunningly deaf to platitude. At the same time, though, there's a major difference between those earlier essays and these three.

The first group reduced literature to message, and the writers showed themselves unable to think with, through, or by means of what I've called "complexity." They made it very clear that they had *some* kind of an agenda, that the agenda had to do with a sense of oppression, and that it necessitated their having, "as writers," *some* kind of relationship with the political structures around them—with, that is, the state or nation. The oppression agenda was inconsistent, the state at some times being oppressor and at other times liberator, the writers thus swinging back and forth between biting the State Department hand that fed them and blindly kissing it. Inconsistent, simplistic, anti-intellectual, nonliterary, and unimaginably narrow, the agenda nevertheless, and therefore the relationship, *were* there and *did* exist.

Now, however, the agenda is absent. The third group of essayists will occasionally allude to it or extend false pieties to it, but it holds no genuine interest for them. Logic says that its absence *should* be a good thing, since as a medium of relationship between the writer and the state, it is fallacious at worst and highly inadequate at best. Its absence *ought* to allow our last three writers, no longer blinkered by the ethnicity agenda, to see more deeply and accurately into the "American writer" question. In this way, they should be able to identify, for better or for worse, what real, actual, or authentic relationship exists between the nation and them, between America and the writer.

The ethnicity agenda's absence, however, has no such result. What happens, shockingly, is that without the agenda—possibly I should say without *some* agenda—not one of the three authors, as I've said, is able to answer the question, with the result that all three fail the assignment. This failure can mean only one thing. It can mean only that they *see* no relationship, *can't* see it. The three writers, in other words, have gone blind.

❖   ❖   ❖

The essay by Sven Birkerts, though wooden ("I felt . . . that I had at last come to grips with the major issues of identity formation") and never particularly compelling, is nevertheless the least overtly dramatic failure in the group of three (Birkerts, Butler, and Ford, Ford being the worst). However dully, the essay at the start actually seems to be answering the State Department's question as Birkerts fills us in as to his having been born (in 1951, in Michigan) to Latvian parents who had been displaced by World War II. All the young Birkerts wanted, we learn, "was to shed every trace of foreignness—otherness—and to become a full-fledged American." He goes on—

> As I ached with all my being for an American normalcy and blazed with ill-concealed shame at the slightest mark of our

difference, I went through my days playing a role, imitating my fortunate friends, wearing one mask after another, simulating in my least mannerism, my every slangy turn of phrase, a belonging I never felt for a moment.

—and eventually comes to the subject of his reading habits: *Catcher in the Rye, A Separate Peace,* Thomas Wolfe, for starters. Then on to *Portnoy's Complaint,* from there to Allen Ginsberg and "Howl" ("my revisionist American Bible"), LeRoi Jones, Frantz Fanon. "The change, the awakening, came," he tells us, when he was in his "late 20s"—that is, in the late 1970s. "I was living in Cambridge, barely supporting myself working as a bookstore clerk, profoundly depressed by the collapse of a long relationship, and utterly stalled in my efforts to write fiction." But:

> If there was any light, any sanity, in my life, it was reading. Always a reader, I went at it with a genuine fervor during this period. Days, weeks, months marched by outside the window while I sat in a cheap sling chair in my little room in the apartment I shared with a young would-be poet, smoking cigarettes and reading novels. More specifically, I read foreign novels, novels in translation, European novels. I read Knut Hamsun and Thomas Mann and Max Frisch and Heinrich Böll and a dozen others, the more obscure the better. I found myself drawn to the settings of these novels, the moods, to everything that made them different from the domestic fiction I had been reading for years. I had no sense, though—none that I recall—of being drawn toward anything that felt like my own culture of origin. I just read and steered my daydreaming self through these strangely kindred atmospheres.

The signs up to this point that Birkerts is getting much of anywhere in his essay aren't good. There's the autobiographical structure again, by no means an offense in itself, as we've agreed, yet seeming here just to be putting everything on hold while the author waits—and waits—to discover whether he'll actually have something to say. Presumably, we're going to learn *something* about the intellectual-emotional state that Birkerts earlier says he felt himself to be in at this point. His "desire to assimilate," he says, had "deepened" his "intuition of difference, of being somehow deeply alien, of not truly possessing those 'inalienable' rights advertised in the Constitution."

Why anyone would use the verb "advertised" in such a context, I don't know. I do know, however, that Birkerts is doing nothing to convince me that he really did ever feel anything like an "intuition of difference," of being "deeply alien." What on earth does he mean? Did he *really* have a deeply felt intuition that, say, the Bill of Rights didn't apply to him? If so, it certainly isn't made felt or real here. Nor is a slighter, merely *social* sense of alienation made evident to the reader—if anything, Birkerts's details make this period of his life seem pleasant, dedicated, centered, even cozy, with those long snug days of reading, working in a bookstore, having a "relationship," sharing a Cambridge apartment with a poet. If there's angst, alienation, or a deep intuition of "difference," I for one just don't believe it.

Of course, it could be true. But the real point is that the writer hasn't shown it, and, as we've seen before, in matters of writing, what's not there isn't there. Whatever the writer hasn't put in isn't in.

And so we come, in this "true worst" group of essays, to the equivalent of the "code" writing that we saw in the first writers. But unlike that group's writing, it isn't a matter here of agenda, propaganda, or message. What we find instead, in some ways an even more perfect example of the erosion and intellectual destructiveness of the Age of Simplification, is *empty* writing.

✤ ✤ ✤

And so, in Birkerts's essay, what happens? Answer: two things, neither good. First, the author rambles on further with his own kind of "code"—writing that *postures* as though it were actually about something but isn't able to show that it really *is* about that thing. After that, there's a kind of strange, discomfiting shudder—and Birkerts reveals that he is altogether directionless, that he, too, has, in effect, gone blind.

The code section first. The author tells us that he got started as a writer of critical essays—that is, had his "breakthrough"—when he "fell into the extraordinary world of Robert Musil's great epic of pre-war Viennese life, *The Man Without Qualities*." What happened, apparently, is that Birkerts fell in love with the atmosphere of Musil's Vienna, read about it widely and deeply, and, as a result, experienced a transference:

> I mean: In living for so long inside this vividly imagined world, I was, in essence, connecting with the story-world I had grown up with. Musil's Vienna—the times, the culture, the brooding baroque *mise en scene*—was in many ways a filter for Riga, for the lives of my grandparents and, to a lesser degree, my parents in the childhoods I had dreamed for them.

After he wrote an essay on Musil, and after that essay had "led to others," Birkerts discovered that he "had staked out a particular literary terrain" as a critic "who would broker between American literary culture and the great richness of literature in translation, mainly European." He follows up these remarks by citing the titles of his first three books of critical essays. And then comes the discomfiting moment.

> I linger thus over my literary resume because it makes what suddenly seems like an obvious point, though one that I was

oblivious to for years: that the whole path of my life—writing life included—has been profoundly conditioned, first by the determined rejection, and then the veiled acceptance of my culture of origins, and that this dynamic has been conditioned at the deepest root level by a very powerful, if distorted, sense of what it means to be American.

The author's flagrant breach of the old rule—"Write with nouns and verbs, not with adjectives and adverbs"—is revealing.[11] As the persuasive ring of plain truth or probability diminishes, the language puffs up, as though Birkerts hopes he can *force* his unshown and undemonstrated idea to be taken as true (or to *be* true) if he can just attach enough hot-air balloons to lift it—"profoundly," "determined," "veiled," "deepest root level," "very powerful," "distorted."

Then, after the verbiage of this inflated non-dog, comes the non-tail that *appears* to be trying to wag it: a "very powerful, if distorted, sense of what it means to be American." The confusion here, the wheel-spinning, the *naming* of the question but not the answering of it, are astonishing. When he thinks we're not looking, Birkerts slips in this neatly packaged little unit and tacks it onto his inflated dog, perhaps hoping that we'll *actually believe it's really a tail* if only for the fact that it comes at the end of the dog.

But it isn't, although it does. The truth is that Birkerts's glib paragraph-ender is as perfect an example of empty writing as one may ever see. Go back in his text, scour it, return to the first of the 2,864 words in the essay, and reread every one of them, right up to the 2,570th word, the one that ends the phrase "means to be American." What you'll find is that *nowhere* in those preceding 2,569 words does Birkerts say, tell, show, define, or demonstrate "what it means to be American." And yet his entire essay, his fulfillment of the assignment given to him by the State Department for display to people all over the world—all of this depends on his satisfactorily clearing up the meaning of "what it means to be American."

What will possibly happen? Birkerts is almost in the end zone: There are only 294 words left in the essay, so if he's going to define what he means, he'll have to be quick about it. Will he succeed?

Let's follow along and see.

The start isn't strong. "I am talking here," Birkerts says, "about the primitive, almost pre-logical compulsion I felt as a son of recent immigrants to merge myself with the world I saw around me, a world which, owing to accidents (or fates) of place and time, took on an absolute aspect."

No definition here of what being American means, but instead just a repeat of the idea from the essay's start, that in high school the writer *really* wanted to be like the other kids—with his language, again, being used in an effort to pump things up, as in "took on an absolute aspect." (And what's the difference between "accidents" and "fates"?)

If the definition is coming, it's crucial that it come now. But it doesn't, as Birkerts again slides away from the needed point: "Interestingly, though, it was not just my chimera. This America [that] I sought mapped [that is, matched] almost perfectly to the stereotype that is to this day prominent, if not dominant, in the global image culture: the prosperous, athletic, decent, white all-American."

Maybe it matched and maybe not, whatever "the global image culture" means. Anyway, we're no closer to what we want. In fact, Birkerts's next sentence all of a sudden goes *so* far away from explaining what being American means that one thinks at first the author may have stumbled into a real breakthrough; that he may have actually glimpsed what his essay is really about.

"In buying the American Dream," he writes, "which I did with such zealous intensity, I was really buying a fantasy spun for me by Madison Avenue."

Can it be? Has the author at this very, very late point, after plowing through 2,677 words, with only 187 more to go, has he now *finally* seen this truth of what it means to be an American in the Age of Simplification—that one lives amidst, is surrounded by, *swims* among, lies? If only he could have *begun* his essay at this point. And, even more to be wished, if only he could have *stuck with* this point for at least some greater *part* of a paragraph or even just a few sentences—but not so. Child of the Age of Simplification, he is incapable of thinking, of *seeing*, for himself. Perhaps for that one single sentence, he does see. But does he even *know* what he has seen? Does he know what it *means* that he has seen it? Impossible. Certainly not. If he knew, he would have stuck with it, he would have explored it and explained it. Instead, in less than the time it takes to read five of these words, he drops it by the roadside and picks up another parallel and prefabricated falsehood to put in its place—all the while thinking that now he's onto the truth.

Watch.

He "bought" the "Madison Avenue" (that is, the mass media) hucksterism and delusion about what being American means, but then he saw that that was "a fantasy." His next sentence suggests that it wasn't exactly *he* who saw through the lies, but that he was "jolted" by the 1960s into seeing through them. ("It took the '60s to jolt me from those complacencies.")

Still, that would be good enough, anyone would agree. In whatever way it comes about, seeing is preferable to being blind, or to being complacent.

Except that, jolted or not, Birkerts *didn't* escape complacency, *didn't* start seeing for himself. And if he didn't do those things, why on earth not? Certainly, he must have *chosen* to see. Certainly, he must have *wanted* to see. The only possible answer is that he *couldn't* see.

Instead, he switches from one fantasy, one complacency, to another, apparently thinking or imagining that he has switched from not seeing to seeing.

Here is the first half of the passage where it happens.

Then [that is, during the 1960s], driven by the contrarian emancipatory energies of the counterculture and the encounters of
experience, as well as by the recognitions of an ever-widening
grasp of domestic and global reality—I set myself against the
tyranny of that stereotype. I fought to reject these most deeply
planted residues, and flattered myself—don't we all?—that I had
succeeded.

If naming things as and for what they actually are is a mark of clear
thinking and clear seeing, the grade here isn't going to be very
high. Whole mouthfuls of words fill space and yet say or name
nothing—"contrarian emancipatory energies of the counterculture"
can't mean much to anyone who doesn't already think that he or
she *knows* what it means, as I'm sure many do think and perhaps
even do know. But "the encounters of experience"? Can experience
not be encountered? And what does he possibly mean? Experience of what? What *kind* of experience? Then there's the phrase
"recognitions of an ever-widening grasp of domestic and global
reality"—a *real* blast from the airbag that boils down to "my growing grasp of reality," or perhaps "my growing grasp of reality at
home and abroad."

But *what* reality? The reality *of what?* What *is* that reality?

These are English 101 sins of the most elementary kind, typical
of the inexperienced or unmotivated student who *always* prefers
the abstract to the concrete for the very good reason that it's so very
much easier that way: Nothing really ever needs to be *named, said,
identified,* or *shown,* and one can write and write without, in actuality, having said or thought through a single thing. The method has a
very familiar old name alluding to bulls and something that comes
out of the back of them, and it works fine in freshman English or in
essay exams in history or literature—until, that is, the paper comes
back with a grade of D– or F. Or used to.

Still, freshman writing is one thing. But what can it conceivably mean about the world we live in, about our nation, academia, the intellectual life of America and its people's ability to think or see clearly, that we find work of this sort coming not from a first-year student, seventeen or eighteen years old and just out of high school, but from a fifty-three-year-old widely published and well-known academic literary figure and essayist in a piece solicited[12] by the U.S. Department of State for distribution around the world on the subject of what it *means* to be an American writer?

Birkerts hasn't yet told us, *or* the world, what it means, and he's not going to, either, in the 116 words left in his essay.

What he's going to do instead is proudly inform us (and the world) that he has rejected one stereotype for another and that he now clings fervently to the new one. This seems to me akin to a man with one wooden leg going into the hospital, then coming out proud to announce that he now has *two* made of wood.

"And indeed," Birkerts continues from where we left off,

> I like to think that whatever I now comprehend as American has everything to do with notions of ethnicity and diversity (obligatory buzz-phrase though it is), and that transformed awareness exerts pressure on my thinking and writing at every turn.

Whatever he now comprehends? That means *all things,* doesn't it? And "has *everything* to do with notions of ethnicity and diversity"? Everything *also* means all things, no? And what does "to do" mean? Does it mean "is caused by"? Does it mean "is associated with"? Does it mean "owes its existence to"?

Since the writer has neither said nor written what he does mean, it's up to us to provide his possible meanings, and those three are the best I can think of. Now that we've got them, let's translate, or try to. Birkerts must mean, then, that "everything in and of and by America—everything American—is caused by, is associated with, or owes its existence to ethnicity and diversity."

But this statement, whether a person chooses to use only *one* of the three verbs at any given time, or to use all three, is simply nonsense. It simply isn't true, is at very best a half-truth. This, however, is no deterrent to Birkerts's fervent embrace of it. It becomes, he explains, a "transformed awareness" that "exerts pressure on my thinking and writing *at every turn* [emphasis mine]."

The only possible conclusion we can make is that Birkerts either *can't* or *won't* think clearly, logically, or for himself. His apologizing ("obligatory buzz-phrase") for the very concept that he embraces "at every turn" makes no sense *unless* a person assumes him to be either mad or a hypocrite. My own guess is that he's a bit of both, and that the cause of his being so is that he's an adult child of the Age of Simplification. Every respectable writer, critic, and literary scholar knows—or used to know—that if something really *is* a buzz-word (or a "buzz-phrase"), then it is to be challenged, mistrusted, and avoided. It's code. It's cliché. It's boilerplate. It's a word used *not* to express thought or thinking, but to express *non*thought, at the very best to express an *attitude* that, though it may once have been thought about, is no longer so. Above all, it is *not* "obligatory" but, if anything, the very opposite.

As we have seen before, buzzwords function in the same way as propaganda and in certain cases *are* propaganda. Thinkers, if they are to remain thinkers rather than blind parrots, must reject and avoid them, as they always have[13]—or have "Until this morning and this snow."[14] For in the Age of Simplification, as we've seen and are seeing again, the intellectual calamity is such that our "thinkers" embrace nonthought and believe it to be thought.

It may be some faint vindication of Birkerts that he himself, at least, seems wholly unconvinced by his own essay, though the arm-flailing free-fall of absurd contradictions and panicky afterthoughts in his closing lines is hardly a sign of intellectual distinction.

Here are those last seventy-four words:

But, truth be told, it [the "idea" that's expressed by the "buzz-phrase"] is not formative in the same way; it is laid on top of the other [that is, the earlier "fantasy"], the visceral. I might wish this otherwise. A different core awareness, a less obsessive investment in these fantasies of WASP normalcy might have made my passage easier, less painful. Alas, intriguing as these surmises can be, they lead us exactly nowhere. We are shaped by what we dream, and there we have no control.

And here, one step at a time, is what the translation seems to be:

1. Although the "ethnicity and diversity" fantasy has replaced the "Madison Avenue" fantasy and "exerts pressure on my thinking and writing at every turn," it really *hasn't* replaced the former fantasy and really *doesn't* exert that pressure. Instead, the "new" fantasy simply floats on top of the "old" one, the old one being deeper—"visceral"—while the new one is . . . well, what can one say? Birkerts, again, hasn't done his own work, hasn't done his own writing, hasn't *said*, so that it's *our* job to guess at what he means. The new fantasy, then, is shallower? Less real? Ephemeral? Even more artificial? But the search is hopeless: I know of no alternative to "visceral" that can complete the apparent thought without compromising Birkerts as either a hypocrite (who says he's had a passage but hasn't had one) or a fool (who thinks he's had a passage when he really hasn't), and perhaps as both.

2. The author wishes he weren't in this absurd situation ("I might wish this otherwise").

3. He wishes he hadn't fallen so totally for the *first* fantasy as he did, for the *first* set of lies, because then his "passage" might have been "easier, less painful." Fine. It's perfectly natural to avoid pain, or wish to. But the pain of his passage to *what*? The options are: (a) the pain of his passage from the first fantasy to the second fantasy—except that he said just a moment ago that he actually didn't *make* that passage but merely laid the second fantasy over the first one—so there can't be any pain from a passage but only

from a *nonpassage*, though that makes no sense; or (b) the pain of his passage to—to what? The question won't go away. Perhaps it's simply the passage to the end of his essay, the end that, like Satan into Hell, he's falling toward now, into befuddlement, confusion, and despair.

4. Thinking doesn't work and can't help anyway. As follows: The writer is in despair ("Alas") and knows that thinking ("these surmises") is pointless ("they lead us exactly nowhere").

5. The author abandons thinking and thought ("We are shaped by what we dream," not by what we think) and simply gives up entirely ("and there we have no control").

Finally, then, here is the message the world heard when the State Department asked one of our leading intellectuals from the Age of Simplification to compose an essay on what it means to be a writer in America, or on the corollary question of what being an American means:

> Being American, or being a writer in America, means being wholly unable to imagine any conceivable way to answer the question of what being American, or being a writer in America, could possibly mean.

Alas indeed.

❖ ❖ ❖

In the essays by Robert Olen Butler and Richard Ford, the thinking is again, as in the Birkerts essay, muddled, evasive, empty, and circular. Both writers *seem* to conclude, à la Birkerts (apparently), that being American means pretty much nothing, but the curious assumptions, avalanching clichés, and certain other embarrassments in the Butler piece make it more interesting than Ford's very foolish, utterly jejune, and almost entirely lifeless piece. Some will remember Robert Olen Butler not only for the fiction he's written but for his strange project, back in 2001, of allowing himself to be "seen" or "watched" on a college website as he "created" a piece of fiction. "Consider what it would have been like," declared a press release at the time, "if English students could have watched live as William Shakespeare composed 'Romeo and Juliet' on the Internet." Shakespeare and Robert Olen *Butler?* Apparently stone-deaf to any sense of the hilarious irony, the press release went on:

> For his "Inside Creative Writing" project, [Butler] will begin with a simple concept for a story and, with no other preparation, will start writing at 9 P.M. (EST) for about 19 days, Sunday through Friday, allowing millions of students and would-be writers a golden opportunity to learn from every creative decision as it is happening. If he comments as he writes, they will hear it. At the close of each episode, he will answer questions e-mailed to him during the broadcast.[15]

In his own State Department essay, Butler himself describes some of how his Internet project came about and, presumably, what it was for:

> I began with a simple concept, and, with no other preparation, I created the story in real-time. My viewers saw every creative decision, down to the most delicate comma, as it was made on the page. Every misbegotten, awkward sentence, every bad word choice, every conceptual dead end was shared and worked over and revised and rewritten before the viewers' eyes.

Readers can decide for themselves whether a comma really constitutes a "creative decision," as they can also ponder for themselves what might distinguish a regular comma from a "delicate" one. A bigger question, though, is the one asking what it was that Butler actually thought his viewers and auditors were seeing and hearing. He himself is no help in providing an answer, due to his own way of being bluntly contradictory. A collector of antique postcards, Butler, the day his webcast was to begin, looked through his collection "in search of the card that had the strongest story hovering about it." The one he chose, described early in the essay, had on it a photograph of a man flying in "an achingly fragile biplane," while the message written on the card explained: "This is Earl Sandt of Erie Pa. in his aeroplane just before it fell."

It sounds like a great choice: I know few who would deny the irony of the card, its suggestion of a tragic event—even though it's already happened—being held off for all eternity, creating the mystery of a calamity forever *about* to happen. But what we're dealing with here isn't the postcard, isn't even the story, inspired by it, that Butler presumably wrote. Our subject, instead, is the State Department essay that Butler composed and that shows us the pattern of his own thinking as he answers the question of what it means to him to be an American writer. And, in this respect, he runs into every bit as much trouble as Birkerts did.

He'd "always assumed," he says, that when he got around to writing a story inspired by this postcard, he would tell it in the voice of the doomed pilot. But that plan "changed on October 30," the day he began the webcast. Here is part of what he says about how the change of plan came about:

> I took up this antique postcard, and my artistic unconscious, my sense of myself as an American, and my larger identity as a human being all powerfully converged. Instantly I knew that I had to write the story in the voice of the man who watched.

It's fair to ask what Butler is talking about in these sentences, two more examples of unwritten writing, of "code" understandable only to those who already know what the writer means. In this case, however, unlike the "political" or "politically correct" code we saw earlier, probably *nobody* knows or ever could know what Butler means. After all, it's one thing to telegraph politically correct, or putatively correct, attitudes or stances by tossing out pre-agreed-upon buzzwords. But *these* code words and phrases are enormous, towering, vast in their generality, philosophically unleashed. Certainly it's a fair question, once again, to ask what Butler's, or anyone's, "artistic unconscious" *is*. Or what the writer means (since he doesn't say) by his "sense of [himself] as an American." Or, in the most abstract and near-limitless case of the three, to ask what *does* constitute or reveal his "larger identity as a human being."

That these three undefined things all came together in a "powerful" convergence might well have resulted in quite an experience—for Butler, that is, since for everyone else the convergence can't possibly mean anything, since the elements making it up are still undefined. And it's unlikely that they *will* be defined, either, since they appear just about at the end of the essay, with only 257 words left to the author out of his total of 2,082.

Knowing that we the readers are thus going to be left in the dark, another legitimate question arises—namely, whether these converging powers, concepts, or entities were defined for the *author:* whether Butler himself knew what he was arguing, talking about, or saying.

As might be expected, the answer is no, but let's follow along anyway to see exactly what happens and, if we're lucky, how and why it does.

Butler's next sentence, after he's written that he "knew" he'd have "to write the story in the voice of the man who watched," begins with the word "because." In other words, what ought to happen is that we'll be given an explanation ("because . . .") of *what actually happened* during the powerful convergence. But no. Here's the explanatory sentence, beginning with that all-important subordinating conjunction:

> Because on September 11, 2001, we were all the ones who watched.

Most people's initial reaction here is likely, I imagine, to be positive, since they're apt to hear in the words a certain moral seriousness—Butler's expression, in fact, of his own awe, compassion, and, if you will, piety at the memory of 9/11. Piety, compassion, and awe, indeed, are called for. They are, indeed, eminently appropriate. Anyone lacking them in the face of the disaster of 9/11 would be not human but monstrous. And yet. That said, there follows the qualification: However understandable, however right, however appropriate piety, compassion, and awe may be and are, they nevertheless do not *constitute* an argument, do not *lead* to an argument, and do not provide any *definition* whatsoever of *any* of the "converging" elements that Butler has told us he is drawing on as he gropes toward *some* kind of an explanation of or *some* kind of an answer to the question that has been asked him by the Department of State.

The one thing alone that is and remains logically valid in the remainder of Butler's essay is the indisputable existence of a *parallel* between the man who wrote on the old postcard and the people almost a hundred years later who may have seen the World Trade Center attack. Both the former and the latter are or would be looking *up*. Both the former and the latter are or would be looking at something having to do with an airplane or airplanes. And both the former and the latter are or would be looking at something that was about to collapse or fall. And that's *it*. That's *all*. I'll admit that it's a *big* "all," that the parallel is a suggestive one, and that the ideas or meanings that *might* spring from it if it were made a part of, say, a poem, movie, novel, or story—perhaps a part of the very story Butler himself wrote—that those ideas could become considerable or even deeply significant.

But Butler's way of thinking—his way of *feeling*, I should say, since thinking, as with others we've seen, has been lost to or abandoned by him, as we'll see more clearly in a moment—Butler's way of thinking allows for no simple *acknowledgment* of the parallel, allows for no permission that it be allowed simply to exist, having or acquiring or achieving such meanings as might be achievable from itself or from the relationships between it and such contexts as it may be given.

Butler, instead, *bullies* the parallel. It's almost as though he closes his eyes and prays at it, a kind of god telling it what it is. And the claims he makes for it, and consequently also for its meaning, have their basis in nothing intellectually rigorous but only in assumption, or perhaps even *presumption*. Not only has he failed to think these claims through, but he has brought them forth under the aegis of ideas that he hasn't defined and that, it's fair therefore to suspect, he doesn't understand. As a result of all this, the claims he makes fall into the abyss of the sentimental and the maudlin. And, like all things guided by those two blind leaders, they fall from the sentimental and the maudlin into the meaningless, and from the meaningless into the fraudulent.

Having begun it by saying that "we were all the ones who watched," Butler completes his paragraph like this:

> From my dreamspace I wrote this story about America of the early 20th century, and in doing so I realized something crucial about that terrible day in America of the early 21st century. The man who snapped the photo and wrote the postcard ninety years earlier felt the same thing that we all did on September 11, and I came to understand that the most profound and abiding effects of that day have very little to do with international politics or worldwide terrorism or homeland security or our unity as a nation. Those issues are real and important too, of course, but it seems to me that the deepest experience of 9/11 happened for us one soul at a time in an entirely personal way. We each of us viewed the fall of an aeroplane under stunning circumstances for which we had no frame of reference, and as a result, the event got around certain defenses that we all necessarily carry within us. And we confronted—one by one by one—in a way most of us never have—our own mortality.

A clearer example of thought from the Age of Simplification could hardly be found: Shortcuts, elisions, assumptions, collapsed logic—that is, unexamined and un-self-conscious thinking—draw a path starting from and leading to only more half-truths and false premises. The "thinker" charges happily down that seemingly (to him) well-cleared path and embraces the elementary-school bromides and homilies he finds there, apparently *believing* them to be both profound and true, though in fact they're neither. Instead, they're inane, wrong, and, again, bullying.

We've granted a parallel between 9/11 and the aeroplane postcard. Now, though, Butler tells us that *because of* that parallel, he "realized something crucial" about "that terrible day," meaning, of course, 9/11. And what *was* that crucial something? Instead of an answer, we get two falsehoods in a row, almost on top of one another. The first is the presumptuous and false assertion that the man "ninety years earlier" watching the plane fall "felt the same thing" that people on 9/11 did. He *did? They* did? Says who? And on what evidence? And what *is* that "same thing," and what does it mean? Is *this*—another "thing"—the "some*thing* crucial" that we're waiting to find out about? So far, it's *nothing*.

Butler may know that the aeroplane man felt the "same thing" as people felt on 9/11, but *I* don't. The aeroplane man himself is long gone and can't tell us. And Butler himself is showing no evidence or proof that he does know what he says he knows. The second of his two falsehoods, however, is worse. Just a few quick words are required to nail it down, and here they are, the emphasis added by me:

. . . felt *the same thing that we all did* on September 11 . . .

I beg your pardon, but just exactly who is this *we*? And what degree of pride or blind presumption does it require for *one* person to tell *all other people in the world what they felt*? Pardon me again, but

allow me to say that you, Robert Olen Butler, have no idea whatsoever what *I* felt or thought on 9/11, and there, as Dr. Johnson was
wont to say, is an end upon it.

I suppose it's possible that Butler really does have pride or
presumption gigantic enough to make him think he's preacher to
the nation. But I doubt it. The impression I get from reading his
essay is that what's at work isn't presumption, but simplification.
The blindness in his case isn't the blindness of certainty, huge ego,
and pride, but the blindness of unseen distinctions, of nonexistent definitions, of failure in focus and logic, in clarity and consistency, that we've seen already as the familiar hallmarks of artistic
or intellectual thought in the Age of Simplification, hallmarks that
come into existence—maybe always, but certainly in this case—as
a result, in the end and above all, of the substitution of feeling for
thinking.

Lacking both compass and rudder, Butler veers and yaws and
drifts and backtracks as badly in his closing lines as Birkerts did in
his. It turns out, he says, that the effects of 9/11 weren't really, in
the end, about "international politics or worldwide terrorism or
homeland security or our unity as a nation," though those things,
he quickly adds, having his cake and eating it, "are real and important too, of course." He then proceeds to contradict himself in a
most damaging way indeed by telling us that "it seems to me that
the deepest experience of 9/11 happened for us one soul at a time
in an entirely personal way"—this after just a moment ago having told us that we *all* felt and thought *the same thing*. Apparently
that pronouncement has now been declared inoperative and has
been replaced with the idea that you can never know what's inside
a person, since we experience things "one soul at a time and in an
entirely personal [that is, unique] way."

Which, do you suppose, it's to be? Are we all the same or all
unique? Well, let's split the difference: that is, muddle it up. On the
"we're all unique" side, Butler reminds us that "*we each of us* viewed

the fall of an aeroplane," and then immediately, as if intent on giving equal time to the "we're all the same" side, switches back to the imperial, papal, editorial we, saying that we individually saw the fall of this "aeroplane" "under stunning circumstances for which we had no frame of reference."

And so, once again: I beg your pardon? *Who* had no "frame of reference"? For *whom* did the event "[get] around certain defenses that *we all* necessarily carry within us"? *Who*, please, is *us*, in the phrase "within us"? And so on and so forth. Butler's essay can't be wrestled down, can't be made to show its hand, because *it itself* doesn't know what hand it holds. The essay can't be held accountable for accuracy or consistency when neither is there. In a single sentence, it suggests that the self is unique ("And we confronted—one by one—"), then that all selves are the same ("in a way most of us never have"), then gets all arch and pushy and preachy again, explaining once and for all what "we" all confronted that morning of September 11 —"our own mortality."

Well, there's no point in arguing. In the Age of Simplification, the writer doesn't *have* to keep track of what he's talking about, doesn't *have* to be consistent. Whether the Age of Simplification writer is *unable* to be consistent or just *chooses* not to be is a question that may be impossible to answer convincingly, certainly not convincingly to all ears. But a skill unused becomes a skill lost, and, as I've tried to show, most of America for a very long time has been discouraged in thinking and rewarded in sloth. Butler himself *appears* incapable of following the simplest syllogistic reasoning. He explains that, through his webcast, "students could see the artistic process directly, in its moment-to-moment fullness." Not long before that, he told us that "art comes from the place where the artist dreams. Art comes from the unconscious." Well, if both statements are true, logic and consistency compel us to conclude that what the students saw during the webcast was in fact Butler's unconscious. That is to say, if what the students saw was "the artistic process . . . in its . . . fullness," and if, also, "art comes from the unconscious," then they *must* have seen Butler's unconscious.

And yet, of course, they saw no such thing. The very notion is absurd. But there it is, part and parcel of Butler's State Department essay, an absurd untruth put before the eyes of the world just as logically as the three-step argument that Ganges is a dog, all cats have four legs, so Ganges is a cat.

A childish business. But what's *really* childish—and something that occurs among college students all the time, at least the ones I've taught over the past three decades—is a refusal to *accept* examples of chopped deductive reasoning of this elementary kind, like the cracked syllogism about Ganges, even when they serve as means of smoking out and chasing down false thinking like Butler's. It's not possible—*is* it?—that Butler was aware of the syllogism he created, since if he *had* been aware of it, he would have edited his manuscript for logic—*wouldn't* he? And if he'd been aware of what he'd created, he'd never have made the comment—*would* he?—that "the unconscious is a scary place," a thought that becomes patently ludicrous once one has been led to understand that this "scary place" is itself the subject and substance of the already risible "webcast," a thing itself that, if not scary, is at least confused.

Like others in the anthology, Butler will say almost anything in order to be able to use many words in the saying of almost nothing. It's as though he sticks out a hand to grab a fistful of just about anything that passes by, then mixes, pushes, and pats what he's grabbed until it coheres, or seems to cohere, in a kind of snowball of meanings that will allow him to say—well, like Birkerts, very nearly nothing, or, worse, nothing at all.

After saying that the unconscious "is a scary place," Butler writes these sentences:

The great Japanese film director Akira Kurosawa once said "To be an artist means never to avert your eyes." [Avert them from

what?] And if the artist truly does that, if she goes into her unconscious, day after day, work after work, and does not avert her
eyes, she finally breaks into a place where she is neither female
nor male, neither black nor white nor red nor yellow, neither
Christian nor Muslim nor Jew nor Hindu nor Buddhist nor
atheist, neither North American nor South American nor European nor African nor Asian. He is human. And if he happened
by birth or choice to call the United States of America home, he
looks about him at the particulars of this place and culture and
finds those aspects of it that resonate into the universal humanity we all share on this planet.

Sounds good and says nothing—particularly if one remembers that
the assigned task is to explain the significance of being an American, or an American writer. Butler's answer, reached by stack-
ing one banality on top of another until the whole towering heap
falls over and dissipates into a mist of Sunday school pietism—his
answer is that being an American or being an American writer
means nothing whatsoever. And what does have meaning? Well,
being *human.*

Fine. Sure. Yup. Of course. And yet anyone who has ever seriously taught writing knows perfectly well that what Butler himself
has written and submitted here is what's known in English-teacher
shoptalk as a "snow job." That is, he's given us lots of pretty writing
that—some would say ingeniously—does anything and everything
necessary to avoid answering the question, in fact to avoid saying
anything at all, concluding with a conventional piety so enormous
and so shameless that the writer is just *sure* the teacher won't dare
attack or contravene it, even though it has *nothing whatsoever to do
with the assignment.*

One of the most important rules of good writing is the simple
and clear one, *Say what you mean,* and Butler's passage is a classic
example of that rule not in the observance but in the breach. The
Kurosawa quote, for example, says that to be an artist "means never

to avert your eyes." Sounds good, but it fails to say what it means, the crucial information remaining unsaid: that is, avert your eyes from *what?* All writers know that it's far easier *not* to say than it is *to* say what you mean—vide Abinader—and Butler plunges forward in the free-fall of that great easiness, filling his whole paragraph with things that are *not*—with what's *not meant*, and with what's *not* an answer to any question whatsoever, including the question that's been assigned. Even his passing nod to that unanswered question itself is swollen, empty, and airy, consisting of filler-syllables—why, except to take up space, the formal "the United States of America" rather than simply "America" or "the U.S."?—itself constituting yet another non-answer. *If* a person (he *was* a female, and now he's a male—neat, huh?) happens to be American, he'll "[look] about him at the particulars of this place and culture," says Butler, once again skating right over what he's supposed to be writing about, namely, what those "particulars" *are* and what they *mean.* But no. Ease and softness govern the Butlerian mind as they do the Butlerian prose, just as the flow of *feeling* replaces the hard work of observation and thought ("those aspects of it" flutters by, another phrase of the unnamed, unobserved, undefined). By no means alone among his fellow writers in the State Department anthology, but superlatively an example of it, Butler demonstrates the intellectual's equivalent of what I earlier called "entertainment rights." In this case, they would be called "writers' rights," consisting of the *right* to say nothing and yet to be treated with the dignities attendant upon one who has said much.

What "those aspects of this place and culture" may be, and *how* they may "resonate into the universal humanity we all share," I simply don't know. I certainly don't know what "resonate into" means. I don't even know what "the universal humanity" that "we all share" *is,* and I'll bet my socks that neither does Butler. What I do know is that even "humanity," like most everything else in his essay, goes by undefined, unobserved, unstudied, just another little fragment of "code."

And I also know that I, for one, am absolutely *not* going to share it, whatever it is, even though Butler says "we all" do. Not true. I myself wouldn't touch it with a ten-foot pole. Not until someone tells me what it is.

seven

Possibly the most sobering thought for someone who has finished reading the State Department anthology is this one: the probable certainty that each contributor did *the very best job he or she was capable of.* With this probability in mind—that each writer thought and wrote as deeply and clearly as he or she could—the failure the anthology demonstrates reveals itself as more dangerous, calamitous, and dismal than ever.

I can imagine someone making the objection at this point that the *writers* aren't the ones who should be blamed for doing poorly, since virtually no one could write a good essay on so insipid and clichéd a topic as the State Department gave. Garbage in, garbage out, such a person might say. The assignment was awful, so naturally the results were awful too.

But that argument can't—mustn't—be tolerated, being itself a product or manifestation of the Age of Simplification. While at one time it was a highly significant and serious thing (or at least *capable* of being, and of being seen as, highly significant and serious), writing has, in the Age of Simplification, gradually been worn down, eroded, and transformed into a minor and by and large powerless art. Only if a person *already* sees writing as weak and insignificant, as being of no substance or consequence—only then can a person dismiss *failure* in writing as itself insignificant, blameless, or without consequence.

In addition, there's the *moral* side of the matter. My own definition of writing is that it's the telling of the truth in a true way, or in a way that's *itself* also true. In the case of poetry or fiction writing, the writer is concerned with the truth of experience, while in expository writing the truth is the truth of ideas. There's obviously overlap, since, for example, *thinking* is itself an enormous part of experience and therefore also a great part of fiction's concern. In expository writing, on the other hand, thought itself is being explored, captured, delineated, clarified, explained, evaluated—and this process, at least when done *in language*, requires a linear, narrative progression.

In both cases, though, the morality of writing lies always in its dedication *to what's true.* To be moral, a piece of writing has to tell, recognize, or realize the truth in a true way about whatever aspect of experience happens to be its subject. Clearly, this standard applies to what we call "serious writing" or "literary writing," not to other things that may literally be "written" or be produced through "writing" and yet that have no interest whatsoever in "the true" as I'm talking about it here—propaganda, for example, advertising, all forms and aspects of the mass media, which have as their sole purpose the furthering of sponsors' monetary interests (whether or not "entertainment" is used in the achieving of that purpose).

But the State Department anthology isn't made up of that kind of writing. It's an anthology, instead, of the serious kind, of the literary kind, and the people who contributed were chosen *because* they were seen, known, or perceived as being serious, intellectual, literary writers, whether inside academia or out, whether poets or novelists or essayists or memoirists, and whether very highly visible or considerably less well known.

All of this being the case, it's clear that there's no feasible option available to pardon any of the anthologized writers on the grounds that the assignment proposed to them was hackneyed, pietistic, or even propagandistic, or that "nobody could have done a good job with a topic like that." Each writer had a clear intellectual, moral, and aesthetic choice: to reject the assignment and be done with it, or to accept the assignment, ascertain and explore the truth in it and of it, and then tell that truth in a way that itself was also true.

I have no way of knowing whether any writers—or if any, how

many—when asked to contribute to the anthology, may have turned the State Department down. I do know, as does any reader who saw the grades I gave, that to my way of thinking the essays written by those who did accept were preponderantly very poor, many of them disastrously so. And I also know that of the fifteen writers, not a single one—excepting possibly Creeley and Collins—got even the least bit under the surface of the question, looked around from behind it, dug into it, saw it for what it was, and answered it in any way whatsoever that could conceivably be of any help, good, use, perception, merit, illumination, revelation, consequence, or practical instructiveness to anyone whatsoever—not to writers, not to readers, not to citizens, not to foreigners, and certainly not to the potential well-being itself of our sick, prostituted, and slowly dying nation.

There has to be a reason for so dismal a showing. My own suggestion is this: So successful, over the past sixty years, has been the programmatic stealing away and adulteration and wearing down of the true, native, individual, independent, thinking self—so complete the alchemical transformation of citizen into consumer—that not only everyone else but even the *writers* in America have gone blind.

Almost twenty years ago, in the *New York Times Book Review* for October 13, 1985, Marilynne Robinson published an essay that I clipped and have held onto ever since because of something in it that seemed to me very important. The essay is difficult, far more demanding, probing, and closely reasoned than *anything* that might be run in *any* section of the same newspaper today, with the exception, possibly, of a review every other month or so by Edward Rothstein. Called "Writers and the Nostalgic Fallacy," Robinson's essay takes up the charge—brought recently, the author says, by "both Robert Dunn and E. L. Doctorow"—that American writers are at fault "for lacking a sense of history, and for failing to achieve what is called political seriousness."

Robinson doesn't dispute the charge, but, instead, she sets out to explain why it's a true one and what's to be done about it—namely, that writers *and* critics and readers need to stop looking at the past nostalgically, thinking of it as if it were a perfect time in sorry contrast to the worn and degraded present. "[The] error of treating the artificial, value-shaped past as an authentic, historical past," she declares, "is as fundamentally naive as supposing [that] our dwarfed and poxy forebears looked like paintings and statues." When read again today, the essay is just as elegant as it was two decades ago ("peculiar to our time is a habit of disparagement [of the present age], persisted in with a kind of obsessiveness that seems like rigor"), though, given the sense of crisis in regard to our cultural and political well-being as it has intensified over the intervening years, the essay does not, it's true, seem quite as directly on the mark as it did then, or quite as helpful in a practical literary way.

Yet even so, at the very heart of it there remains a notion about *language* that's every bit as timely now as it was then, most likely much more so. Near the start of her argument, Robinson says that the criticism being made of writing and writers at the time "is that, like Tolstoy . . ., we could effect good things and momentous things by the use of our pens, if only we could break out of preoccupations [that] we scourge [in ourselves and in our writing] as indulgent, trivial or safe."

The cause of this sense of our own triviality, as I've said, is our addiction to an idea of the past as great, of the present as inferior. Today, in our own anti-intellectual and unhistorically conscious age, almost *any* sense of the past would be more than welcome, which is the reason why the Robinson essay, in this sense, does feel dated, the fault being ours, not its. But in another way, the piece of writing shows itself even *more* applicable and timely than when it was written, and that's in Robinson's comments about language, first as a metaphor for an intellectual habit, stance, or attitude, then simply and purely as language itself.

We're kept minor and trivial, and we keep thinking of ourselves as such, Robinson explains, "because . . . we are enchanted by a myth of history," that myth being, of course, the myth of the Golden Age. For Robinson, this "enchantment" is the result of our use of language in the sense of language as a *habit* or *convention* of thinking: "I think it is the tired assumptions we try to build on and the cumbered and self-referential language we use that keep us in a narrow space, lamenting [about ourselves]." Certainly this sounds, if anything, even more like us today than it did in 1985, with our ever-narrowed categories—our blinkers and blinders—of race, class, gender, and so on that have become a "language," in Robinson's sense, a form of self-imposed myopia that preempts and makes invisible entire previously unproscribed areas or possibilities of independent perception and thinking.[16]

Beyond this idea of language as a metaphor for, say, thought-structure, Robinson also has an interest in language in and of itself, an interest in words and language as tools for seeing and telling the truth. Here is the passage that I have remembered now for almost two decades, all the more apropos to the subject of literary writing today than it was then. For continuity, I include the paragraph preceding the crucial one:

> The literature of expostulation, of Catastrophe, is taken to be very serious. But among people carried along in a canoe toward a waterfall, the one who stands up and screams is not the one with the keenest sense of the situation. We are in a place so difficult that perhaps alarm is an indulgence, and a harder thing—composure—is required of us.
>
> To find a new language for a new kind of novel is a thing I have long aspired to do. No luck yet. When I wrote *Housekeeping* some five years ago, I made a world remote enough to allow me to choose and control the language out of which the story was to be made. It was a shift forced on me by the intractability of the *language* [Robinson's emphasis] of contemporary experience—which must not be confused with contemporary

experience itself. Merely speak the word "suburb," for example, and an entire world springs to mind, prepared for our understanding by sociologists and cultural commentators and novelists, good and bad. The language of present experience is so charged with judgment and allusion and intonation that it cannot be put to any new use or forced along any unaccustomed path. The story it wants to tell I do not want to tell.

The application of Robinson's idea to our own situation is overwhelmingly clear. In the intervening two decades between the writing of the essay and now, the "language of present experience" has become far, far more rigidified, prepackaged, preadjusted for connotation and tone, even *proscribed*, than it was in 1985, even though *then* the language had already become useless to this extraordinarily gifted author[17] who wanted to tell or describe *another* truth than the "truth" that the ready-made and overused language bullied and pushed her into.

The language of contemporary experience, in other words, had become a kind of prison, or, appropriate to the Age of Simplification, a kind of *liar*.

That such a thing had already happened *two decades* ago can only suggest how severely increased the situation may have—must have; has—grown by now. Not only has daily language in and of itself changed further since 1985 in the ways Robinson describes, but language as a metaphor for the *way* thousands upon thousands of intellectuals, writers, and academics *think,* or for the structures and categories that they think *in,* has changed even more obviously and more dramatically, as a glance at so many of the essays I've been discussing will show. "Categories" of thought have replaced thought itself. A certain litany of subjects, or "issues"—race, class, gender, ethnicity, etc.—have not effectively but in actuality have moved *into* the mind, have decided exactly where each room in the mind will be, how large it will be, what it will be *for,* even how the furniture will be arranged. People who have had this happen *won't*—you can read their essays and find out: they won't—think about things or think in ways outside those things and ways already provided in and by those rooms. As far as the existence of *other* rooms is concerned, they *do* exist, but people who have had this happen can't and don't see them. As far as those other rooms are concerned, they have gone blind.

＊　＊　＊

Artists and the arts; writers and poets and literature; musicians and moviemakers: These institutions of the arts, and the people who practice within them, are the *eyes* of a people or nation. The arts are the means for a people or nation to see *through* the false, the clichéd, or the tendentious, to see *through* the propagandistic, the trumped-up, hyperbolized, popularized, falsified, or glamorized, and to see thereby what a people or nation *really* is, what's important about it, what's true about it, what's good and what's bad about it, what characterizes it at its most valued, true, and revered level of being. People and nations are remembered not *only* through the arts, it's true—they can be remembered, too, for example, through wars—but from antiquity onward, the spirit of what peoples or nations *were*—and, now, what they *are*—is known to us saliently through the arts.

Or, that is, when a society is *healthy,* the arts are its eyes. When it's no longer healthy, when it passes into or through one kind of decadence or another, those eyes grow crusted, false, and go blind. And this is what is happening—has happened—to us.

Consider what Marilynne Robinson wrote twenty years ago, and consider how much time has passed since then. Consider what's happened (and what hasn't happened) over that time in movies, music, the graphic and plastic arts, academic humanities, *and* in writing and the literary arts. Consider, then, that the *most meaningful thing* about being a thinker or writer or artist in America *may* be that the all-surrounding "language" of the mass media—the *aesthetic* of the mass media, as I call it, so omnivorous, so omnipresent, and "so charged with judgment and allusion and intonation that it cannot be put to any new use or forced along any unaccustomed path"—that the most meaningful thing to a writer in America is that this "language" robs the self of its very autonomy, drains the self of its individual meaning, and forces anyone who would tell the story that he or she wants to tell rather than the story that *it* wants to tell—that all this forces such a person into a lone, secret, fierce, ongoing battle against that Orwellian "language" for stakes that are nothing less than individual, artistic, emotional, aesthetic, and intellectual survival.

To my way of thinking, and I suspect also to Marilynne Robinson's, that, indeed, is the situation, and that, indeed, is the most meaningful thing about being an artist in America. And why, then, I can only wonder, did not even one of the fifteen essayists write about it, allude to it, or give even the least hint, intimation, or whisper that they'd ever heard of it, been aware of it, seen it, experienced it, or even so much as suspected it, or been so much, even, as simply able to imagine its *existence*?

It must be—mustn't it?—that they didn't and don't see it at all, or, having "seen" it, didn't and don't see it as important, or significant, or harmful, or dangerous, or in any way related to or corruptive of the arts, of the self, or of the nation. The same thing, in other words, as not having seen it at all.

Or take a supposition more political in nature. Consider, once again, what Marilynne Robinson wrote about the language of contemporary experience. Then consider the essential fact that twenty years, two entire decades, have passed since she did so. And *then* consider that for this entire time there has been firmly in place an omnipresent, omnivorous mass media—a "*language* of contemporary experience"—that can and will tell only *one* truth and *one* story, will be forced along no "unaccustomed path," and will remain solely and only in the service of advancing corporate (which is to say also governmental) power and profit—a language that can and will tell the story only of a diminished, enervated, lessened, underindividualized, "softened," consumerized population, a population that serves the *corporations'* purposes and that lives with a blind and adamant faith both in its own *right* to so live and in the *goodness* of its so doing. For someone—like, say, Marilynne Robinson—still able to see through *that* language, still able (or wishing to be able) to see outside of the story that *that* language makes up, for such a person—an American writer, say—wouldn't the most urgent and meaningful thing be to witness and testify to the extent and degree of the *loss*, the extent and degree of simplification of the self and of the mind and of thought itself, inside academia and out, a simplification whose result is that government and the "language of contemporary experience" can redefine experience in whatever way they wish in order to protect the growth of corporate profit—by, for example, taking lies and declaring them truth, taking invasion and declaring it preemption, bringing destruction and declaring it liberation, enacting coups and declaring them fair elections, or exercising tyranny and declaring it freedom, all the while with the population's concurrence because the only language the population knows is the language that tells *that* story and no other?

To my way of thinking, were such a situation to become actuality—as it is becoming, may become, or has become—it would indeed be for me the most important and meaningful thing not only about being American, but also about being an American *writer*. And so I can't help but wonder, again, why not even one of the fifteen essayists wrote about it, alluded to it, or gave the least hint or intimation or whisper of *any* evidence that they'd ever heard of it, seen it, experienced it, even so much as imagined its existence.

If—this, of course, is pure supposition and only that—*if* any of them failed to do so because they felt they "couldn't"—because, that is, they knew that the State Department would refuse to publish any essay written on this particular "most meaningful" subject and so they *purposely* wrote instead on "less" meaningful or "less" true or even *un*true subjects—if any writer did anything of this kind, then, in place of being declared merely unable to think or to see or to write, he or she would have to be declared instead a hypocrite and liar, a traitor to the truth, a traitor to art, and a traitor to our nation.

If, on the other hand, all of the writers failed to write about these most meaningful things about being an American or an American writer because they didn't or don't *see* them, then it seems to me possible only to conclude that evidence does indeed show that the Age of Simplification is real, that representative Americans and American writers have indeed gone blind, have become, like the fish unaware of the water it swims in because it has never known anything to compare it with, unaware of the very intellectual and aesthetic oppression and tyranny that they are in fact living inside of and that surrounds them just as water surrounds the fish.

That is, evidence suggests that 1984 did come, that it is here, the strongest aspect of this evidence being that no one is aware of its having happened. Orwell had it right, except that he had a small error in chronology for us on this side of the Atlantic, where we got to work at it in 1947, a year earlier than in England, where they didn't really get down to business on it until 1948, the publication year that Orwell originally gave as the title of his brilliant but hopeless novel.

If there were a god, I would say, pray for us all.

II

THE DEATH OF LITERARY THINKING IN AMERICA:

HOW IT HAPPENED AND WHAT IT MEANS

The chief cause of false writing is economic. Many writers need or want money.
These writers could be cured by an application of banknotes.
The next cause is the desire men have to tell what they don't know, or to pass off
an emptiness for a fullness. They are discontented with what they have to say and
want to make a pint of comprehension fill up a gallon of verbiage.

Ezra Pound

one

I began this chapter some time ago with the idea that it would serve as an introduction to a book I planned to write. I soon realized, however, that the introduction to that book in itself had to do with a subject that deserved—and needed—its own treatment at whatever length necessary before I could logically move on to the original project.

That project was going to be what I called "a rescue operation." The thing to be rescued was the generally acknowledged body of Western literature itself, whose star had fallen dramatically over the past three decades or so. But it quickly grew clear to me that in order to achieve *that* end, the end of rescuing the books themselves, it would first be necessary to resuscitate, and thus rescue, a literary *way of thinking*. That, after all, is what had begun disappearing first, and its loss—during, and as a result of, the advent of what I call the Age of Simplification—its loss created in turn, or permitted, or catalyzed, the disappearance of literature itself, since people increasingly failed to know, or failed to be *able* to know, what literature *was*, why they should care about it, or what they should do *with* it.

What I call a literary way of thinking—or, equally accurate, an aesthetic way of thinking—is really little more than that way of thinking about the arts that I and others of my age naturally grew up with and then, as students, were trained in. Like most things having to do with the living arts, it's not something perfectly rigid, purely objective, or "scientific" in the way most people think of that adjective. But, at the same time, it *is* based in empiricism, and it *is* very, very definitely *logical*. In simplest terms, it's a matter of letting the artwork, as much as possible, do the talking rather than having someone talk *at* the artwork. In regard solely to the literary arts, it's a matter, again insofar as this is possible, of letting the books, poems, or dramas do the talking, of letting *them* determine what it is that they're "about."

And that's what my postponed book project was going to consist of: It was going to take up the works, from Homer to Beckett, that I'd been teaching for the past thirty or forty years and do with them in written form what I'd done all that time orally and aurally in the classroom—show how to let *them* do the talking, how to find out what *they're* "about," and how to do this without tendentiousness or any unnecessary pummeling and bullying of the books.

I was, and I remain, opposed to the simplistic practice that has come so widely into being of treating literary works as valuable or useful mainly if not solely for their commentary on or their containing of evidence regarding social or political "issues" that in turn are seen as making the works "topical," or "relevant" to the struggles or concerns of today. Perhaps above all I was and am opposed to the relegating of literary works to the subordinate role of functioning as supporting footnotes for the insanely compartmentalized and compartmentalizing pseudo-topics of "race, class, gender, and ethnicity" that I denounced and lamented in my last chapter and will denounce and lament again in this chapter and the one following.

I wanted, in other words, to show again what had once upon a time been so fruitfully shown to me: how to approach literature in such ways as to bring about a perception of its true value—and its true *power* (more on this later)—as well as in such ways as to bring about a perception of how *interesting* it is, how intricate and subtle in myriad ways, and, far from least, how funny it so often is, an aspect of the literary arts now ruinously and routinely missed by my literal-minded new colleagues.

✦　✦　✦

That book, though, has so far gone unwritten, and for what I think is good reason. As I thought my way further into the project, it became clearer that the colleagues I was in opposition to wouldn't be inclined to read it even if I *did* write it. Worse, even if by some fluke they did read it, *it would have no effect on them.* So much of the prestige of literature, and of my kind of literary studies, had already been lost as to make it unlikely that new demonstrations of my approach would find favor with any except those already sympathetic. After all, as we'll see especially in the chapter after this, one of the chief manifestations of intellectual and artistic loss in the Age of Simplification has been a denial of empiricism itself, accompanied by a blindly stubborn resistance to deductive logic. The situation being thus, it seemed to me increasingly clear that I could never, for purposes of conversion or persuasion, reach those with whom I differed *no matter what I did or tried to do.*

And so I gave up the idea, at least for the time being, of functioning as a kind of demonstrating lecturer and became, instead, a diagnostician of the dysfunction itself, of the ill or the deterioration that had brought about the decline and loss of a literary way of thinking in the first place. I would follow and demonstrate the precise and exact etiology of the disease; try to show the full extent of its destructiveness and its potential for still further harm; and live on the hope that any sense of emergency, alarm, or debate that might result could lead at least to a *possibility* of artistic and intellectual renewal.

At the same time, it may already, I'm fully aware, be too late for any such hope of new life or restoration.

two

To start, some definitions and a bit of credentialing. I am now in my middle sixties and have been in classrooms—at the front end of them, that is—pretty much continually since my middle twenties. Partly as a result of what I've been doing all those years, and partly as a result of the time when I started doing it—I got out of college in 1963—a good part of what I mean when I use the word "literature" is what you might expect: books and works that tend— or did tend, until recently—to get taught in classrooms. To my way of thinking, that doesn't mean that such works need necessarily be "classics," nor do I find that word, except on very rare occasions, particularly helpful. Every art, if it's to continue still to remain alive rather than becoming become an ossified and dead form, must have both a past and a present, and both that past and that present must be, and must remain, equally alive. One of the many scourges of the Age of Simplification is the disappearance of this idea, a debility that goes along with a more generally diminished understanding of the past and of an acquaintance with it. The point to be made just now, though, is that in a healthy situation—like the one in existence when I was, say, twenty—"literature" can be understood as something derived from both past and present, something referential to both, and something derived from both, and the word "literary" can be understood as referring to a *quality* that results from a piece of writing's being emergent in this way, from its being related to and born of a body beyond solely itself.

In other words, "literary" or "literature" used to distinguish "art" writing from other kinds of writing, the kinds that didn't have these qualities. In practical terms—and in the way I always used it—it meant that "literature" could be something written today or something written in 850 B.C.

For literary people of my own generation, an awareness of the relationship between then and now, past and present, ancient and modern, was accepted, commonplace, and pretty much ever-present. The two could be thought of as polarities or opposites— as, to some extent, they are—but the much greater, richer, more vital and productive truth is that they're not opposites at all, but that, instead, the past and the present are really one and the same thing.

This idea (largely because it's an *aesthetic* idea and hence anathema in the Age of Simplification) is a tremendously unpopular one nowadays, far more likely to be disdained than embraced. It's an idea also very highly susceptible to being denounced for its possession of qualities declared by those opposed to it to be conservative, reactionary, or right-wing.

Opposition to it comes about not only because the idea is admittedly subtle (that is, not simple), and not only because it is literally true and literally untrue at one and the same time (a paradox, after all, that also can't be allowed into the playground: too complicated), but also because it's an idea firmly and rightly associated with the critic and poet T. S. Eliot, who is far more greatly disdained in the Age of Simplification for his putative anti-Semitism and anti-feminism than valued for his extraordinary and high achievement in literature.

Still, for anyone interested in literary or aesthetic thinking, Eliot's short essay "Tradition and the Individual Talent," published in 1920 in *The Sacred Wood,* remains both pertinent and important—and, if you're like me, even moving.

How can past and present be the same thing? The simplest way to see how may be just to think for a moment about the relationship that exists between opposites. Without the present, how could there be any past? Or without the past, any present? If one is taken away or disappears, both are gone. The same is true of other seeming opposites: up and down, in and out, day and night, warm and cold, male and female.[1]

If this relationship is true in these cases, it must, logically, also be true with time. That is, it must also be true in the case of then and now, that one can't exist without the other, or in the case of past and present. Now, this same relationship can be applied to art: Any work of art, exactly like anything else that's brought into being, can exist only in time, or, if you like, *inside* of time. Therefore something *now*—a sonnet that you've written, say, or a novel—also has to have a "then," or has to have *had* a "then," in order for it to be existing "now."

Logically, in other words, time can't flow in only one direction but must flow both backward and forward in order for it to continue existing. For Eliot, the same is true in the case of art: "Novel-now" can't exist except in relation to "novel-then," or "poem-now" except in relation to "poem-then." This is part of the reason why Eliot wrote, back in 1920, that "no poet, no artist of any art, has his complete meaning alone. His significance, his appreciation is the appreciation of his relation to the dead poets and artists." Then he went a step further, however: Seeming to say that time *literally,* not just conceptually or philosophically, moves backward as well as forward, he added that "what happens when a new work of art is created is something that happens simultaneously to all the works of art which preceded it."

* * *

I can't say I was never given difficulty by Eliot's second statement. I first read "Tradition and the Individual Talent" more than forty years ago, in college, and I remember my excitement at the sense of rightness and truth in Eliot's *first* statement, that art's meaning exists not in itself only but also in its necessary relation with the past. But I also remember my disappointment, almost anger, at his second one, by which I took him to mean that something *literally* changed in works of the past when a work in the present was created. I disliked the idea, and the reason I disliked it was that I didn't believe it, it was clearly artificial, and I fervently wished Eliot hadn't even made it. Defeated by it, I pushed it off into the category of those things that the poet accepted—so I thought—through a "faith" or "belief" of some kind that I didn't, and didn't want to, share. In short, I clung to the first idea, about the past influencing the present, and repudiated the second one, about the present influencing the past.

But that was a mistake. As it turns out, what I thought Eliot meant isn't what he meant at all. He didn't have in mind a literal, mechanical alteration or physical event—nor did he mean anything mystical, either, like, say, tears falling from a stone, or dead bodies stirring when certain things occur in the living world (like Yeats's sphinx, in "The Second Coming," "moving its slow thighs"). What Eliot meant instead is simply that a person's understanding or awareness of a *present* work modifies, enhances, or alters the person's understanding or awareness of *past* work—this being the case so long as the paradoxical relationship between present and past, which makes present and past one, remains in effect, causing art now and art then, also, to be one.

This view, as I said, is scarcely tolerated today, as neither is Eliot himself, a figure scourged by the many not only in regard to the twin charges I mentioned a moment ago, but for what most Americans now might consider equally if not even more heinous, his "elitism."

The decline and fall of T. S. Eliot has taken place more or less over the same years as those spanned by my own academic career. This towering writer, who forty years ago I and my generation admired as greatly as we did any other of the giants then known as the Moderns, has become a writer little valued by the majority of my younger colleagues, seldom read by students, virtually unknown to the common reader, and a figure besides—like the ever-maligned Matthew Arnold—tainted not only by political but by moral wrong. He has become an embarrassment. Simply mentioning Eliot in certain company—like mentioning Woody Allen in that same company now that he has been non-tried in the non-courts and found incestuous and pedophilic—requires great care, immediate qualification, and quick-footed defensive caution, especially if one is referring to him as authoritative in literature. This, needless to say, is hardly a simple situation for me or others like me, who, in spite of qualities that may be lamentable in Eliot personally, spiritually, or philosophically, otherwise still feel about him the way they did in, say, 1963, treasuring his achievement as poet and literary thinker.[2]

What can have happened that so many people's attitudes so quickly changed so entirely? Why and how did it come about that the artist and the art, the man and the work (Eliot as just one example, though an important one) must be taken and judged together rather than singly, separately, and apart? What kind of literary thinking is *that*? And if, as a way *of* thinking, it really is as widespread as it seems to be, how much damage must have been done? How much of value must have been lost?

✦　✦　✦

And so we come back to the Age of Simplification, to its unremitting growth and spread since 1947, this time in order to consider another way of thinking now lost and gone. It hardly any longer requires documenting, this phenomenon—once, almost quaintly, called "dumbing down"—of diminishment in the quality and ways of thinking and feeling among us, in us, and around us. Evidence abounds everywhere, sometimes scholarly (Allan Bloom),[3] sometimes personal and acerbic (Paul Fussell),[4] and always everywhere visible in daily life: One need only look at movies, watch television news, follow education, listen to popular music, observe national politics, read publishers' lists—*or* peruse college catalogs, I hasten to add—to be reawakened to the penury and diminishment that have come into being over the past four decades.

My subject right now, however, isn't the calamity itself, but the toll it has taken on *literary* thinking and life, especially, though far from only, inside academia. And what a toll it is. Who could ever have thought, thirty years ago, or forty, when literary studies made up one of the most varied, rich, intellectually rewarding, sinuous, and reverberant fields that academia had to offer—*and* one of the most popular—that by our own day this same widely generative field of study would have shriveled and degenerated into a largely mechanistic and unimaginative field dominated by a reductively small number of simplistic intellectual rigidities that would programmatically subordinate *every*thing that was *literary* to *any*thing that was "political" or "social"? Who could ever have thought that literary studies would fall victim to, and that its practitioners would grow into perfectly zealous embracers of, the perverse view that all the riches of the world, all the experiences of life and death, all the wealth of existence known and available for exploration by the human mind and heart—that all of these not only *could* be but *must* be reduced, delimited, and confined to one of four small window-less rooms, each with a doorway going in but no doorway going out, these being, of course, the four closets of "race, class, gender, and ethnic identity."

❖   ❖   ❖

And, so, what's happened? What's happened, it appears, is that literary thinking—like that of Eliot and others—has fallen (or been cast) away, and in place of it has been installed something much simpler, said and thought to be *political* thinking, or social, but, either way, thinking of a very simple kind.

Let's have just a glance at exactly how simple by taking a look at two ideas that govern whole realms of academic thinking in the humanities.

The first idea:

Oppression is bad, expression is good. These twin simplistic half-truths (simplistic *because* they're half-truths) provide the foundation for enormous regions of the putative left-liberalism that has taken over academic humanities. Along with them go adulation of "creativity" in favor of "discipline" and the valuing of "self-expression" or "empowerment" over concepts like "mastery" or "knowledge." Along with them, also, on the other hand, goes a general denunciation of all power as *bad*, the sign and tool of political oppression, even though "empowerment" is *good*, so that one of many resulting inanities characterizing much of the thinking in academic humanities today might be, "Power bad, empowerment good."

The second idea:

What people are *matters as much as (or more than) what they* do, *and it's imperative that they be celebrated for what they* are. In this second twinned idea (more analysis to come in chapter 3) lies the foundation for the now-omnipresent programs in and applications of victims' studies and victimology (again, more in chapter 3), while, underlying *that* foundation and supporting it, is our familiar syndrome of feeling first and thinking second (if at all). The implications are many for all aspects of humanities studies. In the case of literary studies, however, the result of this idea or syndrome is that literature, again, is made to serve merely as a kind of sourcebook, providing examples of whatever sort may be needed for demonstrating the truth of whatever "issue" is currently preoccupying the scholars and their students, the provided examples being almost entirely examples of oppression and injustice.

And that's about the extent of it. If put into practice in an essentially unalloyed form, either as pedagogy or as critical method, these two premises or ideas are capable of producing something less justly called education than indoctrination—indoctrination into the richly rewarding intellectual life of half-thought and feel-goodism.

So complete a change in so short a time. It's commonly argued that a situation like ours now has come about as a result of the widespread political radicalizing of so many in academia during the Vietnam era. The argument is that the young people who *then* became political activists have proven themselves unable or unwilling to give up their activism and have therefore brought into academia—now that *they* make up the professoriate—what they first learned, or became, as students who were in open rebellion not only against policies of the federal government but against academia itself on the grounds that it played a collaborationist role *with* that government.

And maybe that argument is valid. In fact, I'm sure it is, to some degree. But it can't possibly account for the entirety of the matter, or for the enormity and the *quality* of change that's taken place. It alone can hardly be enough to account for the whole dreadful picture of what's happened inside academic humanities since 1965, and, specifically, for what's developed—or been lost—inside literary studies.

After all, it seems to me, as it must to everyone, that as people grow, they *should*, in all likelihood, change. As they advance in years, they ought to mature. As they experience more, learn more, and gain in knowledge, they *should* be inclined, and be prepared, to alter their judgments and attitudes accordingly, insofar as alteration is indeed reasonably called for in the light of new experience or knowledge. The people who remain ever the same are—what?— either *very*, very old or deficient in some important way that makes it impossible for them to change, making it their destiny to live out lives either of immature naïveté, on the one hand, or of tendentious orneriness and cootism, on the other.

Or, on yet a third hand, such people—those no longer elastic, no longer respondent—may be that way because they're in the grip of outside forces or external powers, whether perceived by them or not, that have the same effects on attitude as extreme age or other significant deficiencies would have.

I think, for example, of all those writers in the last chapter who appeared incapable of seeing, for themselves, anything of high or true or authentic or previously unperceived significance in the world they live in—and yet who, no matter what, *aren't about to change*. Indeed, as everyone knows, throughout academia there can be found many, many such. Those of my own generation are a good deal older than most of the writers of the first chapter, but, nevertheless, there's no scarcity inside academia of people radicalized in or near the late 1960s who seem not to have changed in any significant way at all in outlook or attitude *over the past thirty-five years*, a length of time easily representing half or even more than half of an average human life.

The radicalization part is more understandable than the absence of change since the radicalizing took place. After all, back in 1967 or 1968, as a result of extreme experiences that they and the world were going through, many inside literary academia concluded that social and political morality and justice were of an importance clearly greater and more pressing than literature or literary study, and as a result they rebelled against the latter (literature and literary study) and embraced, as political activists, the former. So what's the problem? Well, the problem is that here they are now, today—along with the newer generation, who imitate the older— not just still professors in literary studies, but still professors in literary studies *and still teaching that morality and justice, both social and political, are of an importance clearly greater than literature or literary studies.*

Crazy, no? Isn't this a pretty clear example of a "disconnect," as we say? Any normal person would feel very uneasy, after all, going to a dentist who openly professed that toes were superior to teeth. What quality of care could you be certain your teeth would get from such a dentist? Is it out of the question that this practitioner would drill carelessly—all the while snatching desirous glimpses of your toes and dreaming of the surgery that would straighten out those sweet little digits and set them right? Or who, for that matter, would go to a heart surgeon for a thyroid problem, a brain surgeon for a knee problem, or an orthopedist for a rash? No one, of course.

No one would do any of these things, since these things are simply, obviously, and eminently absurd. But why, then, is it that we see nothing whatsoever wrong, or absurd, in the sending of countless thousands of students, all of whom have a literature problem, not to literature-doctors but to politics-doctors—to doctors, that is, of social and political morality and justice?

What's the answer to *that* one? I know of *three* answers, all of them essentially corollaries of one another and all three involving blindness. One is that we don't know what we're doing, are completely impervious to it. A second is that we *think* we know what we're doing, but *don't* know. A third is that we *do* know, but that *we don't care.*

✦　✦　✦

If human beings, as they grow older and gain experience—assuming them to be responsible, ethical, emotional, and intellectual beings—if, that is, such people really can and should be expected to change, then why would a dentist who over a span of *thirty-five years* remained passionately convinced of the superiority of toes over teeth—why would such a dentist not change fields, becoming a podiatrist instead of a dentist?

All right, the question is theoretical, but let me pursue it anyhow. If the dentist failed to switch to podiatry, whether out of weakness, inertia, laziness, or whatever other cause (though *not* from any alteration in attitude, feeling, or view as to the superiority of toes to teeth and the greater appeal of the first over the second), the results might vary, but they would nevertheless remain predictable enough. Such practitioners as the ones in our example, obviously, would understandably and in all likelihood become and remain unhappy in their work, yearning for feet while being required to spend time on the less desirable object, teeth. This unhappiness might be stoically endured and have little or no influence on the doctors' work. On the other hand, if protracted and powerful enough, the malaise could easily be imagined as bringing about one or two probable outcomes.

The malaise might lead a practitioner to careless performance, since while operating on teeth he or she would be wishing for and daydreaming about feet, with a consequent deficiency in attentiveness to the actual job at hand. But we have considered this possibility already. A much worse outcome would be the development of actual self-deception—the dentist's coming to convince himself that he *really was working on feet, not teeth.* Unbelievable, you say? Well, just let me finish. The next step, a serious one indeed, would be when dentists, them*selves,* now believing that teeth are feet, begin to instruct their patients also that this in fact is the case, that teeth are feet and feet are teeth, *and their patients, deferential, submissive, and without recourse, believe them.*

An absurdity, you say, pure silliness, foolish make-believe— dentists who, through inflexibility or inertia or the absence of change or growth through experience, believe that teeth are feet and feet teeth, dentists who instruct their patients in this truth. How absurd! How quaint and fanciful! How childish!

And yet, unfortunately, not so. If only the example *were* quaint and fanciful, merely childish. But our imaginary dentists in truth are perfectly sound and logical parallels to all those in the literary humanities throughout academia who claim to be professing literature or literary studies when in fact they are professing something considered by them to be superior, namely, an applied and practical program—more or less philosophically based, generally leftist or liberal, varyingly faint or bold, in range from the explicit to the merely implied—of social and political morality, ethics, and justice, sometimes broadly and sometimes very narrowly construed indeed. These instructors are, in short, professing *values.* Exactly like the dentists who put bridges and caps on heels and toes, these instructors also show, in a nutshell, that *they don't know what they're doing*. Specifically, although their title may be Professor of Literature, they show that they don't know what literature is, don't know what it's for, don't know why it exists, why it endures, or how it works.

They are, in short, false practitioners, demeaning literature, falsifying it, certainly not letting it speak for itself. In these senses, they are hypocrites, falsifiers, prevaricators, abusers, and misleaders.

Strong charges, desperate words. How could it have happened? And, as Hamlet asked the ghost, *What should we do?*

three

i

The idea of "art for art's sake" has earned an abominable reputation, especially in the muscular world of meat-and-potatoes literature— or in the world of quiche and two-hours-at-the-gym literature— that we appear to be living in now. Artwork without any purpose, especially *written* artwork without any purpose, is a notion that probably more people are more uneasy with and more suspicious of than at any other time in history, at least in the United States.

Why? In America-the-rough-and-tumble, any sign of the mannered or effete in an artwork almost always tends to destine it for a relatively short and airless life, if indeed it achieves much of any life at all. Practicality matters a lot, and books are preferred that *say* something, take a stand, have a position, or at least develop a recognizable attitude—which, if done right, is almost always taken as the equivalent of a book or author's having *said* something.

In American literature, it's not difficult to trace this tendency. Melville failed disastrously with the great if enigmatic *Moby-Dick* after having succeeded previously with books of South Seas adventure and a much simpler exoticism. Hawthorne almost always *seemed* to be saying something—in fact, I argued in my own senior thesis forty-two years ago that he had a hard time writing at all, no matter how much he wanted to, *until* he had something like a message that "allowed" him to go ahead. Emily Dickinson is a genius-struck anomaly, read widely only after her death and subsequent discovery by academics. The naturalists and realists (Crane, Norris, Dreiser, Upton Sinclair, etc.) invariably were taken as having plenty of message, if only by merit of their portrayals of society's (or nature's) cruelties and injustices, as, too, did the so-called proletarian writers—John Steinbeck, Clifford Odets, Jack Conroy, John Dos Passos, Nelson Algren, and so on. Ezra Pound and the Imagist school began in the Dickinson manner—poetry was poetry—but even Eliot himself (published early in Harriet Monroe's *Poetry* magazine, as was Pound) grew to his enormous fame largely owing to message and meaning ("The Waste Land" speaks for itself, does it not, as "statement") in the disillusioned years following World War I. Hemingway, Faulkner, F. Scott Fitzgerald—on and on, the question of what's being "said" or "done" determines how writers are received and is a question unlikely to go away.

Nor should it. God knows that there's nothing wrong with books having meanings, nor is there anything automatically philistine in preferring that they do (though meaning—or message-meaning—is no necessity, as Gertrude Stein, for example, can show). But whether literary works, books, poems, and the like, have meanings isn't what I'm concerned about. I'm concerned about whether they're allowed to have their *own* meanings or whether, with the new professoriate at the helm, they're having those meanings stripped off and tossed away while other meanings—meanings not at all their own—are foisted upon them.

As for the traditional American preference for some kind of meaning that, as it were, you can get your hands on, I mention it only as a way of helping to explain, in some part, how so dreadful a situation could have come about as we now have, whereby "meaning" and "purpose," long favored, have been elevated to a position of greater importance than the very works themselves which the meanings, once upon a time, were understood to have come *from*.

Today, meanings tend to come from preexisting ideas, beliefs, attitudes, theories, or prejudices: Males are killers, the West is evil, women are oppressed, colonialism is bad, racism is too, also anti-Semitism, gays are better than straights, *every*one in the world is the same as everyone else—*except* for those who say they're better than others, and of course they have the *right* to say that. The holders of these preexisting ideas then either impose them upon pieces of literature (*Huck Finn* shows that Twain is racist) or use the works themselves merely to *prove* or *exemplify* the ideas (*Things Fall Apart* proves that colonialism is bad, *The Yellow Wallpaper* that males are insensitive oppressors of females).

Those, like me, who don't consider such proofs, or such gatherings of evidence, to be a compelling use of literature are struck at once by something of rudimentary importance: that reducing literature to the status of message-bearing instrument reveals that the messages it is *capable* of bearing are, at best, childish, simple, transparent, jejune. And that doesn't necessarily mean that such messages are either *wrong* or *untrue*, but, indeed, as I said, merely that they are, at best, childish, simple, transparent, and jejune.

Everyone remembers high school, or junior high school, and the reading-encouragement programs that English teachers made into a unit for at least part of each year, basing this undertaking largely on the old staple, the "book report." *Then*—in, say, the seventh or eighth grade—the "moral" of a book was something I remember invariably being asked to identify. The book reports, often, were to be composed according to a particular form—what is the plot of the book? Setting? Main character? And what did this book mean to you, or, what did you learn from reading this book?

Answer: I learned that you should trust friends only after you have known them for a certain time; or, I learned that you should never go camping or boating without carrying the proper equipment; or, I learned that sports can be dangerous, but team-work makes them less so; or, I learned that you should never auto-matically believe everything a person tells you, even if that person is an adult.

Ah, simplicity! Ah, childhood! Ah, the clarity, profit, and delight of reading!

The truth is, seventh- or eighth-graders *could* learn things from reading, in fact can and did learn things, and I hope still do. Reading is broadening, as the librarians used to say and I imagine still do, although doubtless they speak to many fewer listeners, as the NEA report has shown. But from books, true enough, one learns about foreign lands, customs, mores; one learns about the ancient world, past events, history; one learns about exploration, adventure, loneliness, food, fear, the weather, cities, farms. One learns about pigs, horses, cats. One learns about bow ties, cravats, crinolines, spinets. One learns—or used to—about sex.

But none of this has the least thing to do with literature, though it does have a lot to do with *reading*. It has nothing to do, that is, with the great traditions of literature, and certainly not with literature as a field of study deserving the attention of serious undergraduates—let alone the lifelong attention of full-fledged adult intellectuals. There's an enormous difference between reading for knowledge or information and reading as a literary experience. Needless to say, there's overlap between them—you learn what a coulter is from "The Miller's Tale," the relation between microcosm and macrocosm from *Hamlet*, what the great chain of being is from *Lear*, the importance of René Descartes from *Waiting for Godot*, and the song "I Dreamt That I Dwelt in Marble Halls" from Joyce's story "Clay."

And yet not a single one of these items or pieces of information is the reason, or even one reason, for reading those works, nor is it the reason, or even one reason, why those works have endured. To read for information is fine and good, essential even. But to read works of *literature* for information is mere foolishness, waste, fatuousness, and folly. One learns from literature, yes, but the first, the essential, the *real* reason one reads literature—the only reason, in truth—is not for knowledge but for *experience*.

And what kind of experience is that? Unquestionably, it's one that will vary, sometimes greatly, from reader to reader, just as it will vary, sometimes greatly, from book to book or poem to poem. And, like all experience, its nature and value will depend also to a considerable degree on the readiness and capacity of the one who is having it. So much, though, for the differences. What makes this experience the same in every case, and what accounts for its uniqueness and importance, is that it's not possible for it to be one-sided—that is, it isn't possible for it to be *only* intellectual or *only* emotional. This is true not just in literature but in all the arts, although it's probably more commonly noticed in literary art than elsewhere. But the key fact is that this experience *must be* and in fact, if come upon correctly and engaged in correctly, *cannot be other than a perfect fusion of the intellectual and the emotional.*

A person could name the experience "art-emotion," as in fact Eliot did name it, although in a slightly different context and without the hyphen, in "Tradition and the Individual Talent." I would argue that it could just as accurately be named "art-thought" as "art-emotion," and probably *should* be named "art-thought-emotion." In any case, and whatever it's called, this is the thing uniquely created by human responses to all the major arts: a uniting of mind and heart, intellect and emotion, idea and feeling through a bond that makes the two inseparable. The artwork creates an experience, in other words, that can't be gotten from any other source *than* art—except, very rarely, from certain moments of life itself that, both by chance and by their very nature, sometimes achieve the quality of art.

✦ ✦ ✦

Even though what I'm talking about here is as old as Aristotle, who, in *The Poetics,* tried to define art-emotion in people's responses to tragic drama, it's now nevertheless unpopular in the extreme, inside academia and out. And the charge against the idea of art-emotion is that it's associated—uh-huh, yup, again—with the irredeemable badness of all things conservative, reactionary, right-wing, and elitist.

To which I reply, at one and the same time, "Yes, of course," and, "Don't be utterly absurd."

For indeed it *is* a conservative idea—this preservation and con-servation of the ancient arts in their modern forms—and indeed it *is* an elitist idea, this notion that there are different levels or degrees (of intensity *and* of taste) that artworks can be experienced at, not to mention that these degrees are *not* all the same for everyone or that the means of gaining these experiences are learnable, so that *the experience of art can indeed be enhanced* if the artworks, as I said, "are come upon correctly and engaged in correctly."

Considering the state of affairs that has been reached in aca-demia today—the well-advanced politicizing (from the left) of the humanities and of the humanities curriculum—and consid-ering also the similar state of affairs that has been reached, if to a lesser extent, in general "literary" publishing, I know that I am now touching on raw nerves and inflammatory subjects indeed. Before I go on, therefore, a remark about conservatism versus lib-eralism. Then an explanatory comment about the word "correctly" as I have just used it.

There is no hope for the rescue of literature as it is now "taught" inside the academy, or any hope for the revitalizing of academic literary studies, and very possibly no hope, either, for the arrest of our literary age in general from its deepening slump into somno-lence and mediocrity, unless the recognition can be agreed upon by sufficient numbers of artists, academics, and intellectuals that a difference between politics and aesthetics does exist, and that it's a difference both philosophic and at the same time pragmatic and real.

Unless and until that happens, no radical change in the current and lamentable status quo can possibly occur, and the situation in the arts and in academics will grow only and generally ever more dismal.

The now much assailed T. S. Eliot once famously remarked that he considered himself "an Anglo-Catholic in religion, a classicist in literature and a royalist in politics." It clearly was—and is—not a remark intended to curry favor from the left, or perhaps from anyone. Be that as it may. The significant thing about it now, for our purposes here, is simply its three-part structure. Go onto any college campus and look up the junior or midlevel faculty members in the humanities departments, or visit the offices of any publisher of what we now rather pathetically call "quality fiction" or "literary writing." How many would you find who, when asked to identify themselves intellectually, would even *think* of dividing their answer into two parts, let alone three?

I think I know how many. It would be none.

Almost no one any longer believes, or is capable of believing, that the individual life can consist of or be made up simultaneously of different areas, elements, or categories; and that these elements can (or must) be governed by different rules or assumptions from one another; and, above all, that these different areas, however greatly different, *can still be equal to one another in significance.*

In the world around us today, it's very easy to find plentiful examples of how religion and politics have a way of gobbling people up entirely, on the one hand, and possessing them wholly; or, on the other, of seeming not to touch them at all, leaving them uninvolved, unengaged, and probably uninformed. This is hardly a universal syndrome, but it is a prevalent one. There are religious people, in other words, who tend to see *everything* in the context of their own supposedly spiritual attitudes and assumptions. There are others with this same tendency toward, in effect, the writing of entire symphonies with only a single note, except that their compositional "lens" might be political—left, center, or right—rather than religious. Less common, in fact maybe even disappearing altogether, are those types with *more* than a single intellectual method or means for taking in and processing the life around them—the active and visible public figure, for example, political or not, who has a genuine and serious religious life about which almost no one else knows; the insurance executive who, privately, is an intensely active poet; or even the ordinary person from almost any walk of life who is also a regular *reader* in some kind of regular and selective way—history, classic fiction, social commentary, even philosophy or science.

The rather dismal truth is that in the decades since the end of World War II, during the time of the nation's gradual but steady and now almost complete transformation from a society of common citizens (of whatever class) into, instead, a mass culture, into a "consumer society," during the accomplishment of this transformation, the nation's population has become far, far more intellectually single-dimensional and far more *passive* than ever before. The evidence of it is everywhere, while the results of it are everywhere denied.

I recently came upon a book that has relevance at this point, Hans Zinsser's *Rats, Lice, and History*. Zinsser (1878–1940), an American bacteriologist,[5] says that he wrote his book—a "biography" of typhus—"at odd moments as a relaxation from studies of typhus fever in the laboratory and in the field." So complex, graceful, and literate is the result—Zinsser is at home with literary figures from Irving Babbitt to Ezra Pound and from Laurence Sterne to Gertrude Stein, is a master of European history, makes use of several languages, classic Greek among them, and possesses a warm and considerable wit—so complex, painstaking, and demanding is his book, that a person today would expect it, if published at all, to achieve a certain number of library sales but very few general sales, to be reviewed politely here and there, possibly in a lay science journal or two—and then to drop like a stone.

Not so, however, in 1935, the year it was published by Atlantic Monthly–Little, Brown. Within two months of publication, the book went through five printings, then two more within the *next* two months. Little, Brown, over the following ten years, put it through *seventeen* printings. In August 1945, a month after its last Little, Brown printing, it first appeared as a wartime Pocket Book (from which the quotations here are taken).

The breadth of readership suggested by this printing history would be out of reach for the author or publisher of almost any equivalent book today. Our literary and intellectual world has changed to a near-indescribable degree over the last half-century. Here are two paragraphs from one of the earlier and rather light-hearted sections of Zinsser's book that pertain to the extent and nature of what has happened:

> A friend of ours is a professional writer. By this, we mean a person who makes his living by writing in the same way that a bricklayer makes his by laying bricks, or a plumber supports himself by sweating joints. Writing, of course, like speech, is a method of expressing ideas or telling tales. It is also a means of conveying to others emotions, conceptions, or original comprehensions which might instruct, amuse, or elevate. This kind of writing used to be called art. And once—when only the intelligent could read—writing also needed to be intelligent and artistic.
>
> In our day, however, all kinds of people can read: college professors and scrubwomen, doctors and lawyers, bartenders, ministers of the gospel and trained nurses. They all have the same

ideal of the happy ending of a dull day—a comfortable couch, a bed lamp, and something to read. And there must, in consequence, be writers to supply this need—literature for the intelligent as for the moron—a book for every brain, like a motor car for every purse. (pp. 7–8)

Today, one hardly need point out, Zinsser would be maligned for his elitist stance, whether that be implied or actual (an insignificant detail), as he would be for his unpardonable insensitivity in matters of class, intelligence, and, most certainly, "difference," using the un-euphemized "moron," for example, callously contrasting professor and scrubwoman, even making an arch and subtly disparaging allusion to the famous presidential phrase, "a chicken in every pot": He would, in other words, be seen as flagrantly in breach of one of today's most insistent pseudo-intellectual and pseudo-political dicta, as mentioned before, namely, that *everyone* in the world is the same as everyone else—*except* for those who say they're better than others.

But do something else. Just consider the two paragraphs historically. That is, take them for what they show or suggest of and about their *own* time, and then contrast that finding with equivalent characteristics of *our* time. Doing that, a person can hardly escape recognizing that the massive losses we've sustained since then—socially, culturally, even *as* individuals—are simply extraordinary in dimension and importance.

Reading. We hardly read at all compared with the reading—even just of newspapers—that went on then. And, aside from what's read at work, most reading is done as a time-filler rather than as something meaningful in and of itself, or something to be desired in and of itself. Lots of books are published, and lots of books are sold, but on a per capita basis, those numbers suddenly become quite trivial. Too, the depth, variety, and intellectual energy and independence of most of what's read is, generally speaking, in a state of pervasive cheapness and diminishment. We're terrible readers, really. What we *are* good at, as a nation, in numbers more enormous than could have been imaginable to anyone in 1935, is "watching" things, mainly, but far from only, television.

❖   ❖   ❖

In spite of what on the surface may seem evidence to the contrary—the abundance of "choices" in the daily lives of "consumers," the ease of satisfying certain individual interests and desires—we have, as a people, in the most important ways, grown more and more passive over the past half-century, if only in our willingness to accept ever greater simplification in our daily lives—in our material lives, certainly; in our aesthetic lives, without any question whatsoever; and in our emotional lives, which arguably are the logical product of the first two.

More things are the same as one another than ever before, and the probability, in our "market" and "consumer" economy, is that these similarities will go on becoming more apparent rather than less—in food, houses, highways, cars, the look, feel, and sound of movies, television, radio, music, even books, in all things, that is to say, that are intended to be "consumed" by the "consumer" (or "fed to" by the "feeder"), this "consumption" being a process that becomes more profitable the more controlled, massive, efficient, and *simplified* it can be made. We live, as I suggested earlier and as I argued at length in my first chapter, in an Age of Simplification.

That simplification, however, has proven to be much more than only a *material* simplification. At some point in the sixty years that have now followed V-J Day, even though no single or specific decision was made at any single or specific moment to bring it about, Americans made a Faustian bargain. In exchange for what in the 1950s was presented as or thought of as the "modern" or "efficient" or the "labor-saving"—in exchange, that is, for what has now become our "consumer economy" or "market economy"—

Americans gave away, knowingly or not doesn't matter, a vital, invaluable, possibly irreplaceable inner core of essential independence, privacy, and individual will.

Certain vital elements of selfhood, a person could say, were given away or lost in exchange for this groundswell of affluence, this sea-change in the nature of the individual, or in exchange for what was simply—a convincing argument can certainly be made—a refinement and intensification of patterns, qualities, and elements that had been in our society and in our social economy all along and were now themselves just being "modernized" or made efficient.

Many indeed saw it coming, but no amount of intellectual or socio-analytic commentary could slow the movement of massive economic and corporate forces that had no political brakes—that in fact gained momentum by the removal politically of barriers *to* its growth as corporate, government, and military interests increasingly merged and came increasingly to serve one another. The warnings seem quaintly old-fashioned now, the buzzwords and books, the alarms put out by the then-already-vestigial intelligentsia as it pondered and feared the enormity of what was happening—in books like *The Organization Man, Middletown,* and *Why Johnny Can't Read*—the studied but impotent opposition to developments like the new and manipulative "subliminal advertising," the unnaturalness and waste of "planned obsolescence," and the ongoing alarm at the spreading pervasiveness of "conformity" itself, this last being a character-eroding trait understood to manifest itself both inwardly and outwardly, both socially and psychologically, both in feeling and in thinking.

All of it appears rather distant and primitive and quaint indeed, from the view we have of it now, here in our *true* mass culture, with our *truly* market-driven tastes and habits and fashions and attitudes and food and music and books and clothing, in this brave new world where inner and outer, private and public, artwork and ad, conscience and collaboration have never in the social or political history of the entire world been *less* distinguished from one another than they are now.

Suppose a person were to assume a *normal* state to mean being in control—at least to a certain, acceptably meaningful extent—of one's own private, aesthetic, intellectual, emotional, inner, personal life and of the many and varied choices necessitated by and involved in these aspects of one's individual life. In other words, suppose that to be normal meant to be *independent* instead of conformist, passive, and compliant. If that *were* what "normal" meant, as I think it is, then a person living in our market-driven, mass, consumer society today—somebody like you or me, say, in our daily life, private life, work life, artistic life—would find it necessary to live as an alert, unremittingly vigilant radical oppositionist every instant of every twenty-four hours *simply in order to be normal.*

Redefining "normal" this way, to mean "independent," results immediately in almost the entire population being also automatically redefined, but redefined as *abnormal*. The huge majority of people, that is, having allowed vital core elements of their selfhood to be usurped, redefined, and taken over by the mass media, the controlling market-nation, and all the powers at its disposal; this huge majority of people is now *abnormal* because they aren't any longer independent selves. Meanwhile, those few who really *are* still independent, and therefore normal, are seen by the huge majority as being the opposite, as being the *ab*normal ones. Once this situation has come into existence, with "normal" thus redefined, a number of strange and sometimes terrible phenomena arise.

Among these things, some of them frequently in the news, are increases in paranoia, conspiracy theory, and vigilantism. And, according to our redefinition of "normal," all three of these are in fact normal. The difficulty with them, however—and here we draw closer to the heart of the matter as regards art and literature—is that most of the time they aren't so much wrong, in the sense of erroneous, but that, like the half-truth, they're *incomplete*.

Paranoia least so, and only partly because, unlike the other two, it isn't in itself an *action*. But anyone who is *entirely* free of paranoia in a mass culture like ours, one in which *lying* is the fundamental lubricant and building block for the national-corporate economy—to be *entirely* free of paranoia in such an atmosphere would require a person to be wholly blinded to the nature of the self in contrast to what surrounds that self and to the forces that attempt simultaneously to drain and control that self for consumerist, market, government, and corporate reasons. To reach such a state of nonparanoia, one would need to be transformed virtually into a nonperson, entirely lacking in will *except* such "will" as is encouraged or comes from outside. Such a person as this would, of course, exemplify the figure of the consumer brought to perfection.

In truly normal situations, paranoia in general can be diminished or made to disappear through the introduction of simple information providing rational explanation for such fears as originally gave rise to the paranoia. Paranoid fear of a uniformed stranger who enters the basement of your house once monthly can be dissipated by the information that the person is reading the water meter. Difficulties arise, though, when such allaying information is either unavailable or unbelievable. Or purposely false. In the absence of credible or true information, the uniformed man would, even should, reasonably be feared.

The same tends to be true in the other cases, of vigilantism and conspiracy-theorizing—namely, that meliorative information either doesn't exist, is held back, is untrue, or is unbelievable. Such healing or meliorative information—otherwise known, of course, as the truth—may be twisted, silenced, shielded, obscured, or made unattainable by near-endless varieties of means, implicit or explicit, through omission or commission, by action or inaction, by entities as seemingly dissimilar as 3M and the CIA, or the National Security Council and the Disney Corporation. Writing in the aftermath of the attacks of 9/11, Gore Vidal illustrates such matters and ponders them in most unnerving, paranoia-inducing, yet revealing ways.[6] Though I am myself afraid of vigilantes and self-armed groups and am inclined in general to consider them crazy, still, the wonder to me isn't that there's so *much* vigilantism, conspiracy-theorizing, or separatism in our nation, but that there's so *little,* considering how vast, unimaginable, enormous, and virtually commonplace are the cover-ups we live with.

But things remain generally quiet, since the blind don't rebel.

⁂ ⁂ ⁂

Readers may fear that I've wandered a long way from my starting point, when I declared myself to be setting out on a program aimed at the rescue of a literary way of thinking. The fact is, though, that we're only now nearing the point where we can identify exactly how it is that that way of thinking, or that literature itself, has been made needy of rescue in the first place. It's no surprise that I find the blame lying most immediately with those who, over the past thirty or so years, have brought about the politicizing not so much of the university proper—however much the university proper may need reform—but with those who have brought about the politicizing of the *curriculum,* predominantly the humanities curriculum, and certainly the literary one.

Less readily apparent, though, may be the parallels between these humanities-politicizers, on the one hand, and the vigilantes and militiamen, on the other, even though these two groups— armed militia members and chalk-wielding English professors— may be two of the least likely groups in the world to be thought of as in any way whatsoever comparable. But the similarities, in kind if admittedly not in degree, are meaningful and evident. Both live lives that are a stout blend of cynicism, disbelief, doubt, and rigid conviction. Both are dedicated to an ideal. And both have been brought into existence in large part through having been born and nurtured in and by a world in which true-truth and false-truth— that is, personal and lived truth, on the one hand, and large-cultural or "official" truth, on the other—have come to be more extremely, thoroughly, and programmatically separated from one another than at any other time in history.

✦ ✦ ✦

The elementary level first: Many, many people routinely disbelieve many, many things that their government declares to be true. Some of the time this disbelief is simply the result of paranoia, but much of the time, also, it's the result of experience. Once deceived, twice shy. One hardly need go terribly far in defense of this point—no farther, say, than to reread "Politics and the English Language" and conjecture how Orwell might react if he were to come back to the world of the living for a few days, to watch some television, read some speeches, maybe attend a press conference or two, in order to ponder the extent of our now-achieved expertise in the uses of language as a tool of dodge and deceit, half-truth, omission, and what's nowadays called spin—which is to say, our expertise in the uses of language as a tool for lying.

Any reasonable person should be and hardly can help but be alert to deception in politics and political language; to take any other stance is to be naive or foolish, as people have known since Homer and of course before. But in my own lifetime, two innovations have developed—and have been developed—that have added greatly to the complexities of keeping one's bearings vis-à-vis the true-truth. The significance of these innovations, to any thinking person, can't easily be overestimated.

One of these changes is that government itself—and with it most corollary structures of political thought—has been merged into our system of corporate, market, and capitalist economics, with the result that we govern ourselves—and we are governed—as much by economic forces as by any forms of social or political thought or ideology. This is why there exists what Eisenhower first called—in warning us of it—the "military-industrial complex," and this is also—in an even more radical, devastating, and important change—why we came to be transformed, as if while sleeping through some long-ago and unknown midnight, from a nation of citizens into a nation of "consumers."

The second of the two extraordinary innovations to have occurred in my lifetime is part and parcel of the first. It's that the broadcast media, which indeed existed well before February 27, 1947,[7] were transformed, very largely but not solely through the advent of television, into genuinely "mass" media and thus, in their function as supporting handmaiden to the economy-government or government-economy, grew rapidly into the single most powerful agent for the influence and conditioning of individual attitude, behavior, aesthetic sense, and will ever to have been known on the face of the earth or in the entire history of humanity.

One of my own biggest questions is this one: Why is literature, today, the contemporary writing that's now being produced, published, sold, and possibly even read—why is it so wretched? Exceptional things appear, of course, from time to time. And "wretched" may be too strong a word: I could substitute "middling" or "mediocre," although in matters of the arts—once thought of as the "high arts"—mediocre, essentially, is wretched.

So why is our contemporary literature, for the greatest part, depleted, predictable, imitative, and shallow? To put the question another—and possibly less offensive—way, why is our contemporary literature so extraordinarily untouched by greatness, passion, fierceness, intensity, rage, desire, compulsion, deep seriousness, courage, or even pure, aesthetic *need*—the *need,* that is, to give aesthetic expression to something?[8]

I think I know why, at least in part, though doubtless there are more reasons than one. The "workshopping of America" hasn't helped and in fact has served to diminish the level of intensity brought by writers to their writing. By emphasizing "craft" over genius, by being hyper-egalitarian and democratic—the arts, after all, can thrive in a democracy but can't thrive *if* democratic (more in a moment)—and by falling prey to the same "issue-oriented" and putatively politicized thinking and pedagogy that have preyed on the rest of the university humanities, the writers' workshops have steadily established themselves as more and more widely destructive and pernicious.

In writing courses and programs, this politicizing is even more immediately damaging than in literary studies generally, because it has the result of influencing, if not outright determining, the *subject matter* of writing, thus not only (again) emphasizing what writing *says* over what it *is*, but, even worse, eroding the understanding that writing must have its first origin not in a "subject" or "idea" or "issue" but in and *only* in the *essential, lived, individual experience* of life—this being an experience and concept unavailable if one thinks first in, of, as, or for a group or part of a group (other than the human one).

But there's more to be said about the disappearance of the individual—in writing and in the world—and so I must return to the subject of the mass media.

❖ ❖ ❖

A few moments ago, I just said that the mass media—which now include not only television but movies, books, printed images, advertisements of every kind everywhere, tapes, songs, recordings, radio voices, even our clothing, which is motley with logos, statements, and corporate messages—I said that the mass media were "the single most powerful agent for the influence and conditioning of individual attitude, behavior, aesthetic sense, and will ever to have been known on the face of the earth or in the entire history of humanity."

Can this be true, and, if it is, *how* is it true? Almost without doubt, it can't be proven. Equally, if someone *doesn't* believe it, the chances of my convincing them otherwise are infinitesimal if not nonexistent. I myself have been thinking about this question for more than forty years. And I believe that what I've just said about it is true.

People can become cynical and paranoid because they know that they have been tricked in the past—that their government, for example, lied to them, and that therefore, *if nothing else,* it can't be trusted not to do so again, or even not to be doing so now. We reserve the label of "paranoia" for this pattern of behavior if those exhibiting it are, say, a group of fifty up in the hills declaring themselves a sovereign nation dedicated to individual freedom and willing to shoot any federal agents coming into the hills to tell them they can't do that or to prevent them from doing it.

Probably the most important thing to bear in mind about this situation and others like it is that the people up in the hills are behaving as they do *because they cannot and therefore do not believe the truth of anything the approaching agents or any other representative of their government says.* Now, shift gears and consider another situation that's parallel to this one, though it may not seem so at first. Take American college teachers. Take English professors in particular, the ones I've spoken about before, who repudiate what they would call art for art's sake and see the value of literature instead to reside in its capacity for carrying "message"; who haven't changed the positions and views they formed all the way back in the 1960s; who profess the idea that social and political morality and justice are of an importance superior to that of literature or literary study; and who nevertheless remain, as they have for many, many years, members of the faculties in a variety of departments *not* of social politics but of literary studies, mainly "English."

Readers, doubtless, will anticipate my next step, which is to point out that, like the radical separatists in the hills, these English professors are also skeptical toward government, rejecting the truth of what the government officially says or declares to be true (although their standard of rejection may indeed be less absolute than the hill people's). The professors, however, differ from the separatists in having also *other* sources of authority besides the federal government that they also *do not*—because they *cannot*—believe in as truth-giving. These are literary studies, first, and, second, literature itself.

More needs to be said about both of these, but, first, another word on the parallels between the professors and the militiamen. We agreed that the militiamen are called paranoid for *not* believing—because they *cannot* believe—in the government. The case of the professors, however, is different. For *not believing* in what they don't believe in because they *can't*—these things being the government, literary studies the way they used to be, and literature—we call them not paranoid, like the hill people, but *politicized.*

And justly so, one might think. The militiamen are dangerous, carry guns, can be harmful, at times truly do wreak damage. There's no real comparison. The English professors, after all, aren't *abnormal.* They don't do any damage, any real harm.

And yet, I wonder.

✤   ✤   ✤

I don't know of an English professor who has threatened to shoot people (though a student did once threaten to shoot *me*), and, while I know of many who are anti-government, or at least anti-establishment, activists in various ways, I know of none who have turned to terrorism, arms, or explosives. Dreadful as English professors may be or may have become, none are known to have been involved in anything remotely like the 9/11 attacks or the Oklahoma City bombing. In this sense, clearly, the militiamen and vigilantes are not logically equivalent to the professors.

But it's indisputable, at the same time, that professors hold positions of a certain amount of power, not only the power to influence students' careers, present and future, but the power in some degree to shape and influence their minds, outlooks, assumptions, attitudes, habits, and values. And one can't help but wonder—*I* can't help but wonder—how much damage they may actually do, may possibly have done already, and may be capable of doing.

It's time to turn to the one, central, most radical question in this entire discussion—the question of what it is, in fact, if anything, that literature *does* teach; what the essential element and aspect of literature is that constitutes its unassailable reason for being; what true value and importance it has: what the thing in it and about it is, in other words, that the new professors miss, that they don't perceive and don't understand, and that consequently they can't possibly "teach" but can effectively, in whatever practical terms one might imagine or suggest, only teach *against,* just as the separatist militiamen can function only *against* their government or state.

Many things indeed can be *learned* from literature, but at bottom it *teaches* only one irreducible thing, and it does this, as I said earlier, through the experience one has *of* literature.

History, geography, manners; nations, tribes, people near and far; cities, farmlands, ships at sea; habits, mores; traditions; religions, faith, skepticism, villainy, cowardice, nobility—the list of things to be learned or learned *about* from literature could theoretically go on forever: people, times, places, and events as large as Napoleon's Russian defeat or as small as the beady eyes of Miss Brill's fox fur.

But this kind of learning, however pleasant, useful, or even highly valuable it may be, has virtually nothing whatsoever to do with literature, the art of literature, literature's reason for being, *or* what literature teaches. Indeed, the kinds of knowledge I've been referring to just now are available—and usually more efficiently gotten—from sources of almost every and any kind, written, recorded, taped, filmed, or photographed, not to mention that the simple acts of traveling or touring can and should result in them, too.

In eighth grade, this kind of knowledge-provisioning was presented as literature's purpose and as being, at least very, very largely, its reason for existing, perhaps along with its offering of "morals and civility" lessons of the sort I mentioned earlier. That, however, was in eighth grade, and the use of literature for knowledge, message, and morality has naturally been left behind by readers who have grown, changed, and matured with the passage of time— although, lamentably, that eighth-grade method of reading, as I have said, has now risen up even to college classes and programs under the influence of the undereducated new professors, and has now, for some increasingly grim time already, begun to leach out of the campuses and spread throughout the land.

The one thing that literature teaches doesn't belong to it alone, for *all* the arts also teach it. The literary arts, however, for the simple reason that they're based in narrative—and in words—do this teaching more visibly than is often the case with painting, for example, or music. Literature's teaching occurs, as I said before, when the unique art-emotion is experienced that engages equally the heart and mind, the intellectual and the emotional self. When such art-moments are successful, idea and feeling are in concert, with neither in a superior rank to the other, but each absolutely equal to the other in significance and also in function. Then, when the reader, viewer, or experiencer is simultaneously, equally, and powerfully swept up in emotion and immersed in thought—then, what those who have such an experience will be "taught" is that they are *alone*, no matter how large the human race; that they are each isolated, imprisoned, entrapped in a single, individual body, being, and consciousness, one individual self; and that this individual self is the single most essentially crucial thing in the entire universe—for without it, there would be *nothing else whatsoever.* One is quintessentially alone in the self. Yet only from within this unspeakable limitation, the imprisoning limitation of the single self, *and in no other conceivable way,* can the universal be seen, perceived, understood, experienced—and possibly, even, created.

✤ ✤ ✤

Simple. A simple idea, a simple recognition. And yet at the same time a profound one, a universal one, and one irrefragably connected to the very bedrock essence itself of what it means to exist, of what existence *is,* and even, therefore, what "meaning" *is.* This simple, rudimentary thing—art-experience or art-emotion (it could justly be called *felt-understanding* or *awareness-feeling*) brings into one's awareness the existence of the *meaning-respondent self* and "teaches" the vital, absolute importance, the essentialness, of the self as an entryway to *all other experience,* or, perhaps, to *all other experience that can contain meaning.*

Literature, then, teaches very little, but what it *does* teach, through the experience of it, is of an enormous and enormously humanizing importance and meaning indeed. The lesson itself, as well as the experience of "learning" it, is at once epistemological, cosmological, metaphysical, and, of course, aesthetic. None of these is of much interest to the new professoriate, who are as likely as not to condemn all of those adjectives (especially "aesthetic") twice over, the first time for being "elitist," the second for being of no political or practical use in the bringing about of justice or social reform, but for leading only, as they blindly see it, to the various and indefensible misdirections, indulgences, and falsehoods of "art for art's sake."

That I believe they are gravely in error is obvious by now. But it does need to be declared that the new professors, no more than the militant men in the hills, are in fact not doing what they say and think they are doing—that is, working to bring about justice, individual liberty, and social reform. Instead, unbeknownst to themselves, they are actually laboring for their own worst enemy, the oppressive and not-to-be-trusted political-economic-corporate "government." They are, in truth, actively helping to demean, subvert, and destroy what's genuinely individual in people, and they are helping to replace it with the latest perfected model of the diminished, obedient, passive consumer. They are, from dawn to dusk, collaborating with the very enemy they think that they especially have the wisdom to defeat.

ii

A while ago, I conjectured about the way "normal" and "abnormal" might be defined in a mass culture that, like ours, is shaped and driven by massive forces intended to increase—or to create and then increase—first, conformity, then, resultantly, "consumerism." Everyone has read (and if they haven't, they'd better) *1984*, *Brave New World*, *Darkness at Noon*, and other lesser known but similar works about emotional and intellectual control over people and populations, and for a long time now the question has been argued as to how invasive, extensive, and successful such control has become in the United States. My own impression of the matter has been made fairly clear, I think, both here and in the chapter before this one, and isn't very optimistic. Evidence of the spread of such control seems to me everywhere, certainly in television and popular music but also in other arts, including current "serious" or "quality" literary writing. News, advertising (the same thing, really, just as shows and ads are the same thing), the intellectual level of political speaking and campaigning—it seems to me fairly clear as I look about myself at age sixty-four and compare the view with what I saw at, say, age twenty, that, yes, "dumbing down" is real, has made plenty of headway, and is a grave, grave enemy of the free mind and of a free nation. One thing of enormous importance about "dumbing down" that's not noted often enough is that the phenomenon isn't simply a *result* of other forces but is *itself* one of those forces. That is, the decline into greater and greater ignorance and depravity isn't only a *result* of pervasive, large-scale control over huge numbers of individual hearts and minds, but, once begun, it's itself one of the most powerful *means* of exercising, expanding, and further intensifying that control.

Readers at this point will react in varying ways, I don't doubt, depending on their own attitudes, backgrounds, and experiences. My own reactions are strong enough to have brought me to the writing of this book. They are also strong enough to have increased my pessimism sufficiently that I have now begun doubting whether a turnaround is any longer possible, whether a national enlightenment can any longer occur, whether essential civil liberties, until now constitutionally protected, can survive, let alone whether liberty and justice for all—let "god" do what he, she, or it may—can continue to be protected, let alone furthered.

The essential threat, the true and genuine threat at the heart of all the others, is the threat to the individual. This fact often remains unseen and unremarked. We are, after all, or we once were, said to be a nation of individuals, to value individualism, to pride ourselves on our individuality, and we live, of course, in a nation whose founding was dedicated to the protection of individual freedoms. But so much of that has now been eroded, so much of it has been made a sham, so much has been bent, twisted, numbed, used, channeled, undervalued, pandered to, fawned over, flattered, demeaned, made un-self-conscious, programmatically undernourished, and, again and again and again, so endlessly and unremittingly exploited as an easy means to ever baser and baser and baser ends—that the damage, if nothing else, has grown to the point of having become threatening to the nation's very life.

At a time when the essence of the individual is so endangered as this, so monstrously exploited by economic, corporate, market, governmental, and mass-cultural forces as to be converted into a thing of blankness, ignorance, and above all *passivity*—is it, at such a time, encouraging to find the new professors, who claim to be struggling *against* this very exploitation, aiding and abetting it instead, themselves wholly unaware of what they're doing?

✳ ✳ ✳

If, as I proposed earlier, a normal person is a person as fully in control as possible of his or her own private, discriminating, aesthetic, emotional, and thinking life—if "normal" means being independent in these ways rather than conformist and compliant—then the importance, especially for students and other young people, of the achieving of an awareness of that self through art-experience needs little explanation or defense. Nor is the harm done by the new professors an especially mysterious thing: In making the purposes of literature practical, applied, public, and political, they remove the previously dominant relation—that is, the relation between the *individual self* and art—and replace it with the now-dominant relation of the *group* to art. Further, in reducing literature (or any art) from *experience* to *message*, they transform—reductively, it hardly need be said—the self from being vital experiencer (of the artwork) to being passive recipient (of the message).

That these are pernicious changes is clear to anyone whose hopes and aims are dedicated to the protection, growth, and robustness of the self in the face of a powerfully exploitative culture that aggressively seeks the self's weakening, diminishment, predictability—

and passivity. And how can it conceivably be, one asks, that so pro-grammatically destructive a change should have arisen where it has—inside the place that is the very last place it ever should have arisen, inside the university, the institution more than any other (or so one thought, hoped, and believed) dedicated to freedom of thought and inquiry, its roots in deep antiquity, an establish-ment set on the bedrock of reverence for the individually inquir-ing mind?

✣   ✣   ✣

Before answering that most dread of questions—how the academic humanities became an enemy of us all—let me make an additional clarification about the self as I'm talking about it. This is impor-tant, since I've used "public" and "private" as antitheses, and the meaning of these concepts in relation to the self needs to be made clear.

Most simply put, the "private" self is the part more self-aware and the part more completely or successfully in control of its own actions and decisions. It is therefore the more active and less pas-sive. It is the more autonomous kind of self. It is the more likely to be concerned, whether greatly or little, with its own identity, definition, purpose, and uses. It is the more likely to "see" itself by identifying its distinctions *from* others rather than by counting up its similarities *to* them. It is the more introspective, and the more hesitant to take action without first thinking about the meaning of the action. It more effectively resists conditioning than the other part of the self does.

This more "private" self—or this more private *side* of the self—is the one that tends to be awakened, drawn out, or enhanced through the experiencing of art, or, as I said earlier, through art if experi-enced *correctly*—that is, as art, not message, as an experience of *itself*, not of something brought *to* it for it to "prove" or "exemplify." I know perfectly well that the moment a phrase like "experience of *itself"* appears in an argument (not to mention "if experienced *correctly*"), as it did just now, any new professors, if listening, would roll their eyes as if to say, "I *told* you so," or, "Here we go *again*," and that they would prepare immediately to denounce the effeteness, elitism, and social and political irrelevance *and* exclusiveness of "art for the sake of art," or, in its more familiar phrasing, "art for art's sake."

I think I understand why they would react this way, and I also sympathize with it, for reasons I'll explain in a moment. But at the same time I must condemn their response as a ruinous error, an enormous blunder and misjudgment whose destructiveness may very well, when all consequences have run their course, be immeasurable.

For, if experienced not only correctly but also *well*—or, I might say, if *taught* not only correctly but also well—the art-experience won't awaken the much (and rightly) dreaded kind or sense of self that really *is* elitist, egocentric, superior, and exclusive. That kind of self, in my own view, is largely a public self, often a product of affluence, largely blind to an understanding of its own true nature and identity, and a self *not* brought into existence or caused to grow by the experience of art but rather by the experience of money, property, or prestige that it hopes, in part through hoarding (as a means to being exclusive), to capitalize on in one way or another for its own stature or gain.

That kind of self isn't introspective, self-doubting, or even particularly self-aware, and, as a consequence, it doesn't come into existence nor does it gain or grow through the art-experience—even though it expends much energy in the effort to make itself *appear* to have done so, in the customary form of dilettantism, though producing superficialities only.

The kind of self genuinely responsive to the art-experience, then, isn't the egotistic, vain, snobbish, or narcissistic one, not the one with a built-in sense or conviction of its own superiority or special merit. Instead, it's the self capable of being awakened, through the art-experience, to the simple realization that it, in and of itself, is the only eye through which to see others, the only door through which to join the world. This realization leads not to pride—pride in what? for what?—or vanity or exclusiveness, but more likely to a sense of wonder and awe at a thing's being so slight, small, and inconsiderable and yet of such miraculous, vital, inestimable importance. Everyone in the world is locked away in a prison of one and held incommunicado just as surely as Helen Keller or Laura Bridgman were. The self is eyes to see out with. It is a door to pass through. Without the eyes, nothing whatsoever. Without the door, no touching, ever, of anyone or anything.

Consciousness of the self in this way—as being the sole means to existence, to experience, and to *meaning*—is a consciousness that comes from what we call "education," a word whose prefix means "out" or "out from" while its root comes from the Latin *ducere*, meaning "to draw" or "to lead." Education, therefore, is a "leading out." In the context of this particular discussion, it can be thought of as a leading out from the prison of the self by *means* of the self, by means of an awakening and enhancing of awareness of the nature of, the imponderable limits of, and the limitless *value* of the self.

This kind of drawing out from the self while simultaneously heightening the awareness and understanding of self is what literature, when correctly understood and correctly experienced, is especially good at doing. It is especially good at showing that what the *world itself can be* depends on what the *self* can be—this self that remains the *only way* into experience. The self's being as good as it can be is of immeasurable importance. If the door is narrow, the experience resulting will be narrow; if dark, dark; if twisted, then also twisted. *What the self is determines what you can or will see, and therefore inevitably also what you can or will do, what you can or will think, feel, know, and be.*

In repudiating literature as *experience* and insisting upon it as *meaning*, and in taking literature from its dwelling place in the *private* and moving it to the *public*—in making just these two changes, the new professors have lost everything, and, with the best of intentions, put themselves in a position whereby they are able, for the most part, to do only harm, not good.

✦ ✦ ✦

This capacity for harm, in addition, is a considerable one. The new professors, after all, are no different from other professors in one way: namely, that they continue to send students—as time goes on, entire new generations of them—out into the world bearing marks of what they have or have not "learned" in college, and of how they have or have not changed or been changed.

And yet the new professors, in another way, are quite different indeed. Through their having embraced and then professed a radical and highly influential falsehood about literature, the waves of students they send out into the world will take along with them the dubious gift of diminished and simplified understandings of literature, of what it is and what it does. In this, there is harm enough. Worse, though, is that these students will also be the possessors of simplified and diminished *expectations* of literature, simplified and diminished *desires* for it, and simplified and diminished abilities for *experiencing* it.

And the literary "marketplace," of course, will willingly comply in providing them with what they "want"—and are capable of—as the process moves forward, the more complex being driven out, as I said in chapter 1, slowly and steadily by the more simple.

The new professors, therefore, have their own role—as do, more generally speaking, the colleges themselves—in worsening the Age of Simplification. That such a situation as this could actually have come into being draws attention to a certain fact about these faculty members that can't be overlooked: namely, that they themselves are already a "second generation" in that their own lives, rebellions, and educations have made them into what I believe is a historical first—the existence of an *intellectual class* that is a product wholly of the Age of Simplification.

As such—having lost sight of the true nature of their own field of study (and therefore of the true source of its, and of literature's, power), and most probably also having lost sight of their own private selves—they have turned academically from the advocacy and profession of what is more complex (and more true) to the advocacy and profession of what is more simple (and less true), and have done so with the conviction of belief.

Consequently, it becomes clear that the new professors are on the wrong side and are in fact helping with the work of the enemy—those powers and forces that prefer, and do whatever they can to create and nurture, passive consumers over thinking citizens who may still be in the possession of their own private selves. As the professors go about their inane scholastic alchemy of reducing all human experience into "issues" of race, class, gender, and ethnic identity, of relegating literature to the function and status of baggage-carrier; given this situation, how unlikely is it that the government-corporate powers that stand to benefit from the population's intellectual and emotional compliance and passivity would ever intervene to change the professors' direction or hold them back in their work of helping to fill the world, semester after semester, year after year, decade after decade, with the more simple over the more complex?

The Age of Simplification is well advanced, and plentiful evidence of this fact resides in almost every area of life. There is a grim but real possibility that simplification will continue to increase and flourish to the point where our democratic institutions themselves—for lack of attention, interest, understanding, and support—will grow sufficiently eroded as to collapse altogether. If and when that happens—as I hope it will not but fear it may already have done—the once-great experiment of the American nation will be transformed into a society of the sorts familiar to readers of George Orwell and Aldous Huxley.

I wish I could be stoutly optimistic, that I could declare with firmness, vigor, and certitude that such a thing will never happen. I also wish that humanities education, to which I long ago pinned my own literary, intellectual, and professional hopes, had grown into what it might have been instead of what it has become.

four

Almost anything that can be done to work against the growth and continuation of the Age of Simplification must by necessity be a *small* thing. The battle against the widely deployed forces of the passive and simplified must be made up of innumerable small battles, and each of these must take place where throughout history they have always taken place—on the tiny, isolated field of individual feeling and thought.

Every person, at least at some crucial point, must think alone. And every person, at least at some crucial point, must act alone.

Or so it seems to me, as I expect it would to anyone with a literary training of the same kind as mine—a training that, whatever its flaws, took its stand again and again against the merit or efficacy of thinking by category or group rather than through the agency of the individual and irreducible self, the eye, if you will, of the mind.

And now, in the Age of Simplification, group-think—better named nonthink—appears everywhere, as the eye of the mind falls closed.

✤ ✤ ✤

When I started college, my new classmates and I were required to sit down in a rather elegant old room called Great Hall and listen to three or four faculty members speak in turn about what study would be like in each of their fields and about what they would expect of us if we were to become their students. Reed Whitte-more spoke for literary studies—for "the English major." He asked us to imagine that we'd been given a poem to read, then had been required to submit a short paper on it.

This was the first *adult* literary lesson I'd ever had, and I remember it clearly. Whittemore described briefly a number of the papers he might typically receive—and, after each description, announced that that paper, not being about the poem, still didn't fulfill the assignment.

Admittedly, I had, at that time, a predilection toward writing and reading. I knew what I wanted to study and *had* known it for a handful of years. Nevertheless, it was a modest but thrilling moment: I was about to hear, for the first time, what it *did* mean to write about a poem.

The lesson was simple, essential, and lasting. One person, said Whittemore, wrote about what he or she *felt* after reading the poem. Another wrote about a *memory* the poem had triggered, describing the memory and explaining why the poem had triggered it. Another wrote about *liking* the poem. And so on. What was wrong with such papers? Nothing whatsoever, except that, until a paper provided a descriptive analysis of the poem—or, if you like, an analytic description—the assignment wasn't satisfied. The *poem* hadn't been written about.

At this point, from any of the new professors who may be listening in, I expect more eye-rolling and exasperation, along with the charge that I'm hopeless, a retrograde and reactionary recidivist, turning back to the blind alley that was the New Criticism during the 1940s and 1950s, with its strenuously held position that works of literature must be appreciated, understood, and studied only through *formal* analyses of them, without reference to any external questions or concerns. This was the highly influential approach perhaps best represented by Cleanth Brooks's *The Well Wrought Urn: Studies in the Structure of Poetry* (1947) and by the anthology

Understanding Poetry, first compiled by Brooks with Robert Penn Warren, in 1941, and so widely used as to be known simply as "Brooks & Warren," much as "Strunk & White" has remained shorthand for *The Elements of Style*.

But this is a game I refuse to play—the "What's My Line?" of schools of criticism, an Age of Simplification game that's as inexplicable as it is wasteful and destructive. In 1959, the New Criticism was prevalent indeed, and Reed Whittemore was making use of it in a perfectly sensible way to illustrate for a group of novices the difference between describing a poem as a crafted object[9] and describing other things altogether, such as the emotional *effect* the poem might have on a reader, *associations* it might trigger, or simply a reader's *taste*. There was, in point of fact, nothing whatsoever wrong with the New Criticism, so far as it went. It provided a practical and durable method and vocabulary for describing literary works without judging them *except* by implicit celebration of their beauty, subtlety, sophistication, and complexity. As such, it not only provided a tremendously useful pedagogic method but lent rigor and order to a useful notion of what literary taste could (and perhaps should) be based on. It offered a coherent response, further, to poetry as one main stream of it developed after Ezra Pound and the Imagists, and it served as a major corrective influence on the aging moralisms of the previously flourishing New Humanists such as Irving Babbitt and Paul Elmer More.

The only thing wrong with the New Criticism, to put it most simply, is that it was only one thing. In fact, a person could reasonably compare schools of criticism to areas of specialization in medicine. What's wrong with neurology? one might ask. *Nothing,* comes the answer, except that it neglects the circulatory system. What's wrong with cardiology? *Nothing,* comes the answer, except that it neglects the digestive system. And so on.

The only specialty in medicine, everyone must agree, that could reasonably be considered *bad*—aside from any that actively did harm—is the one that has *nothing at all to do* with the human body or its health. If this is true, returning to the first side of the comparison allows us to conclude that the new professors must indeed be bad because *their* specialty doesn't "treat" literature but, instead, politics and social justice.

We've been over that ground already, but more remains to be noticed about the analogy between medical specialties and schools of critical theory. Everyone must agree that the practice of medicine is very different now from what it was at various times in the past—and everyone must agree that, by and large, the medical establishment has *learned from* that past. There's room for qualification here—it seems clear, for example, that our medical establishment may very well know *less* about some kinds and sources of treatment—herbal, homeopathic, and holistic, for example—than earlier or even so-called "primitive" people did. What we call "science" has made errors enough amid its successes and has sometimes in effect blinded it*self* (readers of Homer, Plato, Voltaire, Swift, and Samuel Beckett are among those who know why).[10] On the whole, however, medical practice has made "progress," has learned from its own history, and has kept sight of its own true subject, namely, the human body.

Then why isn't the same true of literary studies? Why can't the field of literary studies learn from its own past, keep sight of its own true subject, and, like medical practitioners, use specialties for what they are—tools, not ends in themselves?

✤ ✤ ✤

I think literary studies can do that, and have done it, and I know that it's what I myself have tried to do and will continue trying to do. The new professors, however, don't seem so inclined. What power could be at work on them if not the power of the Age of Simplification?

The New Criticism arose three-quarters of a century ago. The

New Humanism's inception occurred more than ninety years ago—almost a century. Back and back it goes—to Arnold, Wordsworth, Coleridge, Pope, Johnson, Sydney, into antiquity through Horace, Longinus, back across the Adriatic to fourth-century Athens and the Platonic dialogues and Aristotle's *Poetics*, written *more than two millennia ago*. That's certainly enough history, and those are certainly enough tools, so that I'm not going to be ruffled if a new professor accuses me of being a New Critic—of going around, as one of them once said to me with disgust, "searching for *ironies*." If my foot hurts, I go to a podiatrist; if my tooth, a dentist; my stomach, an internist. But foot, tooth, or stomach, the true subject of such medical examining as may result is *me*, not just foot, tooth, or stomach, but the whole thing. I can and will adhere at least partially to any criticism or school of criticism, to any critical method, tool, or approach, so long as it honestly serves its subject rather than defacing, deforming, betraying, or abandoning it.

And there's the rub. The new professors have done all four, as have many of the literary theorists who keep company with them. If such people were medical doctors, their patients would be dead, and they, the practitioners (if justice were served), in jail.

✦ ✦ ✦

Who, indeed, especially this late in history, would stick with only one method, any more than a general practitioner would send his patients to only one kind of specialist—our old friend the podiatrist, say—no matter what part of their bodies might be in need of attention or care?

Yet I know someone who is still, now, today, a *socialist* critic, for heaven's sake (does anyone remember Arnold Kettle?). If this colleague were a veterinarian, he would logically have a practice restricted to—what—triceratops, conceivably. On the other hand, the truth is that since as a "professor of literature" his study is in actuality social and economic politics, not books, words, poems, and plays, his veterinary practice would, if parallel to his literary practice, include *no* animals.

If a person's subject is literature, why would that person rule out *any* critical method, so long as the subject of the criticism, too, was literature? Freudian, symbolic, archetypal, structuralist—there are beauties, qualities, complexities, and attributes in literary art to be found, seen, enjoyed, described, and celebrated by means of any of these critical approaches, and by others as well. All I ask is that when a critic's approach or method changes from being a literary one to being an *anti*-literary one, or *non*-literary one, or *extra*-literary one—that that critic practice simple and basic honesty by admitting or acknowledging the change *and* by acting accordingly. If a veterinarian hangs out a shingle saying his practice is limited to dogs and then he *proceeds to kill all the dogs brought to him*— he would be the veterinary equivalent of the literary deconstructionists and certain other of the current—or recently current— theorists. What good is it to the dogs that they be killed? Or what good to anyone else, like, say, the dog's loving owners? What good to the veterinarian himself? Probably the most disheartening and certainly the most unexpected experience of my professional life as writer and teacher has been the generalized abandonment not just of the literary life, inside the academy and out, but the generalized abandonment of the literary *project* overall as I myself understood—and loved—it not only by instinct and predilection but by training as well.

As I've said, I can't find a *central* reason for the calamity's having taken place except from the destructive forces of the Age of Simplification, an era that I fear we may be too far embarked upon for there to be hope of relief or improvement, perhaps *ever*, but certainly not before things get much, much worse than they already are. In 1992, one of the instructors from my own undergraduate days told me that it was just two or three years after my class graduated that "everything changed." Mine was the class of 1963, and by

1965 or 1966, he said, the attitudes, stances, interests, assumptions, tone, even the *manners* of students changed dramatically, and the literary life and atmosphere that he had known from the time of his arrival on the campus as an instructor in 1954 began quickly to fade, pale, drain away, disappear. My class was the last good one, he said. What he meant was that we were the last *literary* class. After that, politics and social justice took over.

And how could that conceivably be bad? Well, it was bad because it grew out of, and happened along with, simplification. Under the emerging new pattern, it appeared not only that people could no longer be more than *a single thing at a time* but that they leaned toward the more simple and away from the more complex. Why else should it have been necessary that the life of social justice and politics drive *out* the literary life, making things poorer, rather than coexisting with it and making things richer? Impossible, it seems, that anyone might, in echo of T. S. Eliot, be radical left in social justice and politics, conservative in literature, and skeptical in religion; or liberal in social justice and politics, conservative in literature, and devout in religion—or any other mixed combination. But not so. Instead, as if the self had suddenly been transformed into a single-party system, it became necessary that a person be radical, radical, and radical; liberal, liberal, and liberal; or conservative, conservative, and conservative.

Simplification of this kind spelled—and spells—intellectual, emotional, academic, and societal disaster.

❖   ❖   ❖

If it's no longer possible, in the Age of Simplification, for people to be more than one thing at a time, then any significant literary life—and any significant literature—is doomed.

Just imagine that you're a serious non-expository writer—poet, novelist, playwright, short story writer. Then imagine that a definition of "serious" or "literary" writing comprises for you (as it does for me) the following three points. The question after each point becomes whether writing of this kind *can* exist in the Age of Simplification.

1. *Serious writing may entertain, may* be *entertaining, even* must *be in some way entertaining.* But it also exists and *must* exist for a purpose beyond entertainment if entertainment is defined as *diversion,* and if diversion, in turn, is defined as pleasure that is received *without there being, in the recipient, an awakening of thought or complicating of emotion.*

In my first chapter, I lamented the vacuousness of "entertainment" when provided as a steady diet and as an end in itself; here, as a kind of corollary, the argument is that a piece of writing *can't* be significant and also be without intellectual content. Only if it's both significant and does have intellectual content can the experience of it result in the "art-emotion" I talked about earlier. In the Age of Simplification, however, if it really isn't possible for people to be more than one thing at a time, the art-emotion can't any longer be experienced. The reason for this is that the art-experience itself requires the recipient to be two things at once, insofar as it necessitates a simultaneous emotional response *and* intellectual response and can't exist without the balance, or the merging, or the symbiosis, if you will, of the two. That is, serious writing, or art of any kind, requires in its recipients thinking and feeling *at the same time.*

2. *Serious writing must have the entirety of reality as its subject matter, and this subject matter must remain as whole as possible throughout the work if the work is to remain serious.* This doesn't mean that every piece of writing must be about everything, but that serious writing must at every moment be as inclusive as is possible while still maintaining coherence. It must push the limit in this regard at every moment or lapse into the unserious. Marilynne Robinson, in an interview, expressed this idea as clearly and wonderfully as, say, Henry James might have a century ago: "Any writer," she said,

"or any moment in writing, when the imagination seems to be *as
alert as possible to everything that can be understood out of a moment
or situation,* seems to me to be when that impulse is being made
into art [emphasis mine]."[11]

The maudlin, sentimental, clichéd, banal, or farcical, therefore,
aren't *in themselves* capable of comprising serious writing because
they are, by their very nature, *incomplete.* The reality is that no
emotion exists without the presence of other emotions (half the
greatness of Shakespeare lies in his complete understanding of just
this complexity), a fact that gives serious writing, which tries to
be *whole,* its feelings of reality, maturity, substance, and humanity,
even when its subject may in other ways be *small.* As Robinson said,
whether the subject be small or large, "*everything* that can be understood out of [it]" must in some way be present in the work (present, I would add, *even if not actually expressed*). All of the policies,
forces, habits, tendencies, and indoctrinations of the Age of Simplification, however, work actively and persistently *against* exactly
this kind of wholeness. The maudlin, sentimental, melodramatic,
clichéd, banal, predictable, immature, "scary," adventurous, farcical, and thin—the *simple*—are the most highly produced, favored,
and cultivated forms of expression in the Age of Simplification
because, by calling forth no awakening of thought (certainly not
new thought) and resulting in no complicating of emotion (and
certainly not *new* emotion), they're the best suited to maintaining
the simple, the passive, and the uncomplex in those who "experience" them. This trend is and has been evident for a long time in
the realms of advertising, film, and broadcasting. But its now being
so clearly present also inside academia and trade publishing is a
strong suggestion of the increased *rate* of decline we can expect to
see in what remains, even now, of serious writing.

3. *Serious writing can't be imitative, but simultaneously it must be
conscious of the traditions it draws from.* It must in some way build
on or respond to those traditions without being enslaved by them
or being simply derivative of them.

Art-writing that has no consciousness of the traditions it grows from can't be serious in the fullest sense, though it may be able to gain richness if and as it gains in consciousness (and therefore in wholeness). Almost all published fiction today is of this traditionless kind, a characteristic that to some extent is produced by workshops, where writing is as likely to be nourished by the work of other students as by the deep roots of literature. Examples of writing that know *part* of their literary tradition and that imitate examples from it are less common yet far from rare. (The stories in Susan Minot's popular collection of 1986, *Monkeys*, are near-clones of Hemingway, Cheever, and so on.)

In other words, as with any art, in order for writing to be serious it must know its tradition, understand itself to be a part of that tradition and a result of it, and understand also that it must—to *be* art—in some meaningful way respond to or build on or rebel against that tradition (as readers of Eliot, again, well know).

Now, then, since serious writing *must* be understood as being in essential ways radically conservative—in the literal sense of conserving vital qualities from and of the past even if altering or challenging them—it follows that the practitioner of serious writing *must also be deeply conservative*. This conservatism, necessary for the production of durable significance, meaning, and seriousness in any art, can in this case be called "literary" conservatism, "aesthetic" conservatism, or even, in Eliot's term, "classicism." It is a conservatism that has nothing whatsoever to do with politics, morality, social justice, or the behavior of nations. It is solely and purely *art* conservatism. Without it, art grows journalistic, thin, light, ephemeral, and dies.

A writer or artist, of course, could also be *politically* conservative and thus be conservative both aesthetically and politico-socially (conservative-conservative), and some writers and artists are so. Among American writers now, however, and inside academic humanities today, as everyone knows, a hugely preponderant number consider themselves, as we've seen, proudly, impassionedly, actively, publicly, and immutably liberal. Fine and good, one might say. Except—what about the arts?

Assume, as is very nearly the actual case, that this preponderance of liberal people also make up the preponderance of those in the nation today who are the practitioners, custodians, and interpreters of serious writing and the literary arts. As such, if they are to reach and maintain literary seriousness, they *must* be not just politically and socially liberal but also aesthetically conservative. If this doubleness of view; if this ability to be two things at once; if the complexity of applying the self in differing ways to differing aspects and areas of life—if this ability has been lost; or if the Age of Simplification has made it no longer prestigious, desirable, *or* possible; if liberal writers, artists, and academic intellectuals have the capacity *only* of being "liberal-liberal" and *are incapable* of being "liberal-conservative"—then the nation *can not any longer* harbor, generate, or nourish a literary life; *can not any longer* build upon, sustain, or further an artistic literary tradition; *can not,* in short, continue to sustain itself as a literary nation, or as a nation with the continuance of a significantly serious literary energy, value, or importance.

✦   ✦   ✦

Evidence can easily be found that this double-disadvantage to the health of literary art is at work and has been so for some time. The double-disadvantage is the disadvantage made up, first, of the Age of Simplification itself, with its programmatic thinning-out not only of the very nature and variety of experience but of available responses *to* experience; and that disadvantage is then doubled by the symbiotic addition to it of the immeasurably pervasive and influential presence of what I've called the liberal-liberal syndrome (itself a child of the Age of Simplification, somewhat in the way that Death, in *Paradise Lost,* is a child of Sin).

Take *goodness,* for example. Never in the chronicles of known history has *goodness* been a cause, source, or determinant of significance in art, certainly not in high or literary art. In mid-twentieth-century writing, books that express, espouse, or celebrate *good* (Pearl Buck, Marjorie Kinnan Rawlings, Harper Lee, maybe John Knowles, and so on) often became popular but were seldom durable or significant in a literary way. Often, and significantly, they became identified as suitable for adolescent readers. Sometimes, too, when a book is said to express, espouse, or celebrate good—as with Anne Frank's *The Diary of a Young Girl*—the claim for the celebration of that *good* rests on willful, false, sentimentalized readings. It can easily enough be seen why this is so—why it is that artworks with *goodness* as their essential reason for being fail in general to gain significance as art—by remembering the necessity for wholeness in the subject matter of literary art, that a piece of writing have "the entirety of reality as its subject matter" and that, in Marilynne Robinson's words, it be *"as alert as possible to everything that can be understood out of a moment or situation,"* where the key word, clearly, is "everything."

The *good,* obviously, can make up only a part, however large or small, of any moment or situation in life. And it's not the part, but rather the *whole* that drives, nourishes, and sustains art—as it's the *whole* that makes art capable of achieving greatness. *The Iliad, The Oresteia, The Inferno, The Canterbury Tales, Hamlet, Lear, Crime and Punishment*—none of these are great or significant because of the *goodness* in them, though goodness there is in each. But these works are significant (along with other reasons, indeed) because of their containing, so far as their own limits permit, *all* of life, or *all* of their subject.

Today, however, in the grip of the Age of Simplification and in the midst of the liberal-liberal syndrome, literary judgments and attitudes have come to be determined increasingly by *goodness* and by the doing of *good,* with the result that our literary age is shallow, predictable, thin, lacking in vitality, and probably doomed.

✤ ✤ ✤

For the last quarter-century or so, "affirmative action" has been a visible part of national life. Its origin, as everyone knows, lay in a desire to bring about change for the good, although the kind or degree of social change that has actually resulted from it is still a matter of often strenuous debate. I have my own hopes, fears, doubts, and views, but, even so, the general subject is outside of my focus here, although I'll take it up again in the next chapter. What's pertinent now is the way that the thinking and attitudes behind affirmative action have had a parallel in literary studies, publishing, and academic thinking.

And the effect of those parallels has, without much question, been more ill than good. This isn't the sort of thing people are able—or willing—to talk about very often, and almost never without discomfiture, guilt, embarrassment, or fear of attack, misrepresentation, or misunderstanding. But liberal attitudes and behavior toward race and ethnicity tend to be one thing while pieties *about* those attitudes and behavior tend to be another. At work here is a very strict manifestation of the liberal-liberal syndrome—in fact, one *so* strict that it leads to the equivalent in thought or logic of saying not, "A cat is a cat," but, "A cat is a dog."

Fifteen years ago—in the spring of 1991—my department held a series of meetings to discuss what changes, if any, should be made in the reading lists for our required core literature courses—courses that filled a college requirement but remained under the English Department's jurisdiction. They were survey courses modeled on and derived from Columbia's "great books," or "lit hum," course, with a span that reached, over two semesters, from the classical world to the midtwentieth century.

The meetings were called because of murmurings of discontent in the department about the book lists, and, indeed, at the first meeting I attended, someone said that the lists should include "more works by women and people of color," especially in the second course, which began in the eighteenth century. I commented that I thought the books should be selected not through political criteria but by judgment of their aesthetic merit and interest, their influence, and their historical significance.[12] At this point, a third colleague took sides with the first. She rejected all my criteria, including historic—or literary—significance, judging them to be no more valid than the criteria of authors' sex, race, or ethnicity. She closed the "argument" by declaring that "all criteria are political, anyway. Everything is political."

It may be that my criteria were no more valid than hers: but they were, nevertheless, *different* from hers. But that difference, you can be sure, was not about to be explored, acknowledged, or evaluated.

It was a perfect example of the liberal-liberal syndrome. Since *doing good*—in this case by countering injustice toward women and minorities—was my colleagues' highest priority; and since their private selves had been simplified to the point where they were *capable of being only one thing at a time;* they had therefore become liberal-liberal (or social-social, political-political) rather than (as could have been possible in another time) liberal-conservative (that is, liberal in social questions but conservative in literary ones, or liberal in political matters but conservative in aesthetic ones).

Depressing and wretched enough: as if, with a single snap of the fingers, there had been caused to vanish, perhaps forever, literature, literary history, the literary life, literary studies, and post-secondary education in the arts. Presto bismo. Gone. Still, possibly worse is the crudely simplified logic used by my colleague to *defend* such a position. This is reasoning born of the Age of Simplification, when a catchy, sophomoric half-truth ("everything is political") is ignorantly or disingenuously posited as a whole truth, in fact as an absolute, with the effect, in the half-truth-teller's own well-intended and possibly sanctimonious eyes, of *justifying whatever it is that the half-truth-teller thinks ought to be done.*

Such trammeling of whole realms and regions of history, tradition, culture, and art—the waste and loss all brought about and defended in the morally irreproachable name of doing *good.*

Pieces of writing selected by the sex, race, ethnicity, or sexual preference of their author: even to *question* the practice of selecting works by these means is to open oneself to attack, misrepresentation, calumniation, and seemingly deliberate misunderstanding. Merely speaking against this mode of selection or evaluation will be taken—in the minds of the simplified—as an implicit expression of disdain for and prejudice and hostility toward whatever gender, race, or ethnicity a selected author may belong to. The logic? It can be followed only by the simplified: That is to say, it can be followed only by those for whom the social and the literary are one and the same thing; only by those for whom the political and the aesthetic have come to be seen as, or come to *be,* identical; and only by those for whom being *free of oppression* has come to be seen as identical to (1) having one's literary work in print or (2) having one's literary work included on course syllabi in "history" or "literature" courses in colleges or, even better, in high schools.

And maybe they're right. Maybe oppressed sexual, ethnic, religious, or racially identifiable groups are indeed better off, less oppressed, and less likely to *be* oppressed in the future due to pieces of writing having been (1) brought into print and (2) adopted for use in school curricula *because of their having been authored by members of such groups.*

But I very much doubt it, and I doubt very much, too, that the matter is anywhere nearly that simple. I doubt that dignity and equality for an oppressed group of any kind whatsoever can be achieved through condescension, paternalism, or the putting into place of a double standard.[13] Further, no one I have ever heard or spoken with or read anywhere, ever, in any language or any nation, has ever made a good case for the argument that the merit of a piece of literature can or should or has been or will ever be determined by the racial, ethnic, or sexual identity of its author. If anyone knows of such an argument that in fact is an effective one, I hope that they will bring it to my attention.

The aim of achieving social justice and equality under the law for all, for every individual, is desirable, laudable, correct, mandated by the very spirit and history of the nation, and to be supported. The aim of achieving social justice and equality under the law for all through the use of literary or artistic quotas or representationalism, on the other hand, is false, bankrupt, counterproductive, demeaning, paternalistic, and destructive, destined only to bring about the diminishment of individuals and, worse, only to serve and empower further those forces whose interest lies in bringing about and increasing the simplification of every thinking person in the land.

✦ ✦ ✦

Through the workings of a long social and intellectual history, publishers and academics emerged more or less equally as those upon whom the responsibility fell—and to whom the prestige was given—of serving, by and large, as custodians of the national literature and as overseeing midwives to its future. This arrangement achieved its mature, most recognizable form probably near the period of the First World War or somewhat before, and it remained in place without *fundamental* change for a span of perhaps fifty years—until sometime during the middle or late 1970s. Then, the changes that we have been talking about began to take place, both as a *result* of simplification and politicizing and, in turn, as a cause of *further* simplification and politicizing of the arts, literature, and academics.

That no single person, group, entity, event, or even *thing*—like, say, television—can be seen as solely responsible for the onset of such vast and destructive ills should be clear to everyone. For their *continuation*, however, now that the ills are evident and visible, now that their importance, dimension, and significance can be seen and measured: *now*, responsibility, for action, reaction, even for inaction, is very, very great indeed *for* and on the part *of* every individual, group, institution, government, and even of the nation itself.

Literary questions may seem wholly insignificant against the scale of emergencies gripping entire governments, nations, and regions of the world. But governments, nations, and regions are made out of people, and therefore the way those people *think* is a question of great importance, as are the questions of how *well* they think and what they think *about*. Literature, the literary arts, serious writing—call it what you will—has an enormous role in these matters. A nation's literature reveals a great deal indeed about what that nation has been. And its literary *habits*, equally, reveal a very great deal indeed about what it continues to be.

And if the custodians of our literature—regardless of whether the original blame lies with the age they live in or with the custodians themselves—are in fact going to continue simplifying literature by reducing it to message and putting it in harness like a donkey that they think does *good*, they—and we all—will suffer the consequences.

If, instead of the complex, we are going to have the simple, then we ourselves will grow slowly also more simplified. If we are going to have art-messages instead of art-experiences, we ourselves will grow slowly less understanding of the relationship, first, between intellect and feeling, less understanding of what each of these can do and of what the two can do together; and, second, we will become gradually less subtle in our understanding of the experience of life itself and, even worse, less complex in our expectations *of* that experience. We will be pushing ourselves only further toward simplification both inwardly and outwardly, jogging along ever more dumbly into the reverse womb of our own *Brave New World*.

If such thoughts create an apocalyptic tone, let it stand as a suggestion not only of how far I find these dire patterns to have developed already, but also of how high a value I place on education and how much I believe depends on it. Most education that takes place today is in fact *anti*-education. This is, thank god, least true in the elementary grades, more true at the high school levels, and—certainly so if the new professors are taken as paradigm and model of what goes on there—more true still in the college years. Where it's *most* true, however, is in advertising and the mass media—which is to say, in a huge and even preponderant part of most people's waking, and probably sleeping, lives. The influence of advertising and the mass media is *anti*-education because the end being sought is the simplification and diminishment of experience, and of people's *expectations* from experience, through the simplification and diminishment of their inner, private selves, the final aim being to make them not more autonomous but more manipulable and passive—thus, eventually, bringing about their perfection as "consumers."

If exactly that same process of simplification and diminishment is taking place in baccalaureate education, on whatever scale or with whatever degree of thoroughness, how lamentable, heinous, and despicable a thing that is—and if it occurs in humanities studies, especially literary ones, where many of the archives of human independence of spirit and mind have traditionally been stored, then all the more the betrayal. There was a time when "education" took place regularly and originated from multiple sources, often throughout life—a time when community and social existence entailed and required personal engagement with institutions of various kinds, all of them in one way or another both formative *and* informative, bringing about and often requiring social, cultural, even intellectual experience and intercourse.[14] Not all of these institutions, by any means, were equally "good," or for that matter equally desirable or acceptable to everyone. Church, for example, became for a certain kind of person something to rebel against, as did the institution of the neighborhood or the small town itself, its repressive demands for conformity and contentedness making it a force to be escaped for the bigger and more open world of the city or even of other countries. But oppressiveness of those kinds is endemic to all society and all social organizations, and, in that sense, is perfectly normal. The situation we're in now is entirely different.

The social and cultural institutions that informed most people's lives during the period, say, from 1890 to 1950 or so differed obviously from the electronic and mass media that inform and surround our lives now. It's true that there are *fewer* social and community institutions now than there were in earlier periods, and that even some of those are largely moribund, so that we are likely to be less thoroughly interknit with whatever community we live in than might have been the case in earlier periods.[15] But equally important, and perhaps of paramount importance, is the fact that while earlier institutions did indeed exist for the purpose of influencing, or trying to influence, behavior, they didn't, as the media do now, attempt first to alter the very *nature* of people in order to achieve that influence. The appeal for conformity and good behavior in earlier periods was made to people's community ethos, if you will, to their presumably common desire for the stability and betterment of everyone through the stability and betterment of the community, their presumably common desire to ensure a good life and sound future for their children, and so on. Now, however, while a certain feeble power may still reside in the old pieties, allowing them *some* ongoing contribution to the common weal, the *true* power exerted to bring about conformity of behavior comes through a completely new means, one unique to our own age. The attempt is first made, that is, through simplification and diminishment *of the person*, in order that then the desired behavior will follow accordingly. The aim is not, as before, to achieve the betterment, stability, and soundness of the community and its future, but the aim is simply and solely to keep the corporate-economic government in power and *growing* in power. That requires, of course, a continuously expanding economy (or "military-industrial complex"). And that continuous expansion, in turn, requires continuous manufacture and sale of goods and material, whether through continuous warfare—as Gore Vidal argues—or through continuous and wasteful civilian *consumption*. Or both.

This is why we have been transformed from what we were in earlier periods, a nation of citizens, into what we are now, a nation of *consumers*.

Consider the problem. To what ideal or value, after all, might an appeal actually be made in urging people to become *consumers*? To be a consumer is to be an intaker, devourer, feeder, absorber. It is to be a mouth or a stomach. It is to be an *intestine*. What might convince people that they ought to become something so demeaning? It's one thing to make sacrifices for others by being a part of the community, by pursuing an education, holding a job, raising a family, staying informed, voting. Doing such things as these— not only for oneself but for the sake of others, for stability, peacefulness, the pleasures of everyone, and a better assured future— is unlikely, except in the sociopath, to create a sense of having been demeaned. But to serve the community, town, or nation by becoming an absorber, intaker, or consumer; a mouth or intestine; by being made akin to the catfish that with its pulsing mouth vacuums up the river bottom's decay, or perhaps to the snail that sucks algae from aquarium walls—these, to any grown human being with the least gifts of reason and pride, would indeed create a sense of having been demeaned.

Much more practical and efficient, therefore, to make changes *beforehand* in those who are to be transformed into consumers.

Much more practical and efficient, beforehand, to diminish and simplify them in order that their resulting pliability and passivity can make exploitation far more easy to achieve than any appeals to altruism, stability, dignity, or community could ever have hoped to do. Once in place, the program is kept going and in fact expanded by unremitting repetition and simple continuation. Misinform them, degrade them, condition them. Spoil and trick them into taking *pride* in the banality of having lives that exist solely in order for them to consume.[16] Make them ever more controllable by simplifying their *expectations* from life, thus making them feel that they are being sated while they're actually being starved; that they are the world's elite while in fact they're its docile and programmed hordes; that the world around them is gorgeous in its detail and proportion, when in fact it grows uglier daily; and perhaps above all that it's their *right* to do what they're doing as consumers, so that, *because* it's perceived now as a right, they may be expected, should it become necessary, to fight to the death for that right and all that it subsumes: for the right to waste things, squander them, ruin them, overuse them, poison them, destroy them, deplete them, devour them, absorb them, ravage them, consume them, preempt them, and, finally, turn first them, and then the world, into garbage.[17]

✦ ✦ ✦

Some way back, I proposed a definition of *normality*. Being normal meant being as highly and independently conscious as possible of the complexity of life, both actual and potential, and being conscious of the valid engagement of one's own will in meeting that complexity. *Not* being normal thus meant being, either radically or relatively, simplified in one's consciousness of complexity in life and, concomitantly, passive in one's acceptance *of* that simplification. The point back then, the same as now, is that, in a country like the one ours has become, anyone wishing just to remain normal will find it necessary to dedicate him or herself to being *an alert, unremittingly vigilant radical oppositionist during every passing moment of life.*

In 1984, normal is getting *away* from Big Brother, though almost everyone in the novel *sees* it as normal to remain in the sight of and under the jurisdiction of that controller. In our case, equally, what almost everyone *accepts* as normal isn't normal at all; and what they think of as the state of normality is in fact a state of being limited, simplified, acquiescent, and passive. Because the new professors are among this huge, accepting majority (along with, it must be said, the new publishers, new readers, new booksellers, and so on), the literary life is being lost, literature is being lost, literary studies are being lost, and what I call art-emotion or aesthetic thinking is being, or has already been, lost.

The pattern is evident throughout the humanities, but in literature—and in graphic art—it stands out with great obviousness, being observable in the highly visible process of works of art growing steadily weaker and weaker instead of stronger and stronger as, like thoroughbreds harnessed to the plow, they are pressed by the new professors into the service of the simplified and misguided program of doing *good.*

Literature *can* make people better—at feeling, at thinking, at knowing and perceiving and judging—but beyond that it can't, never has been able to do, and never will be able to do any kind of practical or political *good* at all. Still, as has been the case for generations, many of those drawn to literature and literary studies are rebellious sorts, of an idealistic and meliorative bent, people hoping for the betterment of the world and usually thinking of literature, at least in general, as some kind of a force for good. And it is such a force, as I've just said, but only in the *ways* I've just said. After all, the more people the world has in it who are better thinkers, feelers, perceivers, and judges, the better the world itself will end up being. But plans or programs of *good,* campaigns or missions of any sectarian or practical or applied kind, are another matter. The activist or radical element, usually, resides in a literary school or *group* rather than in the literature itself that may be produced by individual authors of the group, unless, of course, what's produced is radical in a *literary* way, like *To the Lighthouse* as a "product" of the Bloomsbury "group"; or John Dos Passos's *U.S.A.* trilogy as a "product" of the author's early leftism; Yeats's poetry of his Irish nationalism; or Ezra Pound's verse of that poet's well-known, maverick, and even treasonable radicalism.

The *literature* exists of, by, through, and for its own merit and interest, not its politics or even whatever concrete social or political influence it may once actually have had or exerted. Most often, literary works that do have an influence of this kind, however huge, fade away afterward by merit of holding little innate interest once their moment has passed. Obviously, they may well continue being of interest historically, like, say, *Uncle Tom's Cabin* or Upton Sinclair's *The Jungle*, while being otherwise all but void of literary energy, life, or interest. In the context of this point, one of the most revealing things about the new professors is their tendency to do exactly this, to turn more and more often to literature of the second and third rank as they switch from the teaching of literature to the teaching of social and political history, using "literary" works—like Stowe and Sinclair themselves, along with their more modern, everywhere-available, and invariably second-rank epigones—as supporting evidence of the "truth" of what they're "teaching."

A natural consequence of such conceiving of literary works as footnotes for historic truths—slavery existed, slaughterhouses were unclean, workers suffered, there was colonialism—is thus a slide toward the mediocre, a trend that itself not only further weakens literary studies as a discipline (by showing the discipline to be unnecessary) but weakens and diminishes the quality and intensity of such art-experience as it will even be possible for students to have.

Wanting to do good is desirable and admirable, but not when the impulse produces more damage than gain, or even *equal* damage and gain. The loss to everyone when literature is reduced from experience to message is bad enough. But a further damaging and perhaps even more cruel result occurs when literature is reduced to a tool for making people feel *good, important,* or *"empowered."*

Long ago, in 1966 or 1967, I remember one of the instructors in the Iowa Writers' Workshop making a comment at the end of a long fiction-writing class to the effect that the workshop, as opposed to the straight academic side of the graduate program, was the better place for a developing writer because, in the workshop, "at least" a person wasn't faced all the time with "literary giants" and "great works."

In other words, it was less intimidating, less discouraging—more *comforting*—for a writer to be brought up under the tutelage of works and authors from the second rank than from the first.

The remark may have been more involuntary than I thought it at the time, something the person might quickly have wished he hadn't said. Knowing him, however, I lean toward its having been a simple statement of something he'd thought before and meant at face value.

That was almost forty years ago, and, looking back, the remark seems prophetic. I thought, then, that it was a shocking thing to hear. Now, it expresses an idea that has been put into practice everywhere around me.

It was depressing and disconcerting then, and so it is now. Who could be content with studying under the second rank when they knew that the first rank not only existed but was *available to them?* Who could prefer the second rank to the first on the grounds that the second was less challenging, and thus less intimidating—unless it was a person who was either *afraid* of being, or who for some other reason *chose* not to be, of the first rank?

Now, there's nothing wrong, certainly, with the second rank—

nothing wrong with choosing it and nothing, either, with being afraid of the first rank, if such happens to be the case. But it seems to me that the remark made so long ago by my old instructor raises another issue, or another facet of the first one. He *was*, after all, not a student, but an instructor in a widely celebrated graduate writing program. And he *had*, after all, admitted—or said, revealed, let slip—that he preferred the company of the second rank to that of the first, the implications being as follows: that he preferred *learning* from the second rank rather than from the first; that we, as subordinates to him and under his tutelage, should by his example thus feel free, even encouraged, to have and indulge the same preference as his; that we ourselves had been studying, were now studying, and would continue to study through the use and under the example of the second rank; and, finally, that, after all was said and done, the second rank was *good enough*.

Aha. Now *that's* very interesting. And it shows how important it is that something further be added to the sentence that began the paragraph before this one. Thus: there's nothing wrong, certainly, with choosing or settling for the second rank, *as long as doing so doesn't entail denying the existence, or the superiority, of the first rank.*

Even though I enrolled in one, I was skeptical of writing workshops, and I am still, although no more skeptical of them than of academic humanities in general under the new professors. But workshopping and the later, more generalized, decline are in fact part of a related syndrome. If great writing, as Plato and Shakespeare attest, really is the result either of madness or genius, then workshops never *were* a good idea, since genius *can't* be taught and it's hardly permissible to teach madness. The example is frivolous, yet at the same time it's also relevant to the conceptual and structural weaknesses that from the beginning tended to drive workshops—and writing itself—unrelentingly toward the mediocre. The bigger and more widespread the workshops became, the less possible it was for them to avoid teaching down, or to the middle, rather than to the top. By the nature of things, only few among us are great, yet the workshops contain, and must serve, multitudes. Their faculty and staff can hardly hope to keep enrollments up by continually emphasizing to their students how *not great* they are. A considerably different message is much more effective in achieving institutional survival. The very least a student will want to hear in order to feel rewarded, or in order to feel inclined to make another, and then yet another, tuition payment, is the message that he or she is *good enough*.

The task of making everyone who *wants* to be a writer *into* one, or of making as *many* people into writers as possible, is obviously made easier by simplifying the idea of what writing is, a measure that also makes more manageable what it is that's going to be "taught." From the start, a workshopping strategy of this kind took the form of a focus on "craft," since "craft" was thought to be teachable, and, indeed, it is. The turn toward craft, however, goes along with an equivalent turn away from the things of greatest importance, namely, from the very essence, meaning, purpose, and nature of writing. The loss is obvious: As all turn toward craft, none turn toward essence. Writing workshops, popular, lucrative, omnipresent, and *very* much at home in and as a part of the Age of Simplification, are reminiscent of, say, offering a course in late Gothic architecture by setting the students to work cutting stone and mixing mortar. Many of the writers discussed in the first chapter of this book can serve as examples of the result.

Embracing the second rank over the first because it's "teachable" (as in the workshops), because it better conveys "message" about social and political justice (as in the literature courses), and because it therefore more effectively serves the new professors' perceived desire to do *good*—for reasons like these, the powerful drive toward mediocrity continues and, appropriate to the Age of Simplification, continues also to be seen not as something bad but as something good.

Imagine a parallel development taking place not in the humanities but in another kind of program, perhaps a program in medical training. Would anyone consider it a good idea for a medical school to provide its students with exposure to anything other than the first rank of medical research or theory? In anatomy courses, what would people think if medical schools used only cadavers of the *second rank,* those, say, somewhat damaged or decayed and thus obscuring certain subtle anatomic elements—so the students would end up with an *okay* or a *not great* knowledge of anatomy? Or what about the study of any other aspect or area of medicine— trauma, surgery, pathology—should knowledge of these be as good and complete as possible, or would *good enough* be fine?

Most people will quickly agree that, no, *good enough* wouldn't be fine. Even the new literature professors will agree that the only standard in medical training that can be justified is the *very best standard available.* That, after all, is only reasonable and right.

But if so, why isn't the same also true for the humanities?

five

But enough; lamentation will bring nothing back. The fact is that literary thinking can't be recovered—nor can the benefits it's capable of bringing—until such time as we once again recognize thought and feeling not just for what they *are* but also for what they're *not.* As things stand now—in America, in academia, in the mass media, in the arts—feeling is doing the work of thought, and doing it very badly indeed. Thought, meanwhile, is hobbled and hamstrung by the cords of feeling it's bound up in, with the result that most of the time thinking can hardly be said to be taking place at all. John R. Searle, straight-faced and without irony, wrote well over a decade ago in the *New York Review of Books* that "one of the most depressing things about educated people today is that so few of them, even among professional intellectuals, are able to follow the steps of a simple logical argument."[18]

In the case of academia, what's most commonly said is that the humanities faculties and curricula have been "politicized," which is indeed a truth but not a whole one: It doesn't get to the level of *cause,* for one thing, and, for another, it looks at academia as much more separate from the mass media and the mass culture than it really is. The new professors, after all, can't be understood *except* by understanding that they themselves, as we saw in the previous chapter and will see again in the next, are children of the mass media and of its omnipresent, all-surrounding, and all-permeating aesthetic.

And, as products of that aesthetic, with its many, subtle, and skillful means of bringing about indoctrination and conditioning of kinds that serve government-corporate interests and no others—as products of this aesthetic, the new professors, like all other products of it, are conditioned and prepared in such ways that they will mistake feeling for thought. The desire to *do good,* for example, is perceived by them as an *idea,* as a *concept,* when in fact it's no such thing, but is and must always remain solely and only the thing it is: a desire or a *feeling.*

What happens in the next step is equally misconceived and misbegotten—and equally devastating, certainly to the arts, immensely so to the *literary* arts. Here is the way it goes:

The *desire* to do good, being mistaken for a thought or idea, is acted upon *as if* it were a thought or idea. Though the reasons are too complex to go into right now, an understanding nevertheless exists that the good to be done is to be done to *others,* and these others, in the case of the new professors, are of course their students. Now, in order to *do* this good *to* the students, the procedure is to show them examples of *good* things and examples of *bad* things so that, with whatever clarification or nudging may be necessary, the students can then *choose* the good and *reject* the bad. "The Yellow Wallpaper" will be read, for example, and the students can conclude that paternalistic oppression of women is *bad,* or *Things Fall Apart* will allow them to conclude that colonialism is *bad,* and so on. If an echo should come to the reader's mind at this point— "Four legs good, two legs bad," for example, or, "Oppression is bad, expression is good"—it shouldn't be surprising, since the procedure we're describing must and can take place *only* on a very simple level. The instructor, after all, in using books in this way—as *examples* of good and bad intended to lead students then to *choose* between good and bad—must surely not perceive the books to be *more* or *more complex* than simple "living examples" (which, significantly, appeal to their readers' *feelings*) of good and bad that then permit choice to be made *between* good and bad. For the instructor, anything more complex would in fact destroy the entire undertaking and ruin the lesson or even the semester—something so simple as mere *ambiguity* in a book, for example, could complicate or even derail the making of the good/bad choice, thus becoming not an aid but an *obstacle* to the instructor's desire *to do good* by leading his or her students to *make the "right" choice.*

This isn't education, but anti-education.

✤   ✤   ✤

Or at least, as a part of any presumed *literary* education, it's anti-education. Consider what's happened. First, the literary work itself is no longer the feast to be devoured, but merely the vassal who waits tables, *bringing* the meal, or perhaps it's even simply the dish that *holds* the food that itself, presumably, is the content of the meal. And what is that content? Well, the content is not an object but an *attitude*—anti-colonialist, pro–liberated women, anti-racist, anti–gay bashing, and so on.

And, asks someone, what's wrong with that? Nothing's *wrong* with it, I answer, but it's a mighty thin diet to go to *college* for. These are, after all, the materials less of a college education than they are of a kindergarten one—basic, obvious, unarguable, well intended, decent: Don't cheat, don't lie, be fair, treat others the way you want to be treated.

They are, in short, perfectly laudable moral and ethical attitudes. And yet they become part of a corrosive and ruinous project of anti-education at exactly that moment when they themselves become the thing studied, when they themselves become the *subject* and *content* of the curriculum. Exactly at that moment, there occurs one more shift away from *edu*cation, one more step in the direction of *indoc*trination, this shift bringing with it yet another degree of *simp*lification. What choice would any student have, after all, in a classroom of this kind, except to submit to the feeling or attitude that has now become the subject and purpose of the undertaking? The point is not that no student is likely to demur anyhow, declaring him or herself to be biased in favor of colonialism, misogyny, or the brutalizing of peoples. No, the point is that no student would be *free* to differ or demur.

At the moment when feeling or attitude becomes *itself the subject* of any part of the curriculum, that is the moment when education steps out the door and coercion steps in. It isn't coercion if I assign *Hamlet* and then, on their *Hamlet* exams, fail those students who haven't read it. It's coercion, though, if I tell them that the play is misogynistic, or that Shakespeare is misogynistic, and then fail those students whose exams reveal that they don't—or won't—agree.

The example may seem too simple, but it's not. In the one case, what's being studied is the play *Hamlet*, the art-object itself, the words on the pages. In the other case, what's being studied is a pre-existing attitude or feeling toward or about *Hamlet* the play. In the first case, the play itself will do the talking, and such ideas (or feelings) as may emerge from the play's "talking" will then be taken

as empirical guides toward the forming of ideas, feelings, and attitudes about the play and toward it. In the other case, any "talking"
in or from the play that fails to support the preexisting attitude
toward it will be silenced, repressed, misconstrued, or ignored,
thus blinding, distorting, and brutalizing the play.

In the curriculum of the Age of Simplification, however, the
play has *already* been subordinated to certain feelings *about* it, so
the brutalizing of it is presumed, by those doing it, as having very
little significance, if any at all. Along with the brutalizing of literature, though, another kind of brutalizing—of *people*—takes place
in the coercive classroom, with implications both dreadful and far-
reaching. Most notably, the confusion between feeling and thinking
leads to the actual reinforcement—the "teaching"—of exactly the
same *passivity* in students that the mass media create and maintain
in the consumer culture generally.

I argued earlier that the only real or true or genuine or endur-
ing reason to read works of literature is for the *experience* of
doing so; that this "art-experience" is unique in that it both
creates and requires a perfect balance or merging of the intellectual
and the emotional in the person who has or achieves it; and that
the experience can, should, and often does result in an awareness
and understanding of the enormity, inviolability, and unique value
and indispensability of the individual *self* as the sole entryway that
exists for any of us into a consciousness of our own existence and
an understanding of such meaning as that existence holds. All of
this means that "studying" pieces of art or literature has got to be
an active undertaking and can't be a thing achieved passively. It's
not a matter of "entertainment" but a matter of *experience,* and of
an experience, further, that can come into existence or occur only
if both the artwork and the person reading or experiencing it do
their part. The *particular meaning* of the experience can't be known
until the experience itself is brought into existence (along with its
meaning), although part of the experience's meaning and a very

great deal of its significance lie in the fact that it can be achieved and known only by the single individual self, and that *without* that single, individual, invaluable, and inviolable self, the experience couldn't exist and couldn't even be *known* to exist.

The art-experience, in other words, awakens the self to the *nature* of the self, both as to its limitations and its abilities, as to its loneliness and its universality, and certainly as to its absolutely singular *value*, since without that self there is nothing at all, whatsoever, anywhere.

But when art is reduced to message, there can *be* no experience of the kind I'm describing, and therefore there can be no awakening of the unique existing self to an awareness of its own significance.

The meaning known *ahead* of time—"*Hamlet* is a misogynist play"—is an agenda. The *unknown* meaning—"Let *Hamlet* talk to us so maybe we can discover what it means"—is an experience.

The agenda is received. The experience is earned and taken.

And the effect of accepting the agenda is not that a person becomes in any sense *realized*, but only that a person becomes one of a *group*. The person becomes attached to the group of putatively "like-minded" others, and the aim of the new professors is to make this group as large as conceivably possible. The corollary thus emerges, that the aim of the new professors is to make the group of *passive recipients of the agenda* as large as conceivably possible. And so we see that their aim is exactly the same as that of the mass media.

The effect of earning and thereby *having* the art-experience, on the other hand, is that one becomes aware simultaneously of being isolated, alone, and separate from all else and all other people; yet that one becomes aware, at the same time and even so, of having had an intense recognition of *oneness* with all else and all other people. One becomes aware of the irreducibility of the single, lone, individual, isolated self; aware of its autonomy and of its sheer inviolability (except through its destruction); and becomes aware of the inestimable value and the utter indispensability of the self as the sole eye or doorway through which any of us can think-feel or feel-think our way into an authentic experience of life and to an understanding of what the experience of that life means and *can* mean.

And *that's* about as far removed from the aims of the mass media as it's possible to be.

✦ ✦ ✦

The corporate-state, with its policing and proselytizing arm, the mass media, wants, in all citizens, to create and maintain passivity, lack of individual thought, and as low a consciousness as possible of the nature, meaning, and full potential of the individual self. And if this is so, how can it be, how can it conceivably have happened, that the bringing into being and the nurturing of those very same deleterious qualities and characteristics—rather than their desperately needed and deeply undervalued opposites—could have become the routine business even of the intellectual, academic, and artistic classes in the nation?

Complexity and confidence of individual perception and thought alone can equip or enable anyone to begin to resist the smothering and destructive conformities, diminishments, deceptions, and simplifications of thought and of self that serve the interests of the corporate-state in its exploitation of the population and of the republic itself. But where, in the face of this unutterably alarming truth, is to be found the needed leadership that can represent, identify, speak for, and encourage the kind of independent thought and strategy needed for resistance? Certainly, such leadership *should* be expected to come from intellectuals, artists, writers, academicians, and literary publishers. And yet, even from these crucially important elements of the population, as we've seen already in academic humanities, comes nothing of the kind, but only, instead, still more simplification, still more self-referential "categories" of thought in place of real thought, still more labels and agendas and codes, all with the numbing and diversionary effect of filling, as it were, the mind's eye up with darkness, blinding it to the realities of the life that exists not only everywhere around it but also inside the unseen, unexplored, and steadily diminishing self.

The evidence is everywhere, inside classrooms and out, much of the time in the very *language* of simplification. The website of the *North American Review,* for example, is typical in what it suggests not about "literature"—too simple, direct, clear—but about what, speaking in simplification-ese, it calls "the literary experience." The website's "Note to Prospective Contributors" goes as follows:

> The *North American Review* is the oldest literary magazine in America (founded in 1815) and one of the most respected. We are interested in high-quality poetry, fiction, and nonfiction on any subject, but we are especially interested in work that addresses contemporary North American concerns and issues, particularly with the environment, gender, race, ethnicity, and class.[19]

And there it is, the automated, code-word litany of narrowing, proscribing, predigested categories of permissible *seeing,* as if these few agenda items were all that's left of life, the rest having fallen off somewhere into darkness. Consider the history of American intellectual and literary life, two and a half centuries holding a vast aesthetic and social chronicle of burgeoning, impassioned achievement, of probing, often haunted, sometimes obsessed, at other times revolutionary productivity and exploration in literature, from Anne Bradstreet and Jonathan Edwards to T. S. Eliot and William Carlos Williams, from Benjamin Franklin and Thomas Jefferson to William Faulkner and Marilynne Robinson. Until *now,* that is. Until 1947. Until thirty or forty years ago. Now, it seems, that entire glorious chronicle, that entire history of heart- and mind- and soul-driven courage and risk and dedication and accomplishment has suddenly withered away, been simplified, reduced, denuded, and diminished, until *now* the artistic and intellectual life no longer has to do with love, life, death, being, nothingness, progress, fear, passion, childhood, birth, hope, desire, beauty, rage, terror, metaphysics, the role of human beings and nations, history itself, salvation, fate, the cosmos, or madness—to cite only a few examples of the stuff of art. No longer, it seems, is *life* what calls out to the artist's mind and heart, but, instead, what compels the creating self are "subjects," "concerns," and "issues."

Such standardized vacuity of concept and expression, such agenda-driven category-think as this, then, is what we have come to. Change of this kind is something that we have *allowed to* happen. Things of this sort show what *has been done*—to us, to literature, to the way we're *able* to look at the world, to the very *way* we think. We think in abstractions first, with life itself tagging along behind, if it's lucky, whereas what *should* happen is this: Art should originate from a germ of life, no matter how small, but so alive that the artist is incapable of *not* beginning with it. Today, in simplification's paint-by-numbers and begin-with-the-agenda manner of literary "thought," where is *life? Passion? Originality?* The life-is-issues idea may well have been brought into being by the energies of a moral and ethical commitment and, as with the new professors, a concomitant desire to do good. But that originating morality is weakened, enervated, cheapened, and transformed into secondhand, stained, and shopworn goods when it's put piggyback on the frame of its own natural superior—literary art—and *then* given the blind temerity and self-serving gall to declare *itself* the driving force rather than the true force that's carrying *it*, although at the same time that true force is quickly dying, since the rider on its back is in reality thin-souled and poisonous, narrow-visioned and righteous, giving neither food nor energy to the thing it rides on, the tradition of literature, but simply beating it to death instead.

The sheer penury of such "literary" thinking is both obvious and pernicious. Why should race, class, gender, or ethnicity even be summoned or evoked as "things" fit or desirable to inspire or nourish *art?* What do *issues,* anyway, have to do with art in the first place? Could Dostoevsky name the "issue" that brought any one of his novels into existence and sustained it? Art comes not from issues and abstractions like race and gender, but from forces and feelings like mystery, rage, sorrow, loss, and ecstasy, or it comes from the unbridled, the angry, the selfish, the unleashed, the miserable, the grief-stricken, the hopeful, the doomed, the yearning, the desiring, the blissful, the ecstatic—in every case this originating embryo or germ of emotion, existing *in life* and not in abstraction, is then *married* with intellect and thought, creating the art-union of feeling and thinking that in turn results in meaning and significance, a meaning and significance *that can be created and expressed in no other way than through that marriage.* The moment an "issue" or the agenda comes first, the moment it's declared the originating thing, the writer is reduced to the status of hireling, akin to an ad writer, in service to the issue, not to life *or* to art. Race, class, gender, ethnicity—where, one asks, is *all the rest of life?* What about those who have no interest whatsoever in the agenda or its attendant issues—could *they* submit their art to the *North American Review?* Where is Walt Whitman? Could *he* submit to it? ("Till the gossamer thread you fling, catch somewhere, O my Soul"—where are race, class, gender, and ethnicity *there?*) Could Emily Dickinson? ("With blue, uncertain, stumbling buzz, / Between the light and me"?) Thomas Wolfe? Gertrude Stein? Virginia Woolf?

What, in other words, about *real writers?* What about the *entire rest of the universe?*

But, oh, not so. These aren't questions of the kind you hear any more in classrooms or writing workshops or cafés or even in interviews with writers, and they aren't questions of the kind, either, that you hear *implied,* peeking out silently and yet irrepressibly from between and behind the words at readings, not even in the words that *are* read.

The Age of Simplification is real, and the confusion between thought and feeling is real. Where thinking should come first, as in the classroom, feeling does instead. And where feeling should come first, as in the vital germ of life inspiring a piece of writing, abstraction takes the lead instead, akin to a plow-horse stepping on a rosebud. The loss, the vacuity, the error, the *inattentiveness,* the unawareness, the waste, the *damage.* Consider the importance of classrooms: Classrooms are places where the older, wiser, and more experienced have charge of the younger—have charge, that is, of the *eyes* of each individual self, looking out from its place among the rows of seats, these being the future eyes of the nation, the nation whose very fate depends upon what those eyes of the new generation will *see* and *be able* to see. And what is it that happens in the classrooms of the new professors in the Age of Simplification? These eyes get poked out one by one, made harmless, obedient, blind. As for the literature itself, meanwhile, there will continue to be less and less of the great and more and more of the imitative, mediocre, uncomplex, and derivate, *not* the literature that can bring vision to eyes and power to hearts.

If I were a student again now, finishing high school—if I were, that is, fifty years younger than I am—I think I would skip college altogether and find some other means of becoming educated. The very notion is quixotic, admittedly—how could any kid at sixteen or seventeen know enough to make such a decision, and where would he or she *turn* for education? Where, indeed, which is a question that makes one feel only the more intensely how egregious, alarming, unforgivable, and utterly ruinous it is to see academia, instead of *awakening* the self, becoming a purveyor of *un*-self-consciousness, and, instead of breadth and depth and beauty and wonder, purveying narrowness, passivity, groupism, the dimming of sight, shallowness of perception—doing exactly those things, and doing them *perfectly,* that the corporate-state itself most treasures and most delights in being helped along with. And the intellectual classes, blind and simplified, are only too happy to lend a hand.

To put it another way, when I think of all the students being instructed all over the land year after year by the new professors, being raised on a diet of the second rank, the tendentious, and the simple, being led to think that literature is message and the arts are social commentary—I can't help but think that, when someday they realize what happened to them, the way they were patronized and treated like children, were not shown the best, the most real, the highest things, in effect were *lied* to—that then, they'll be bitter and angry and vengeful and will despise their old professors.

On the other hand, if the Age of Simplification succeeds, if it all works out the way the great plan begun in 1947 intends it to work out, such a thing will never happen. Their very *selves* having been deprived, narrowed, indoctrinated, and blinded, the students, no matter how old they get, never *will* come to such a realization, never *will* find out about all the greater and bigger and fuller and freer things they could have known, and could have *been;* never will, in a word, ever, ever find out what they have missed.

III

CONSUMERISM, VICTIMOLOGY, AND THE DISAPPEARANCE OF THE MEANINGFUL SELF

Why does society exist, if not to accommodate our lives? Jefferson was a civilized man—clearly it was not his intention to send us on a fool's errand. Why do we never imagine that the happiness he mentioned might include a long supper with our children, a long talk with a friend, a long evening with a book? Given time, and certain fading habits and expectations, we could have comforts and luxuries for which no one need be deprived. We could nurture our families, sustain our heritages, and, in the pregnant old phrase, enjoy ourselves. The self, that dear and brief acquaintance, we could entertain with a little of the ceremony it deserves.

Marilynne Robinson, "Family," in *The Death of Adam*

one

One of the most alarming aspects of daily life in America, particularly since the election of 2000, and even more so since 9/11, is that it has become impossible to discuss politics in anything approaching an even faintly meaningful way. There are a number of reasons for this blindness, or paralysis—the metaphors aren't easy to choose between—and not only are all of them almost equally, and immeasurably, important, but they're intertwined in exceedingly complex ways.

A place to start may be with the notion of the "unreal." According to the OED, this word itself dates from at least 1605,[1] and, as all know, it has taken on varieties of meanings, including "incredible," "fantastic," "amazing," and even the recently hyperpopularized "awesome." Just three or four decades ago, the word gained another and even more interesting meaning: namely, "true," so that, for example, when the Kent State killings took place in 1970, highly shocked people would say *"unreal."* What they meant, of course, was that the killings were *true*, that they were *all but* unbelievable, yet that they had actually happened.

Now, though, there's been another turn of the screw, and either that short-lived meaning of "unreal" as "true" has changed back again to the previous meaning of "not true," or—which I fear and suspect—people have simply begun refusing to believe the evidence of their senses. Faced with intolerable ideas, or with intolerable acts, people in very large numbers have begun simply denying them, declaring them "unreal" and thus with a word striking them out of existence.

Americans, in other words, are turning their backs on empiricism as a means of perceiving the truth and of acting on it reasonably. Whether they're *willfully* shutting their eyes to things they don't *want* to see, or whether they *really don't see* things that *are there* to be seen, I'm not entirely sure, and the question may not really be a matter of either/or. Perhaps there is a psychological mingling, instead, of *true* blindness, on the one hand, and *willful* blindness, on the other. But the pattern itself of *not seeing* is inescapable, evident to anyone who looks.

Although there are exceptions, which I'll get to in a minute, the observable pattern is simply this: Huge numbers of people *will not talk* about great political matters that are unprecedented or of the most towering and important consequence. For example, they *won't talk* about the possibility of interpreting the Supreme Court's intervention in the 2000 election as the equivalent of a coup or the installation of a junta. And they *won't talk* about the possibility that the Bush administration knew that 9/11 or something like it was coming but did nothing to prevent it since it would be useful to their own political interests. That is, people *will not even entertain the possibility* of such ideas.

But why on earth not? I'm not asking for agreement on any such questions, but I *am* asking—no, I'm imploring—that it be permissible to *consider* them. To make it something *not* considerable seems to me the equivalent of willful blindness and very dangerous. I have an acquaintance who is an internationally recognized and highly honored senior professor at a major—no, an illustrious—university. Admittedly, he is conservative politically and considers himself so, but it seems to me that conservatism is one thing and denial another. In an exchange, I asked him whether or not law is built on precedent. Yes, he said, in extremely large part. I asked him if the Court's intervention in the 2000 election was a first-time thing and unique or whether it had a precedent. A first-time thing, he said. So I asked: Doesn't the Court's action then stand as a precedent in this area of law, making it more rather than less likely that the Court might again enter into a similar electoral matter and that a parallel or corollary finding might be handed down again? No, he said: It doesn't and it won't.

Even my acquaintance's deep conservatism can't explain this

simple, brute stubbornness: After all, he's done something akin to saying "A dog is a cat," or, "A dog is not a dog." He would never admit that he'd done so, but hasn't he, in effect, said, "A precedent is not a precedent"?

On the face of it, an absurdity. But I think I understand it, at least to some extent, just as I think I understand the refusal of my colleagues, friends, and other acquaintances even to *entertain* the notion that the Court's action could conceivably be understandable as a coup. And the reason is that the very thought is unbearable. It is unspeakable. In a word, it's *unreal*.

Indeed it is. And yet that's the *very last* reason *not* to speak of it.

✢ ✢ ✢

Without any doubt, something is seriously wrong in our national politics and has been growing more and more wrong, in a long downward spiral, since sometime around 1947. But for this situation to have come about, something also has to have gone seriously wrong in the population itself—in the national self, if I may call it that, at least for the moment. Between the two—the ruin within and the ruin without—the dread and unspeakable situation has come about that, following the attacks of 9/11 and the passage of the Patriot Act, we are in fact living no longer in a free country but instead in a police state. For the comfort of us all, I could rephrase this to say that we are now "technically" living in the "equivalent" of a police state. But the result is euphemistic only, bringing no difference whatsoever in meaning.

This police state, however, isn't what I want to discuss, at least not exactly, or yet. What I do want to discuss is the phenomenon, as I've said, of that topic and other topics closely related to it having become effectively impossible to talk about.

Earlier, I said it was impossible to discuss them "in anything approaching an even faintly meaningful way," and it's time to clarify what I meant. It's clear to everyone that in fact there's plenty of "discussion" going on: campaign speeches being delivered, polls being taken, grassroots organizations being formed, marches on Washington being staged. Fine and good. But the trouble is that, unless the *truly* important matters can also be exposed, addressed, and responded to, none of the rest of this activity matters very much at all—if at all.

It can be said with some truth that everything is important. But, at the same time, distinctions can be made, and, if they're made carefully, they can be enlightening. For example, if we were to distinguish between types of political issues on the basis of their "scope," we might come up with a statement like this: Political issues of *true, obvious,* or *immediate* importance are those that have to do with the life and death, survival or destruction, of entire peoples or nations.

A corollary statement then becomes this: Political issues of *less* obvious or immediate importance are those that have to do with the individual or with groups of individuals smaller than the *national.*

This isn't a distinction likely to earn me friends among the new professors or among those—in effect, almost everyone—who are allied with them or think like them. I'm touching on, after all, the fraught issue of *rights*, the value-concept lying at the very heart of the new professors' thinking. And what I'm saying about rights is that they're of secondary importance. There are two reasons why I'm saying this.

The first reason, which will get a very, very great deal of attention later in this chapter, is that the concept of "rights" as held by the new professors and others like them is, if not entirely then very largely, a bankrupt and falsified concept: Too much of the time it isn't honestly or genuinely a concept that has to do with rights at all.

And the second reason I'm saying that "rights" are of secondary importance is that the political claims to such "rights"—no matter that the thinking behind them may be false or compromised—

are what *do* get discussed, presented, insisted upon, aired, written about, haggled over, and litigated about at the expense of other and, I would argue, greater political subjects.

Some readers, I'm sure, will conclude at this point that I'm a troglodyte reactionary without feelings, vehemently opposed to any and all programs having to do with human rights and dignities. Of such readers, I ask only that they hold their judgment until they've read the rest of this chapter—*and* that they give greater weight to what I *do* say than to what I *don't* say.

I'll never say I'm against human rights or any programs that protect human rights when the rights or protections are honest, true, principled, and fair. I *will* say, however, that there's a kind of schizoid double standard in place when talk of rights regularly trumps talk of other and arguably far greater matters. For example, when a college president putatively "disrespects" a black scholar by judging that his scholarship is weak, the matter gets printed, *as news,* in the *New York Times,* while at the same time the absence of *wing holes* in the side of the Pentagon that's said to have been hit by an airliner on 9/11, along with the absence of aircraft parts or wreckage at the crash site, is a thing passed off as the hallucinatory raving of a few "conspiracy theorists" and kept out of the news, in effect denying people of the right to read—or to think, or to know—about it.

❖ ❖ ❖

A disconnect—this is the word that comes to mind, in its recently acquired psychological sense. For the American mind does seem to have been *unplugged* in regard to certain things, unable to see them or, as I've said, even to entertain the possibility of them. The word "junta," for example, *can't* be used, *can't* be taken as being even remotely or conceivably applicable to anything that is happening or has happened in the United States. It's unreal. But what if we define "junta" as a power group that takes office by non-electoral, pseudo-electoral, or extra-electoral means and then passes laws depriving its citizens of liberties and freedoms that were previously guaranteed and that, if such now-curtailed liberties and freedoms were in fact exercised, could be obstructive to the interests of that power group?

In other words, a definition of the Bush administration. If one uses the word "junta," on the other hand, the idea immediately seems crazy and unbelievable, since the word brings with it powerful connotations and associations that have nothing to do with the condition, flavor, or atmosphere of daily life in modern America. "*Junta?*" a person on the street might respond. "No, of course it's not a junta. If it were a junta, things would be weird, strange, extreme, crazy. But everything is normal. Everything is regular and familiar. Everything *looks* the same as always. So it can't be a junta."

And there, indeed, lies a very big problem. Insofar as things *appear* to be the same as always, they're likely to be taken by people as *being* the same as always. This kind of assumption, up to a point, is a matter of perfectly natural common sense. If someone looks and sounds healthy and claims to feel fine, we're likely to assume that that person *is* healthy, even though there may be a disease within, asymptomatic and hidden. But we've got to look at the question of the determining power of the familiar, and at the question of judging things by their looks, much more deeply than just on the commonsense level if we can ever hope to understand what Americans see—and what they *don't* see—and why.

That is, we've got to go back to what I called, in the first chapter, the *aesthetic* of the mass media and the fruits that that "aesthetic" has born after its almost sixty-year existence. Governed by its only purpose, of protecting and increasing corporate profit and national economic growth, this aesthetic—that is, the whole of the mass media—has never from its inception had any allegiance to truth, but has, in effect, for almost six decades, consisted essentially of all lies all the time. The big central lie, ever present and subtly interwoven among all the small and middle-sized lies, is the single and fundamental lie that *everything is simpler than it really is.* Products, the effects they'll have, the things they'll achieve for you, life's social elements and personal affairs, all of these and myriad other things are incessantly portrayed and unvaryingly presented as simpler than they really are. Even beyond this, the *look* of things, the sense, the shape, the aura, the *feel* of life are all made to seem simpler than they really are. The result of this unbroken program of falsification and simplification, kept indefatigably at work over a period of six decades, all the while enjoying the ever-increasing attention of an ever-growing audience and taking advantage of an ever-improving technology allowing its ever more effective, powerful, and thorough delivery—the result of all this is that *people* no longer decide for themselves what's to be taken as real or true, but the media do this choosing and deciding *for* them.

The simplification itself is part of what comes to be taken for reality, and, as this quality of simplification throughout daily life and thinking becomes more and more familiar, it comes also to be taken more and more automatically or unthinkingly as *normal.* One outcome of the entire process is that complexity begins to disappear: It fades away, tends to be forgotten, disappears as a *habit* of thought, expectation, or seeing. Simplification thus feeds simplification, the simplified becoming the *normal.* The entire process brings about another outcome as well, which is that *thinking itself diminishes.* This is partly because thinking is, of course, discouraged and unrewarded while impulse and desire—throughout the system of consumerism—are *en*couraged and putatively *re*warded. But there's an even worse outcome in regard to thinking and thought, and this is that thinking as it was once conceived of essentially begins coming to an end. This is because intangibles begin falling away and falling out of use and becoming less and less familiar, replaced by the far simpler phenomena of tangibles, which themselves come to be relied upon more and more. Finally, "thinking" occurs only *without* the aid of abstractions or intangibles, not *with* the aid of them; it occurs, once this point has been reached, *only by and through and in response to tangibles, things seen, externals, and surfaces.*

Consumers might be said to have come to a point of perfection once they've been brought to this condition, since now they are freed of the ability to see beyond the surfaces of things, freed of the *habit* of doing so, and freed of the *desire* to do so. Once large enough numbers of the population have been brought to this condition, neither politics nor national elections as they were once known can any longer exist, since ideas can't be a part of an electoral contest, but only looks and appearances. This is why one candidate will invariably look, talk, behave, or act essentially like another. What has happened is that *the familiar itself has become the true and is to be accepted,* while all else is untrue and not to be entertained. This explains why, for example, nothing new must ever appear on television, or nothing unlike things that have appeared before. Only the familiar can be allowed, and, in this sense, there must never be *news,* because real *news* would, by definition, be unfamiliar.

two

Hand in hand with the Age of Simplification goes the gradual collapse, as I've suggested, of nothing less than empiricism itself as a means of thinking. This collapse, partly because it knows no social boundaries, but reaches even into the intellectual classes, may be the aspect of simplification that's most damaging and paralyzing to whatever humane or productive future we can or might hope for.

In the May 2004 issue of *Harper's,* Lewis Lapham devoted his monthly editorial, or "Notebook," to the abandonment of empiricism, though without using that word itself. "The postmodern sensibility," he wrote,

> is a product of the electronic media, which lend themselves more readily to the traffic in dreams and incantations than to the distributions of coherent argument. As the habits of mind

beholden to the rule of images come to replace the systems of thought derived from the meaning of words, the constant viewer learns to eliminate the association of cause with effect.

Part of what I call simplification, Lapham calls "magical forms of thinking," adding that these ways of "thinking" are a part of a "broad retreat into the forests of superstition"—away from empiricism, that is to say—and of a "flight into the self-referential landscapes of wish and dream."

Ours, says Lapham, is "a society in which fewer and fewer people know how to think," while we have become a people for whom "nothing necessarily follows from anything else," and for whom "what is important is the surge and volume of emotion, not its object or its subject," as we live lives of narcissism and inconsequentiality in which "the time is always now."

✤ ✤ ✤

My own impression is that the decline of empiricism—and the rise of unexamined "rights"—began accelerating in the mid-1970s, a time when the atmosphere in classrooms, at least in my own, was also changing, with "disruptive behavior" on the increase. I still remember my first clear experience of empiricism's failing as a means of argument or communication. In one of my composition classes were two young women—girls, really—who, from the term's beginning, sat in the back row and tended to talk with one another whenever they liked, whether class had started or not, whether another student was speaking or not, or even whether the instructor—that would be me—was speaking or not.

This, to me, was a departure. In my own undergraduate days, a mere comment, maybe even just a *signal*, from an instructor was enough to end behavior of this sort and prevent its return. And as I had experienced, so I taught. But it became clear right away that any requests I made of these girls, in class or out, or any comments I made *to* them, would have no effect. Maybe for a time they would seem to pay attention, but before long, whenever the impulse struck, they'd be back at it again.

Then, once, I lost patience. I interrupted myself (and the class) and demanded that once and for all they stop talking. And this was how I found out about the erosion of empiricism.

The girls *denied absolutely that they'd been talking.*

They were adamant, and my insisting that they *had* in fact been talking made them only more outraged at the gall of my accusing them, at the falsity of my authority, and at the injustice of the whole thing.

✦ ✦ ✦

A simple example, a quarter of a century back—antiquity!—almost too minor to have much meaning. But it was a marker and symptom of a world losing its sight.

In their particular form of self-absorption, where were those girls dwelling, after all, if not in Lewis Lapham's "eternal present"? For them, "the time was always now." For them, the force that drove behavior was a desire for gratification that could *always take place*— that is, it could take place *now*—because the girls' "self-sense," or their "me-sense," *overrode* their empirical sense, either wholly or selectively, so that at one moment the classroom full of other students simply "disappeared" for them, *was not visible to them,* and at the next moment the fact that they *had been talking* disappeared in turn from their radar, the self's interest and gratification now being served not by the gratification of talking but by the gratification of escaping accusation. The girls had their "gratification rights," and among those rights was the additional right to be nonempirical whenever being so might serve to protect and preserve the *other* rights. What the girls had claimed for themselves, or what others in the Age of Simplification had created and then claimed *for* them, were, again, "*me-rights*" or "*self-rights.*"

This period—the middle or late 1970s—was in fact the period

of burgeoning "rights" movements and their entrenchment in academia, publishing, and the arts generally—black rights, Puerto Rican rights, women's rights, gay and lesbian rights, and so on. During my own decades as an instructor, I've watched this movement—or perhaps I should say these movements—push their way into the political structure of academia and then into the curriculum itself, and from there into the minds of whole segments of the intellectual classes. My own two talking students were simply an early example of what the movement would lead to. After all, they were only exercising one of their newly minted 1970s-style rights. Doing so made them quite nasty, it's true, but part of their new possession was, if you will, "nasty rights." And their high dudgeon, their pointed taking of offense at my hollow tyranny in attempting to exert authority over them—yes, they were merely exercising their "righteousness rights." From the outset, it quickly became clear that there *could be no appeal* against the exercise of these new rights, since their freedom from empiricism in effect made them absolute.[2] Such rights were the apotheosis of a kind of emotional solipsism that resulted in the right of the *self*, subject to no check or appeal, to be taken, accepted, and celebrated for what it *is*, no matter what that may be. It didn't matter. In Lapham's words, the important thing was "the surge and volume of emotion, not its object or its subject."

The *self*, as if by fiat or edict, had become the measure of everything. But this self was—and is—a false one, meager, misconceived, shallow, opportunistic, even hypocritical. Its overshadowing of the genuine self, its elevation in place of the genuine self, has been not only a failure but a catastrophe for the entire nation and for much of the world as well.

✦ ✦ ✦

Still, nothing comes from nothing, and a fair part of what happened in the 1970s had its beginnings elsewhere and came from afar. To look into the origins of the "rights" movement, in fact, necessitates looking into other American cultural forces, one reaching far back indeed—that is, seventeenth-century New England Puritanism— and another much more recent—namely, the development of the mass media through the twentieth century.

The joining of these two historic elements into one hyper-powerful cultural stream has had remarkable—and ruinous— results. Over a period of not much more than thirty years, the union between them has come close to destroying American higher edu-cation, has reduced whole ranges of American literary culture to insignificant and self-contented pablum, and has made a sham-bles of the American political system. Once the envy of all who loved and sought dignity, justice, and freedom, our country has been transformed into a tyranny that's more despised, by the free and shackled alike, than any other nation or power in the world.

✦ ✦ ✦

Seeing a parallel between my two disruptive girls back in 1975 and President George W. Bush today may seem, at first glance, absurd. But in fact it's an absolutely sound comparison. Both the girls and the president—they in regard to their talking in class, he in regard to yellow cake, weapons of mass destruction, Saddam Hussein's connection with Al Qaeda, the benefit to the poor of massive tax cuts, and so on—again and again assert things to be true even when, by means of empirical testing, it is apparent that they are not.

In this sense, to put it bluntly, both the girls and the president are incorrigible liars. However, because we live in the Age of Sim-plification, there's more to it than that. Because we live in the Age of Simplification, the question arises immediately as to where the fault lies for their being liars—whether it lies with them or elsewhere—or, in fact, whether their being liars can even be con-sidered a *fault*.

When I told the girls that they had indeed been talking and

that there was empirical evidence of that fact, my remonstrance made no impression. When I pointed out that I and others in the room had *heard* them; that we had *seen* their lips moving and their heads bowed together; and that if any of us had touched a finger to either of the girls' larynxes, we would have *felt* the vibrations of vocal cords—none of this made the least difference to the girls. And the reason is that they were no longer functioning—except perhaps selectively—by means of the processes of observation, reason, and empiricism, but instead solely by claim to *right, solipsism,* and *belief.*

Rights—individual and inalienable—as everyone knows, are built into the very foundation of our republic, a fact that has had a powerful role in allowing America to grow great, and certainly to grow free. But something is happening, or has happened, that the founders did everything they could to prevent when they shaped the nation—when, that is, they not only did everything they could to distinguish *between* belief (or faith) and reason, but did all they could to keep the two *apart* from one another. Never could they have imagined that a time like the Age of Simplification would come. Never could they have imagined that a time would come when belief and reason were to collapse together into one, or a time when this would happen for other reasons, *primarily,* than through erosion of the wall so carefully built between church and state. No, what the founders could never in a thousand years have imagined, and yet what has begun to happen now, is this: Like the founders, we, too, cling to the powerful value of individual rights and their inalienability, but we do so—something the founders could not even faintly have conceived—*without any longer adhering to empiricism as the determining basis of either our logic or our thought.*

The famous phrase—"We hold these truths to be self-evident"—is a statement fully appropriate to its era, the period known as the Enlightenment or Age of Reason. But the words "self-evident" don't really mean "self-evident" at all. Most people hearing these words used together in this way would probably take them as meaning something like "needing no proof" or, perhaps more commonly than you might imagine in this time of extraordinarily but not inexplicably burgeoning evangelism, as meaning "dictated by god."

But "self-evident" means neither of those things. What these words mean, instead, is: "We hold these truths *to be empirically demonstrable.*" In other words, *observable evidence* is what proves them to be true. The truth of the founding period that's simplest to demonstrate as having an empirical basis is also the founders' most sweeping one: This, of course, is the truth that "all men are created equal," and it is a sweepingly radical truth because, followed to its logical conclusion, it destroys the institution of nobility by birth, replacing it with the institution of advancement through achievement and the institution of *earning* rather than *inheriting* merit.

But what exactly *is* the empirical evidence that proved convincing enough to sweep away king, count, and czar as it showed itself able to do, for example, in 1776 and 1789? This question, for me, has come up annually for the past thirty-four years as one after yet another fall semester has begun and, with it, another reading of Voltaire's *Candide* (1759).

The casual simplicity and familiar bawdiness of Voltaire's famous tale make it popular among students, but they're often surprised to discover that the story, beyond being a comedy, is also a study of the revolutionary significance of empiricism. Readers will remember that, in it, the young and attractive Candide is kicked bodily out of the castle of the Baron Thunder-ten-Tronckh for the offense of kissing the equally young and attractive Cunégonde, the Baron's daughter. For the rest of the tale, Candide travels the world in search of his beloved Cunégonde, experiencing and observing atrocities, pains, calamities, and human abuses the entire way.

Now, Candide's unpardonable offense doesn't lie in his *kissing* Cunégonde, but in his kissing her when he is insufficiently elevated in the ranks of the nobility for this familiarity to be permissible. In short, the story is a studied satire of the injustice, unnaturalness, and negative human consequences of the institution of nobility by birth, and, as such, like Voltaire's writing in general, was prerevolutionary, helping clear the way for 1789.

As for the relationship between empiricism and revolution, then, one need only imagine what I've grown accustomed to calling "the nakedness experiment." In this imaginary experiment, a classful of students, aided by plentiful but equally imaginary grant money (from the U.S. Department of State), would travel in time to a chosen place and moment in France toward the middle of the eighteenth century. There, half of the students would travel around for a week or two finding fifty nobles and fifty commoners who, in exchange for a designated stipend, would agree to congregate, on a warm summer day shortly afterward, in a designated meadow, glade, or lea. There, they would all strip entirely naked, wearing nothing except for a badge or piece of paper around the neck with an identifying number, the lowest being the number one, the highest one hundred.

As the naked people mingled among themselves or walked about the lea, the literature students who had *not* helped select and organize the group would each be given a pen, clipboard, and sheet of paper. The sheet of paper would have lines on it numbered one through one hundred, and, corresponding to each numbered line, there would be two boxes, one labeled "Noble," the other "Commoner." The task would be to identify each of the one hundred people as one or the other.

The point is clear—that the experiment is destined to fail entirely. In the absence of clothing and other accoutrements normally signifying rank or class, there would be no empirical, observable evidence whatsoever by which noble could be distinguished from commoner or vice versa, and no way that any statistically significant result could come from the marking and then tallying of the boxes.

Of course—as students are always quick to point out—there would, or might be, identifying marks or traits left among the hundred as the result of poorer or better diet, more or less physically demanding occupation, greater or less protection from the elements, and so forth. Perfectly true: The institution of nobility by birth *produces* empirical evidence of class and rank, but no empirical evidence exists to justify that institution in the first place. In selecting the group of one hundred, care would naturally be taken to avoid extremes—the rickets cases on the one hand, gout on the other, or extremes of obesity or emaciation in either subgroup. Too, the experiment would obviously have to be conducted in silence: Speech would be an instant identifier of class or rank.

❖ ❖ ❖

So there you are: The reason the United States is a democratic republic dedicated to principles of freedom and individual rights isn't because it was decreed to be such by god, but because, when they're naked, or when they're born, people are all alike. By substantial and significant empirical evidence, a naked king and naked plowman look the same. And when they're *born,* the empirical evidence of the sameness of the son of a king and the son of a farmer is overwhelming.

What each may become later in life—what each may *amount to* in life—is of course another matter altogether. But that they were created equal is shown by plentiful empirical evidence.

Nakedness, therefore, is revealed as being *every bit as important to human society* as clothing and other appurtenances are, though we tend not to think of it in this way often, if ever. This is because custom takes over, and when custom takes over, we stop *thinking.* Custom is obedience or habit, not thought.

But, of course, in order to know what *not thinking* is, you need to know, first, what *thinking* is. When, over the past thirty-five Septembers, I would ask a class to define "reason," most students would respond that reason is "logic" or "logical" or what's "true." If in turn I asked them what *made* something logical or true, they would usually, at first, go in circles, saying, for example, that if something is true, it's logical, and if it's logical, it's true—a trap of redundancy. Luckily, someone would almost always offer at about this point that a thing is true if it's a "fact"—and the moment would have arrived to introduce the familiar old example of the dog and, through it, syllogistic or deductive reasoning:

> Ganges is a dog;
> all dogs have four legs;
> therefore Ganges has four legs.

But not:

> Ganges has four legs;
> all dogs have four legs;
> therefore Ganges is a dog.

And not:

> Ganges the dog has four legs;
> all cats have four legs;
> therefore Ganges is a cat.

People quickly understand that for a syllogism to be valid (like the first one), its first and second premises must themselves be valid and true, and must, further, be in a valid and logical relationship *with one another.* When all of that is true, the deductive conclusion (Ganges has four legs) will also be valid, true, and inevitable.

Task completed? Well, no. It seems clear that we can now declare it a "fact" that Ganges has four legs, but we still don't know what the *foundation* of our deductive reasoning is—in other words, our original question still hasn't been answered, namely, what *makes* something valid or true? How do we *know* that Ganges is a dog or that all dogs have four legs?

At this point, students sometimes grow impatient, shouting out, *"Because it's obvious!"* But, no, I'm sorry, it *isn't* "obvious," even though it may seem obvious to us. Was it "obvious" to everyone in 1759, when *Candide* was published, that monarchy was not just, reasonable, or natural? Or was it "obvious" that "all men are created equal"?

By no means was any such thing taken as "obvious" by everyone in 1759. Nor would the following perfectly sound syllogism have been universally acceptable:

1. All men are created equal.
2. The king and the plowman, both being men, are equal at their inception.
3. Therefore, either one of them may prove the better suited as leader of the realm.

So unacceptable was this deductive logic, in fact, that two wars, beginning only thirteen years apart, were fought to decide its validity. These, of course, were the American and the French Revolutions, and both, as all know, were won, albeit with many complications, by the defenders of the syllogism's validity. And the syllogism's validity, in turn, couldn't exist without the support of a prior foundation—and that, of course, is the foundation of empiricism.

At this point, we come back to our original question, and now we're able to declare that the answer to it is this: The only way we can conclude that Ganges is a dog, or that Ganges has four legs, or that all men are created equal, is empirically, *through observable evidence—evidence that can be seen, heard, tasted, smelled, or touched—demonstrating the validity or truth of each assertion.*

Common sense? Well, yes, it's common sense, but it's empiricism first. We're so accustomed to empiricism—the scientific method—that we scarcely need the word any more, and many people no longer even have it in their vocabularies. In these senses, yes, it's "obvious" that Ganges is a dog.

But in these senses, too, the "obvious" happens just now to be a subject of far, far more than routine or customary importance. In the Age of Simplification, after all, empiricism is both under attack *and* in the late stages of abandonment and neglect. In place of it, we have, more and more perversely and more and more pervasively, equivalents of Lewis Lapham's "magical forms of thinking" and "retreat into the forests of superstition." Ours is a time when one element of the population after another willfully replaces empiricism with *conviction* (American academicians included), a time when zeal, belief, and "sincerity" programmatically outrank reason and logic, and when feeling outranks and obscures thinking or knowing.

Precisely because of substitutions like these, extremely important and extraordinarily destructive things occur. Indeed, the United States at present is the military invader and occupier of a previously sovereign foreign power, a state of affairs that has come about through zeal, conviction, opportunism, and desire—anything *but* empiricism. Everyone is all too familiar with the litany of things un-existent and unseen but *believed* in as justifications for this calamitous, muddled war: yellow cake uranium *not* being sold by Niger to Iraq; weapons of mass destruction *not* being stockpiled throughout the latter country; there *not* being weapons capable of launch against other nations within only *forty-five minutes* of the decision to launch; there *not* being ties between Saddam Hussein and Al Qaeda; Iraq *not* being a haven for terrorists from around the world; and so on.

In his *New York Times* column of April 27, 2004, Paul Krugman conjectures as to why the Bush administration is *so* intent, at seemingly almost any cost, on keeping secret the composition of Vice President Cheney's energy task force back in 2001. It's a very good question. Krugman speculates:

> The real mystery is why the Bush administration has engaged in a three-year fight . . . to hide the details of a story whose broad outlines we already know.

One possibility is that there is some kind of incriminating evidence in the task force's records. Another is that the administration fears that full disclosure will highlight its chummy relationship with the energy industry. But there's a third possibility: that the administration is really taking a stand on principle. And that's what scares me.

But what principle would that be? And why is it frightening? No offense to the courageous and observant Paul Krugman, but the reason it's frightening isn't really because it's a principle at all, but because it's a *right,* which is really what Krugman means anyhow. If it's a *right*—the same as my students' me-rights back in the classroom—*then there's no appeal to it.* And that, indeed, is the frightening part. Why? Let Krugman explain again:

> What Mr. Cheney is defending, in other words, is a doctrine that makes the United States a sort of elected dictatorship: a system in which the president, once in office, can do whatever he likes, and isn't obliged to consult or inform either Congress or the public.
>
> Not long ago I would have thought it inconceivable that the Supreme Court would endorse that doctrine. But I would also have thought it inconceivable that a president would propound such a vision in the first place.

And so we're back to the junta again, the very idea of which, now as earlier, is unspeakable, disorienting, and appalling. Krugman remains polite enough to qualify the dread word "dictatorship" with the happily democratic adjective "elected," but his good manners are in themselves a subtle jab, for in truth, after all, the Bush administration *wasn't* elected but came into office, as said before, by pseudo-electoral, or extra-electoral, means. Krugman, thus, is calling the current presidency a dictatorship.

And if the administration is a dictatorship, why is there so little alarm? Why is the unspeakable not spoken? The answer is this: because we are now living deep in the Age of Simplification. I've already said that the dictatorial "principle" governing the administration's behavior isn't really a principle at all, but a *right*. Suppose, now, that we go further and *identify* that right, give it a name, say what it's a right *to*. Indeed, why not assert that it's the right *not to be empirical?* That's the same as the *right* to behave by impulse, belief, superstition, desire, or will. And we know, as Lewis Lapham has also pointed out, that *most* Americans have already developed, have been given, have been indoctrinated into, or have devolved down to the state where they are holders of *that very same right.* And so just exactly how is a non-empiricist going to go about criticizing someone else for being non-empirical? How is a non-empiricist even going to be able to *see or know* that another person *is* an empiricist or non-empiricist?

Non-empiricism is, after all, a form of blindness: There are certain things that, except through empiricism, can't be shown and thus can't be seen. Nor can they, therefore, be contested. A government that is non-empiricist will revert to—or, by definition *be*—a tyranny. A *people* that is non-empiricist will be governable only by appeal to desire, by appeal to the voluptuary or sensate, not by appeal to *idea.*

In the United States today, we have both a non-empiricist government and a non-empiricist population. The situation, as Lewis Lapham put it, "doesn't hold out much promise for the American future." In the absence of essential change, stability can't be relied on for much longer, certainly not stability in any remaining context of liberty or freedom. As for revolt, it may no longer be possible for it ever to come. It *certainly* won't come in the immediate future, since most things still *look* normal. Most things still *look* regular and familiar. Things don't look unreal, so nothing's alarming.

And that's *really* alarming.

three

Compared to the subject of dictatorship in America, my "naked-ness experiment" may seem trivial and truly inconsequential. But in actuality it has depths and applications that we ignore at our peril—and that we *are* ignoring, and are being programmatically *encouraged* to ignore, in the dreadful stage-managed conformities of the Age of Simplification that lead ineluctably toward the totalitarian.

The "experiment" isn't mine, really, beyond its being a kind of template I invented to help illustrate a central idea in Voltaire's satire and also in that of his great near-contemporary, Jonathan Swift. Both of these Enlightenment writers, after all—not unlike the American founders—addressed themselves assiduously (and empirically) to the radical and radically important question of what a human being *is*. The answer to that question is both radical and radically important for this very good reason: that it is absolutely necessary for the answer to be understood, and abided by, if there is to be any successful and meaningful resistance to tyranny.

Our own greatest emergency now, an emergency that has been growing since at least 1947, is that the Age of Simplification is doing all it can not only to make us blind to that answer but to make the answer itself disappear entirely and forever. If that happens, the administration of George W. Bush is only the slightest early example of the horrors standing in the wings, waiting for their cue to step out onto the ruinous stage of an unimaginably dreadful and vicious albeit yet-unknown history.

❖ ❖ ❖

So what *is* the answer to the question, What is a human being? There's a moment early in Voltaire's tale when Candide, penniless and starving, approaches an orator who has just been speaking on the subject of charity. Instead of being charitable and giving Candide something to eat, however, the hypocritical orator berates him cruelly for not being sufficiently anti-Catholic ("'My friend,' said the orator to him, 'do you believe that the Pope is antichrist?'").[3] The incident takes place in Holland, a land of fierce doctrinal conflict between Protestantism and Catholicism. Even the zealot's wife gets in on the act when, from an upstairs window, she empties out a chamber pot on Candide's head.

Help comes, however, in the person of the "good Anabaptist Jacques," who, passing by and happening to see the "cruel and ignominious" way that "one of his brothers" is being treated, comes to the rescue and sets forth to feed, clothe, and house Candide.

There's much more to the story, of course—including huge helpings of both pathos and hilarity—but the thing here and now most pertinent to our question is Jacques' definition of a fellow human being, or "one of his brothers." According to Jacques, who takes his definition from Plato, a human being is "a two-footed, featherless creature with a soul."[4]

Anyone with an understanding of empirical thinking, an understanding of how we ascertain that Ganges is a dog, can have a pleasant moment with this curious and rather delightful definition.

It consists, really, of four assertions. I'll list them, and then test to see how many can be shown, empirically, to be true. They are:

1. That a human being is two-footed
2. That a human being is featherless
3. That a human being is a creature
4. That a human being has a soul

First, we can tell by sight and touch that a human being is two-footed, just as, second, we can tell by sight and touch that a human being is featherless. We can assume that by "creature,"[5] Voltaire means not just "organism" but "mammalian higher organism"—

that is, an organism that eats, digests, evacuates, breathes, and sexually reproduces. Corroborative evidence then can come through virtually all five senses, *seeing* these organic processes occur, *hearing* them, feeling them, even *smelling* them—particularly, one hardly need say, smelling results from the process of evacuation.

And so, like Swift and Voltaire themselves, we step, as my old Sunday school teacher might have said, into the gutter and embark upon a certain amount of dirty talk. For reasons soon to be explained, it's necessary to do so *if* we really want an answer to the question of what a human being is. The truth is that if Enlightenment thought hadn't itself descended to a consideration of what we're here calling the "dirty," there never could have *been* an Enlightenment, never could have *been* an American or a French Revolution, never could have *been* the rise of the modern democratic state as we know it.

Before seeing why not, however, a brief word about the soul. Separation between church and state in our nation's founding documents didn't come about *only* because the founders knew only too well how much bloodshed and tyranny had resulted in European history through the workings of the nonsecular state. The separation came about also because the founders knew very well that the soul's existence had no basis in empiricism, since no observable evidence could be found to verify it. The soul couldn't, and can't, be seen, smelled, tasted, touched, or heard. It could only be *believed*, or be believed *in*.

As a consequence, it couldn't be considered a part either of the rational self or of the known self and accordingly had to be set off from the affairs or considerations of any state government. For that matter, the soul could not logically or justly *be* governed by any human agency larger than the individual, and so, whether it did or didn't exist, the soul could not and was not to be part of the state.

The Enlightenment, however, was quite able to garner observable evidence of the human being's possession of *mind*, along with possession of the mind's product, reason. That evidence occurred when reason-based action had results that could be seen as improving the condition of life—as, for example, the bringing of an end to the institution of nobility by birth and a consequent turning toward egalitarianism that brought with it, say, diminishment in rates of starvation and disease.

It would be no distortion of Voltaire's position or intent, then, for us to change the good Anabaptist Jacques' definition of a human being to "a two-footed featherless creature with reason," and herewith permit me to make that change.

The United States was brought into existence during the Age of Reason, by men of reason who had trust in the power of reason to make human life better. All of the powers of the Age of Simplification, on the other hand, are aimed at the limiting, demeaning, and simplifying of that same element of the individual self—the reason—while encouraging, amplifying, and stimulating the feeling, voluptuary, and self-directed elements. In consequence, the nation itself, its art and culture, its historic achievement as a model of humane and enlightened governance—all of these are doomed if the individual mind cannot find some means of resistance, cannot be defended, saved, and nurtured into robust well-being. Lewis Lapham concludes his own recent lament on the subject with this same idea, commenting that "the republic's best and only chance for survival rests on its freedom of thought and force of mind."

✤ ✤ ✤

Though Voltaire died in 1778, too early to see the storming of the Bastille, he nevertheless had a major influence in paving the way for the revolution—and he did it to a good extent through so-called dirty talk. Another way of saying the same thing is this: He had an enormous influence in preparing the way for the revolution *by looking at things as they are.*

That is to say, he looked around him, at inherited institutions and at matters of *custom,* with the eyes of an empiricist.

The opening line of *Candide* immediately shows Voltaire's method through his choice of a name for the august personage who kicks Candide out of the castle. This person, of course, is the Baron Thunder-ten-Tronckh.

The name gives anyone who cares to take it a good opportunity for a visit back to certain old high school matters about words and poetry—connotation, for example, and onomatopoeia, even the bedrock question of what words *are* or are *for*.

First of all, the name Thunder-ten-Tronckh *sounds* funny, and of course it's intended to, since it's meant to ridicule the custom or institution of nobility by birth. Anybody can sense *that* aspect of it immediately. But a closer analysis of the satire is richly rewarding indeed.

Tronckh, obviously, is a made-up word that won't be found in dictionaries. Whether this means that it isn't really a "word" is a matter of opinion (and definition), but, in any case, it's undeniably a real *sound*, or the suggestion of one. And so the reader, beckoned by onomatopoeia, is invited to produce that sound for him or herself, or a sound that seems near the suggested one. And what is this sound that one hears in the third part of the baron's name? Is it a grunt? An elephant's trumpet? The honk of a goose? A duck's quack? Well, it could be any of these—or even, my own personal preference, the fart-sound.

And so, we're back to dirty talk again, but dirty talk in the service of the revered and central revolutionary principle that our nation is founded on, that first of the "truths" that the founders held to be "self-evident," which is, again, the empirical truth that "all men are created equal."

Because it so distinctly has three parts—or two parts hinged together by "ten" (having the same meaning as "of" or "von" or "de")—it's easy to think of the baron's name in association with the image of a chemist's balance, or the scale of justice, like this:

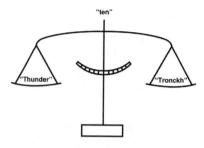

Suppose that "Thunder" and "Tronckh" are each placed on one of the pans of the scale: Which one, having the greater weight— or dignity—will raise the other upward? A glance at connotative meanings is helpful at this point—and for many student-readers that glance makes it seem obvious that "Thunder" easily outweighs "Tronckh." What are the connotations of "Thunder," after all, if not those of awesomeness, power, fearsomeness, augustness, and dignity, all exemplified, for example, by the fact of thunder, or lightning and thunder, which have been associated with gods and leaders from Zeus on up? On the other hand, the associative meanings of the fart-sound, the duck's quack, or the goose's honk are just as obviously low, undignified, base, fleshly, primal, and animalistic.

So there's no contest at all, it would seem. What king, leader, ruler, or even president wouldn't infinitely prefer being called, say, President Thunder over President Honk or President Quack or President Fart-Sound?

And yet anyone who evaluated the baron's name in the way we just have would be wrong indeed. Such a person would not only have failed to understand the whole of Voltaire's meaning but would reveal him or herself to have fallen straight into the trap that that witty writer and thinker cunningly set.

After all, is the nakedness experiment so quickly forgotten, with its empirical evidence that all men are created equal?

Voltaire's baron is indeed a fool. But that he's a leader (connoted by "Thunder") isn't what makes him a fool. Nor is he a fool because he's a two-footed, featherless creature that eats, evacuates, and reproduces (all connoted by "Tronckh"). No, he is a fool for one reason only: He is a fool *because he believes that, having been born a baron, he is superior to others.*

The baron, then, who believes himself innately superior to those of low birth, would see the relationship between noble and common, or himself and others, this way:

$$\text{Thunder} > \text{Tronckh}$$
or
$$\text{Tronckh} < \text{Thunder}$$

In other words, the baron would hold the fact of his nobility to be a value greater than the fact of his mere physical existence as a human being. A revolutionist, on the other hand, if he happened to be blinded by a zeal that caused him temporarily to forget all about the empirical basis of the concept of equality, a zeal that imbued him with a passionate belief in the superiority of "the people"[6] over the nobility, would see the relationship as just the opposite, this way:

$$\text{Thunder} < \text{Tronckh}$$
or
$$\text{Tronckh} > \text{Thunder}$$

And Voltaire? He is, of course, lambasting the baron as a pretender and a fool, suggesting that, although the baron *thinks* he's elevated and mighty in *kind,* he was in fact created in no different way from any other two-footed, featherless creature. The mind of a man is as essential to life as is the body of a man, both being of equal importance. If one is to be a human being, one must both be a "creature" *and* have a mind. If one is to be a true and just leader, one must possess both authority *and* the essential, bodily, animating humanity that bonds the leader with those led. And so Voltaire would show the relationship like this:

Thunder = Tronckh

or

Tronckh = Thunder

four

Abraham Lincoln's ringing, stately, and beautiful phrases in the Gettysburg Address—"that government of the people, by the people, for the people, shall not perish from the earth"—arise from the same revolutionary assumptions, with their roots in empiricism, as do Voltaire's barnyard jokes and indefatigable political satire. Whether the literary style is high or low, elevated or irreverent, the political-philosophic *matter* is the same. The baron is a bad leader because he is not *of* the people being led. And since he is not *of* them, his leadership can't be *for* them, but it is, rather, for himself. Obviously, it can't be *by* them.

When empiricism became the basis not only of scientific method but also of social, philosophic, and political thought, the idea stopped any longer being welcome or tenable that a people could or should be governed by any force, institution, authority, or figure that wasn't *of, by, and for* that people. Because of the revelatory powers of empiricism, especially when applied to political thought, the institution of nobility by birth was disestablished, and in its place was put the empirically based concept of the equality of man. At that same moment in history, and resting on that same brand-new foundation—a foundation back in currency again, that is, for the first time since antiquity—our own nation was brought into existence as a modern democratic republic.

It's now more than two hundred years later and time to come back to the subjects of the George W. Bush administration and the two students in the 1970s who had become so unconnected with empiricism as a method of thought that they *didn't know when they were talking and when they weren't.*

This may be the moment, first, however, to return, not to the nakedness experiment itself, but to a corollary of that experiment's empirically derived, once revolutionary, and now axiomatic principle concerning the equality of man.

The corollary is simple but in no way whatsoever is it any less far-reaching or profound in its implications for justice, freedom, political thought, and human dignity than any other seminal ideas the Enlightenment helped bring into being. It is this:

> If all men are created equal, it follows that all men are equally susceptible to and equally capable of feeling pleasure and pain.

It's no accident that, on the one hand, Voltaire lets Jacques provide us with the extraordinarily humble definition of human beings that he does ("two-footed featherless creatures with a soul"), and, on the other, that the founding fathers of our own republic, in the grand and ringing cadences of the Declaration, should have felt it appropriate *and necessary* to include among other "self-evident" truths and "inalienable" rights something so basic, homely, simple, and plain as the fact that one of those inalienable rights is "the pursuit of happiness."

We've heard these and other of the founders' phrases so often and for so long that, indeed, we do tend to take them for granted—something that, as everyone knows or should know, is a dangerous thing to let happen. Think of it—the founders actually *equated* the right to be allowed simply to remain *alive*—the right not to be killed—with the right to try to find, achieve, and perhaps even maintain *happiness*.

What could possibly have given rise to such a "self-evident" equivalence if not the empirically based understanding that all men are equally capable of feeling pleasure and pain?

Consider for a moment, too, just how revolutionary this understanding really *is*. The baron would never and *could* never be concerned either with the lives *or* with the happiness of his subjects, since he *is not one of them, is superior to them, and is different from them.*[7] That the baron should be concerned for the happiness of his peasants is as out of the question as that a seabird should be concerned for the feelings of the fish it eats.

Indeed, the baron's concern for his subjects or for their "happiness," insofar as that did or might exist, would in actuality be a concern only for *his own well-being,* since the state, for him, is a device, machine, or possibly organism, intended solely and only to serve that end, the end of his own well-being. Anyone depending on a device, machine, or organism for his own well-being would naturally wish that it be kept in the best possible running condition. His wish, however, would be not for *its* sake but for *his.*

After the rise of empiricism, as we know, this concept changed, and the relatively mechanical conception of the state that accompanied the late monarchies (that is, the post-empiricism monarchies) was replaced with the more integrated and organic concept of the rulers and the ruled being the same: the same by merit of their having had the *same equal origins,* and the same by merit of the profoundly formative corollary understanding that *no human being differs from any other in the capacity each has for feeling pleasure or pain.*

It was a time of extraordinary optimism, this revolutionary era, however much it may also be understood—correctly—as having been war-torn and bloody. But in its humane political philosophy and in its estimation of the rational powers of the mind as an aid in the improvement if not the perfectibility of life, it offered steps that there hadn't been any clearly equivalent model for since fifth-century Athens or republican Rome. And the United States was at the very center of it.

Useful and to the point is this brief passage:

> **ENLIGHTENMENT**, term for the rationalist, liberal, humanitarian, and scientific trend of 18th-cent. Western thought; the period is also sometimes known as the Age of Reason. The enormous scientific and intellectual advancements made in the 17th cent. by the EMPIRICISM of Francis BACON and LOCKE, as well as by DESCARTES, SPINOZA, and others, fostered the belief in NATURAL LAW and universal order, promoted a scientific approach to political and social issues, and gave rise to a sense of human progress and belief in the state as its rational instrument. Representative of the Enlightenment are such thinkers as VOLTAIRE, J. J. ROUSSEAU, MONTESQUIEU, ADAM SMITH, SWIFT, HUME, KANT, G. E. LESSING, BECCARIA, and, in America, Thomas PAINE, Thomas JEFFERSON, and Benjamin FRANKLIN. The social and political ideals they presented were enforced by "enlightened despots" such as Holy Roman Emperor JOSEPH II, CATHERINE II of Russia, and FREDERICK II of Prussia. DIDEROT'S *Encyclopédie* and the U.S. CONSTITUTION are representative documents of the Age of Reason.

Those phrases—"human progress and belief in the state as its rational instrument"—from *The Concise Columbia Encyclopedia* express the logical conclusion of much of what we've been talking about so far. And, on a slightly more personal note, they've been helpful also to many a September's worth of college students embarking upon readings in Voltaire, Swift, and Blake, students who have been helped to see that the "little society" at *Candide*'s end, with its foundation in empiricism, is itself a "rational instrument" with the potential for bringing justice and humane improvement to life in political systems.

Now, however, those same phrases have a different purpose, serving to return us to our own endangered present, to the administration of George W. Bush, to the similarities between the president and my two non-empirical but rights-endowed students, and to the very real possibility that the republic we have enjoyed for two hundred years may not be the one we will have for much longer, and may not even be the one we have now.

✤ ✤ ✤

The question, now back some ways, was whether, in order to get the war started, the president lied "outright" to the public about yellow cake, weapons of mass destruction, forty-five-minute launch times, Saddam Hussein's relations with Al Qaeda, Iraq as a terrorist refuge, and so on. That is, did he lie outright or did he, "declaring the false to be true," actually *believe* that the false was true?

The latter possibility, as we've seen, is the more frightening one to Paul Krugman, as it is to me and as it should be to everyone. The former possibility is grave enough and, on the surface of it, offers grounds for impeachment.[8] If, on the other hand, the president *actually did believe* he was telling the truth, as opposed to lying knowingly, then the situation is even more dire, since then we are dealing not with unscrupulousness but with derangement. Either way, the apparent look of the situation is inescapable, that the president has set about to employ the entire might and structure of the nation to bring about the furtherance of his *own* interests, accompanied by the personal interests of his corporate backers. It will take more than easygoing postmortem panels about "intelligence failures," more than attenuated competitions in finger-pointing among agencies, to bring out a clear answer to the questions of exactly what did happen and, equally important, exactly what *didn't* happen during the end of the 2000 election, during the time before 9/11, during 9/11 itself, in the immediate aftermath of 9/11, and in the subsequent and unrelenting drumbeat of forced march to the invasion of Iraq. Obvious in all of these events, and obvious *to* all who are willing to see it, is that there have been failure and deception, either or both, of virtually unbelievable degree, extent, and continuousness on the part of an administration that seems to have no capacity for guilt, to be incapable of embarrassment, to be unaware entirely of its own accountability, and to act as it chooses, both militarily and economically, not in the interests of the nation but in the interests of itself and its immediate supporters.

In other words, we now have behavior on the highest levels of national leadership that is demonstrably identical in kind to the behavior of my two rights-driven students, in whose eyes the world existed to serve them, not they to serve the world.

✤ ✤ ✤

There are two questions that, it seems to me, any concerned and observant person must, and can't help but, ask:

1. Why did all of this happen and what does it mean? (Put another way: How *could* all of this have happened and what does it mean?)

2. Why is the response to it so limited, the expression of outrage so meager and so weak, the demand for accountability so nearly nonexistent? (Put another way: Why, given the enormity of the situation and the potential it holds for disastrous outcomes, is it *all but impossible even to discuss it publicly?*)

All *but* impossible. Some time ago (June 3, 2003) Paul Krugman devoted his column to the subject of the Bushists' use of deceit for purposes of getting the war rolling. Krugman didn't see it as merely probable or possible that there *was* deception; he saw the use of it, instead, as typical of the administration's customary pattern of behavior:

> Suggestions that the public was manipulated into supporting an Iraq war gain credibility from the fact that misrepresentation and deception are standard operating procedure for this

administration, which—to an extent never before seen in U.S. history—systematically and brazenly distorts the facts.

Like Voltaire, Krugman is nothing if not refreshing in his candor and in the directness of his language, as when, later in the column, he accuses "some Democratic politicians" of "[offering] the administration invaluable cover by making excuses and playing down the extent of the lies." After all, what can possibly be gained by euphemizing that last short little word? And it's no good, either, justifying the war after the fact by celebrating the riddance of the tyrant Saddam, whom, it's true, no one could wish back in power. But that has nothing whatsoever to do with the subject of the prior lies, as Krugman makes clear:

> It's no answer to say that Saddam was a murderous tyrant. . . . [For] the important point is that this isn't about Saddam: it's about us. The public was told that Saddam posed an imminent threat. If that claim was fraudulent, the selling of the war is arguably the worst scandal in American political history—worse than Watergate, worse than Iran-contra. Indeed, the idea that we were deceived into war makes many commentators so uncomfortable *that they refuse to admit the possibility.* [emphasis added]

So there it is, the idea from the very start of this chapter: "[Refusing] to admit the possibility" of a thing makes it impossible to discuss that thing. And what, exactly, is the difference between *refusing to admit* the possibility of a thing and being blind to it? When the stakes are so extraordinarily high, that question takes on more than just an academic or semantic importance. Krugman continues:

> But here's the thought that should make those commentators really uncomfortable. Suppose that this administration did con us into war. And suppose that it is not held accountable for its

deceptions, so Mr. Bush can fight . . . a "khaki election" next year. In that case, our political system has become utterly, and perhaps irrevocably, corrupted.

If the stakes—as Krugman suggests and as I believe—are really this high, if our political system is at risk of being *irrevocably* corrupted, if American government of, by, and for the people is at risk of vanishing from the earth—then why is it that this crisis is being met, as I have asked before, by so remarkably *little* sense of emergency? It's true that a presidential campaign is going on as I write these words, but it's not true that John Kerry offers significantly greater freedom from the demands of corporate support than Bush does; nor is it evident that the campaign is offering any more elements of truth-telling to the public than at any other time—with the result that, yes, the campaign goes on, but, no, it's not departing in any significant way whatsoever from the business-as-usual model, dimension, or incisiveness of, say, the election four years before. In this sense, given the intensity of the emergency, on the one hand, and the grievously pedestrian insignificance and vacuity of the campaign, on the other, isn't it as though what we're *really* hearing is not a battle for ideas and an insistence upon restatement and restoration of essential values and fundamental principles, but, instead, a yawning, huge, extraordinarily dangerous—in effect, a complicitous—silence? If all of this is true, if the election is this far away from so much as even *looking* at the urgent matters of greatest importance to the maintaining of a free republic, it becomes understandable that certain people might conclude, not that the republic is in danger of being lost, but that it has been lost already.

five

Earlier, talking about the proliferation of the "absolutist rights" that started back in the 1970s and are, more fully grown, with us still, I said that the roots of that "movement" were deep, going back all the way to the Puritan seventeenth century. I was referring, of course, to America's tradition as a haven for those fleeing persecution or intolerance, notably those seeking the right to worship as they chose. Also, as we've seen, the founders' concepts of tolerance and natural rights grew out of the empiricism of the seventeenth century and were strengthened further in the eighteenth century. The notion of *rights*, indeed, as it should and must be, is woven into the very fiber and bred into the very sinew of our nation and has been so from its origins.

And so what could possibly be the problem with the "rights movement"?

The problem is that not until our own poor, lost, dangerous, and demented age, which began sometime within five years after the end of World War II, have we *as a nation* ever before fully abandoned, and become entirely blind to, the foundation of empiricism that alone gave and could give those rights their *meaning.*

We continue to cling passionately to our "inalienable right" to "inalienable rights." But at that point our thinking stops in its tracks. We go blind, turn inward, drop all empiricism, philosophically speaking, and become solipsists: Politically speaking, that's when we become "consumers."

And, as solipsists and consumers, we do exactly what we're expected to, which is this: We remain essentially passive in all things *except for our passionate insistence upon individual rights.* Beyond that point, however, we do not go. No longer does it even occur to us to ask, in any meaningful way whatsoever beyond the emotional, sensual, voluptuary, or hedonistic, what it might conceivably be that those inalienable rights in fact *are for.*

❖ ❖ ❖

In a free country, of course, they don't have to be *for* anything. In mainstream thinking, John Stuart Mill's attitude has long passed as general currency—that a person is free to do (or not do) what he wishes with his life so long as he brings no harm to others. But we're speaking here not just on a moral or ethical level, but also on a political one. We're talking about what it means to be a citizen in a free, representative, democratic republic. And in such a republic, one of the things that a citizen's inalienable rights are *for* is to protect and preserve the very republic itself and the rights and freedoms it guarantees. If citizens do *nothing* beyond the voluptuary or consumptive with their rights (beyond the bestial, that is, as Hamlet would put it),[9] then they may indeed lose both rights *and* republic.

And exactly this, it appears, is what's happening now and may have happened already.

✦ ✦ ✦

Because we have, over the past half-century, gradually but surely abandoned empiricism as our fundamental tool of thought, we now tend for the most part to drift around blindly in varyingly lost, puzzled, confused, and aimless states, veering most often between the equally grim emotional poles of rage and sloth, those psychological twins that dwell in the breasts of almost all cases of ennui or unacknowledged despair.

The rage is known and seen everywhere—in "road rage," in "going postal," in the dumb, hulking wrestler's walk affected by American men (feet wide, elbows out, threatening paws open and at the ready). The sloth is equally visible, especially but far from only in the young—in the parade of absurd, baggy, bum-and-prisoner clothing; in the maddening, shuffling slowness of gait that's affected; in the soft-boned slump of seeming exhaustion that has replaced upright posture; in the flopping or draping of the body instead of the seating of it; and, familiar to everyone who reads the papers, in the nation's epidemic of obesity.

Readers at this point may take issue, arguing that what I'm

naming are nothing more than random and anecdotal signs, unrep-resentative of any true national condition or malaise, and that if I'm going to start making sweeping claims about ennui, despair, rage, and sloth, I'd better become a sociologist or a psychologist and at least get scientific about it.

Fair enough. This may not even be the place for a discussion of the relation between the outward *look* of daily American life and the inward psycho-emotional wasteland it reflects. But the cen-tral point remains, and it's this: The Bush administration, again and again, declares things to be true that are not true; takes the nation into a war on the basis of lies and doesn't admit having done so even when exposed; gives to the rich, steals from the poor, and drives state governments to insolvency, all the while declar-ing that these policies are for *everyone's* good; and not only fails to explain its—and the U.S. Air Force's—extraordinary and suspicious behavior[10] during the first hour and twenty minutes after the hijack-ing of *four* commercial jetliners on 9/11 and the first crash into the World Trade Center, but actively does all it can to *stop* investiga-tions into its behavior on that day. The Bush administration does such things and continues doing them, and yet in the American public at large there are no significant signs of fear, alarm, dis-pleasure, or consciousness that something is fundamentally and radically amiss, and little or no reaction of any truly significant or visible kind against such behavior.

A simple but terrible question: *Why not?*

✦ ✦ ✦

One of the grim points that must be understood in an effort to answer that question is this: that in truth the inalienable rights of the people effectively no longer exist—beyond the level of the bodily or voluptuary—for the perfectly good reason that the people, beyond those levels, don't exercise them.[11]

Most people, as everyone knows, don't vote. Most people don't read. Most people pay little or no attention to the news, and, if they *do* keep up any exposure to affairs in the world outside the self, they do it mostly through *television,* which, by this late date in our national devolution of consciousness, has been brought to a point of near-perfection as an instrument that—through distortion, omission, simplification, and many devices and methods (all of inestimable value to television's corporate controllers)—tells, shows, and promulgates far, far, far more lies than truths about the nature of being alive, the actual range of experience open to human beings, and the complex and manifold purposes either of life itself *or* of the possession and exercise of "inalienable rights."

This is very old news indeed, the influence of the mass media; this news has been with us for at *least* half a century, getting worse all that time, until now no one even talks about it anymore. But no thinking or observant person who has been alive since the World War II era—or who, as I said earlier, was alive and observant in 1947 and is *still* alive and observant—can be unaware of the breadth and profundity of change that has been brought about in both our national and private lives by the overwhelming and penetrating influence of the omnivorous and largely ungovernable mass media (and, one hastens to add, by air conditioners and automobiles). The very ways we act, speak, feel, and socialize (or *don't* act, speak, feel, and socialize), even the ways we *think,* have undergone changes far greater than could conceivably have been the case during *any other fifty-year period of our entire national history.*

In a word, mass culture came into existence in the decade or so following World War II. Since then, it has changed not at all in its essence, but instead has become, year by year, more and more perfectly defined, achieved, and, of course, exploited by those people and organizations in positions to gain from it.

The result is that we now live in and under the authority and defining powers not of a representative democratic republic, as we once did, but of the extraordinarily powerful, profoundly oppressive, and demonically efficient corporate-economic-political ganglion that Wendell Berry calls the "total economy,"[12] Gore Vidal the "National Security State,"[13] and George Orwell "Big Brother."

How could it have happened?

Well, it took half a century of conditioning (through advertising, largely), half a century of "market research," half a century of de-education and at the same time of anti-education[14]—with the result that the population at large has at last acquired exactly the characteristics desired of it by the power-seeking corporate-state.

Chief and foremost among these characteristics is, of course, passivity, of the kind so clearly seen now in the absence of public reaction to the deceit, manipulation, and tyrannies of the Bush administration.

Pliability and passivity of the kind now all around us is, obviously, of great importance to the corporate-state, not only for political reasons but also for economic ones: Each person must be transformed in such a way as not only to remain indolent in the face of leadership's tyrannies and injustices, but also to adhere to his or her role as a cog, if you will, in the vast economic machine that keeps the whole state going. Each person, that is to say, must be transformed in such a way as no longer to be a citizen but, instead, to be a consumer.

The ideal consumer could be identified as the person who never votes but always buys, who never thinks but always wants. This wanting should always be kept, insofar as possible, on the sensory, emotional, and voluptuary level: It must be, as with food or sex, a desire that results in its own gratification but awakens again as desire soon afterward.

In the 1950s, the pattern was called "keeping up with the Joneses," and in that now seemingly quaint decade "consumerism" was born to stay. The next and most obvious and influential change, on the other hand—the replacing of thought with feeling—began taking place in the middle and end of the following decade, with the rise of the hippie movement, the increased use and popularity of recreational drugs, and the extreme fervor of the antiwar movement. All three of these, but primarily the antiwar movement itself, both gave rise to and in turn were fueled by a very strong idealism. This idealism, under direct attack by what was perceived as the rightist and intransigent state, soon enough began seeking an armorlike protection by letting itself become permeated with absolutism, making its cause stronger by merit of its being held as unnegotiable. This adoption of the absolute did indeed have a practical and focusing effect, politically, for a certain time. Then, however, the political situation changed, but those in the movement didn't: Their intransigence at that point stopped being a matter of politics and became zeal instead. What had begun as thought came to be rigidified into *belief,* into *attitude,* into *feeling.*

This change was an extraordinarily critical moment on the road toward the crisis we now face. Exactly when that crucial moment took place is a matter almost of choice, but without question it happened sometime in the 1970s. During that period, what took place was this: The political left set about destroying itself through a kind of intellectual suicide, doing so in the name of all that it considered good and also in the wrong belief that it was *doing* good—though, in fact, as we now can see, it was doing incalculable and irrevocable harm by removing liberalism from the active political-intellectual field altogether (and putting it in the realm of feeling and righteousness), thus leaving a vacuum for the right to fill, which the right began doing immediately and without the least hesitation.

In my estimate, there has never in the intellectual history of the United States, from the Declaration on, been a greater calamity than this spectacle of the liberal-left intelligentsia setting out to destroy itself. My own thirty or more years as a literary professional inside academia gave me a ringside seat from which to watch, and, as I described in the first chapter of this book, the process I observed was one of zeal and certainty replacing reason, feeling replacing thinking. My literary—and other—colleagues in the humanities, in subscribing to these changes, revealed themselves *already* to have been transformed into intellectual or artistic versions of the "ideal consumer," not necessarily into the template of one "who never votes but always buys," but definitely into the template of one "who never thinks but always desires."

What my colleagues *desired,* to their credit, was to help bring about *good*—to have all things in the world be fair, to have all things be just, and, above all, to have nothing be *harmful* to anyone or anything anywhere. That these wishes, though laudable, are naive and idealistic is testament only to the extent to which positions among the newer ranks of faculty—by the middle or late 1970s—had been filled *already* by those molded and conditioned by the methods and simplicities of the mass media and consumerism. Since they had already been intellectually diminished through having spent their lives and having received their educations under the ever- and omni-present influence of consumerism and the corporate-state, it was quite natural for them—not a dislocating or wrenching step at all—to allow the complete and final replacement of thought by feeling in the new arrangement that then passed for "reason" but was really a rigidification based in the certitudes of a morally committed feeling that was essentially absolutist.

The academics now in this newly compromised intellectual condition remained no less dedicated than ever to the doing and bringing about of *good*, but because of the emotion-based thought-world they now lived in, and because of their zealous conviction that this thought-world was *correct,* they tended, as thinkers, to demonstrate mainly a stubbornly fixed passivity in their intellectual-emotional lives rather than any ability to be intellectually inventive, interpretive, or active.

As a result, and as a result also simply of time passing, their "thinking" took on the increasingly Manichaean simplification in which things are seen as pure opposites. In this view, their own moral feelings were assumed unquestionably to be all *good,* the corporate-military-economic state to be all *bad.* The extent to which each of these premises is a half-truth is significant but doesn't need concern us here. What has to concern us, though, is the inherent danger that arises when any strenuous or pure dichotomy considers feeling ("I *know* I am right because I *feel* so due to my moral sensitivity") to be superior to any putative *absence* of feeling ("I know that all those responsible for the oppressive corporate-state are *bad* because they are insensitive and have no feelings").

Expression good, oppression bad. Feeling good, thinking bad.

And now, having reached this point of visionlessness and muddle, we must return to those two students back in the mid-seventies who *didn't know* they were talking in class but who knew with absolute conviction that they had *every right* to do so.

✢ ✢ ✢

No one—no one—can contribute successfully to the commonweal or help successfully in the husbanding and protection of the republic or its merits and freedoms if they remain empiricists in only certain parts of their thinking rather than in all parts.

The two students, whether they knew it or not, were indeed empiricists as far as the *determination* of equal rights was concerned—they accepted the empiricism of the nakedness project, and, still as empiricists, they accepted the truths that all men are created equal and that all men are endowed with the inalienable rights of life, liberty, and the pursuit of happiness.

In regard to what goes on *after* the granting or determination of those rights, however, they were not empiricists in any way whatsoever: Their "thinking" after that point took place solely and entirely in the regions of belief, faith, zeal, feeling, and superstition, as they remained wholly blind to any and everything except what was on the solipsistic, voluptuary, sensory, or emotional level.

In other words, having abandoned empiricism *after* the granting of their rights of equality, they paid no heed whatsoever to the matter of what they did, made, or achieved with, from, or as a consequence of those rights.

One can't, first, accept the blessing of empirically derived human rights, and then, second, abandon empiricism altogether as a means of judging the quality, goodness, truth, nature, or meaning of what one does in life *from that point onward*. Or one can't do so and hope to be in any way consistent or admirable philosophically, intellectually, or ethically.

But so what? To do this very thing is what we've been trained, indoctrinated, and conditioned to do for the last half-century or longer, a period during which the nation has been unremittingly and programmatically urged and conditioned, by near-countless means and methods—electronic, propagandistic, commercial, political—to feel rather than think, to seek gratification immediately rather than delay it, to judge life's meaning by the measure of wanting things, having things, and then showing things off, meaning, of course, consumer "products" and possessions. Never in human history have so many people through such powerful methods over such a length of time and with such vested and intensely concerted interest been led so consistently to become simpler rather than more complex, to be more childlike rather than more adult, to live for and to value the superficial rather than the profound, the obvious rather than the subtle, the physical rather than the intellectual, the dumb rather than the smart. And never before have so many people been so thoroughly indoctrinated in the merit and justice of asserting righteously and insisting vehemently upon their unquestioned, inalienable, unexamined *rights*—the right (just as the ads, the schools, the correspondence courses all say) to be anything they wish, the right to do anything they want, and, above all, the most inalienable right of all, *the right not to be disrespected*.

This final "right," which I've preceded intentionally with an appropriately Orwellian modifying phrase ("the most inalienable of all"), is, of course, not only the "new" right most widely and frequently insisted upon these days, but it's also the most obviously post-empirical of the lot. This can be shown—that it's egocentric and energized by the sensual and not the intellectual—by noting that it's *not* the right to be respected *for what I have done, achieved, or accomplished* (or even for what I am doing, achieving, or accomplishing right now), but that it's *the right to be respected for what I am, as I am, whatever I do, or whatever I don't do.*

The abandonment of empiricism and its replacement by this kind of brute insistence on an *ur*-solipsism began long ago, and Tom Wolfe's coining of the popular and revealing phrase "the me decade" (in 1976) deserves a nod. But "me-ism" has by this late date moved much, much farther into a widespread intellectual pathology that has brought about, already, untold damage and destruction.

Academia, again, may be the easiest place to see the real extent of this perversion, which has resulted in a blindness and decay whose virulence threatens everything—including, as we'll see, the very future and stability of the nation's freedoms and political structure.

With a country in such intellectual shambles as ours, it's no wonder we have George W. Bush for president, along with his law-breaking cabinet. We get what we deserve. May the gods help us.

❖   ❖   ❖

If one has the right to demand respect simply for *being,* as opposed to respect for a judged value of what one *has done* or now *does,* then all humans are truly equal indeed: not just created equal, but equal completely and totally and for the long haul. After all, in the absence of empiricism, there can't even *be* any judgment of the meaning, merit, or value of what a person *does,* since that person could do something good, something bad, something utterly neutral, and none of it would matter, since the person would and could still demand respect just for *being*. Without empiricism, all being is equal, categorically. Only empiricism can determine whether bank robbery is more or less advantageous to society and the self than, say, the development of penicillin. Only empiricism can determine whether shooting people from a bell tower is more or less advantageous to society and the self than, say, bringing about the construction of humane, attractive, and durable low-income housing. From the founding, the right to life has been understood as inalienable, but what that means is the right not to be killed, *not* the right not to be disrespected if you do something disrespectable or fail to do anything *r*espectable.

I'm reminded at this point of those students who, when I asked how it's known that Ganges is a dog, said, impatiently, that it was "obvious." It was once "obvious," also, that monarchy was "natural," that rulers were something other than "of the people," and that they possessed divine right. Only empiricism, as in our imaginary nakedness project, allowed the disposal of that view as being a "natural" one and its replacement with what in turn did become known as "natural law," this time based on an empirically observed and thus proven equality.

Over the past half-century, we have seen the concept that "all men are created equal" degenerate (or be degenerated) into the far simpler, untrue, and utterly egalitarian idea that "all men *are* equal." The founders would never in a thousand years have agreed to this degenerated version of the "created equal" truth that they had declared "self-evident." We, on the other hand, have in just over half a century let that real truth be stolen from us—by advertisers, the marketing industry, the mass media, the corporate-state that wants us passive and consumptive—and be replaced with rotten goods, which we, in our happy ignorance, now embrace with passion, anger, and vigor.

"Rotten goods" may rightly be declared a stylistic lapse indulged in—by me—for its purgative effect, and I will let it stand, though

I must also add a clarification. Exploitative manipulation of the individual—whether one at a time or in masses—by the corporate-state is indeed demeaning, offensive, repressive, and dangerous. But my focus just now is not on that state but on those living under it, however spoiled or deformed they may have been made *by* that state. The Declaration's famous words themselves aren't rotted or decayed: It's our way of taking, interpreting, or accepting them that is. And this is why it's a decayed way of taking them: because in taking them to mean that "all men *are* equal," we have abandoned the very empiricism the Declaration stands on and have replaced it not with any real manner of thinking but with the purest feeling. There is, for the empiricist, no conceivable way that "all men are equal" can be taken as a statement in any way either valid or true, since there's no end of observable evidence to the contrary: Some men are vile, some laudable; some are murderous, some Hippocratic; some are thieving, some philanthropic; some are loving, some sadistic, some benevolent, some demonic. These differences are all and in every case known by means of observable evidence (that evidence being what each person *does*) that allows the empiricist to accept the differences as valid and true—and to reject the *denial* of those differences as invalid and untrue.

My argument at this point, admittedly, holds together only if the "inequality" between people is determined by what they *do* rather than what they *are*. For non-empiricists, however—including so many of my academic colleagues—the distinction between what people *do* and what they *are* is unhelpful. The non-empiricist is one who greets, judges, and lives in the world not through the agency of thought but through the agency of feeling; consequently, not being *able* to judge people by what they do, the non-empiricist chooses not to judge them at all but instead to *embrace* them.

The syndrome of emotions that brings about this desired sense of oneness among all, however, is deficient in one way only. The liberal thinker who becomes metamorphosed gradually into the liberal *feeler* and, under the sway of the powerful emotional force within, reaches out in an embrace of all mankind—well, such a person will come face to face very quickly with an extraordinarily serious problem: namely, that he or she will find himself or herself embracing not only *good* people but *bad* ones as well; not only soul-brothers and soul-sisters of universal humanity but also those monsters of depravity who feed off the flesh and blood of the people, like Bush and Cheney; not only boon companions but satanic enemies as well, including even the despised titans of industry and the military and the masters of the very corporate-state itself.

Clearly, *some* means of distinguishing between the right people and the wrong ones remains a necessity even for the non-empiricist, but it must, of equal necessity, be a very, very simple means, for the non-empiricist, indeed, has lost, been deprived of, or given over almost the entirety of any natural ability (or inclination) to *make* intellectual distinctions of any considered import or substance at all.

Preferably, in fact, this means of distinction would have no intellectual basis whatsoever, but would itself have an *emotional* one. And this is where we must turn again to my hypothetical nakedness project of some time back, and, more specifically, to the corollary that grew from it. The nakedness project demonstrated an empirical basis for concluding that all men are created equal. The corollary that derived from it—one that was perhaps even *more* important in bringing about government of, by, and for the people—was that all men are equally susceptible to and equally capable of feeling pleasure and pain, and that all men alike, therefore, will seek the one and attempt to avoid the other.

This corollary was powerful in helping break down the institution of nobility by birth and therefore also in making it self-evident that a leader *cannot* be other than *of* the people, since to be other than of the people would require him or her *to be something other than, or something different or separate from, human—* as, for example, nonbodily, beyond the merely physical, or, that is to say, divine.

A brief observation is appropriate here, about something that will have to be returned to later, when I come back to the subject of the Bush administration and its programmatic hypocrisy, deceit, and crime. To some, what I'm about to say will seem merely a matter of semantics, a splitting of hairs regarding a certain word's definition. To me, however, it seems much, much more than that.

The point is this: Inside an empirically based, representative, democratic republic, a coup from the right wing cannot occur, the reason being that the instant it *does* occur, that empirically based, representative, democratic republic *ceases to exist.*

That is, in the very instant that its leader is no longer *of* the people, the republic, by definition, disappears. The extraordinary importance of this fact in today's politics can be seen simply by considering what kind of leader could possibly head the state and *not be of the people.*

One possibility, of course, is that it could be a monarch, a figure who, by very definition again, could not be *of* the people. Another possibility is that it could be a god, although this may well be seen as identical to a monarch. A third possibility is that it could be a dictator or tyrant—that is, a putatively superhuman figure who would hypothesize himself or herself as being above normal human susceptibility to pain, and who then would rule in *any way necessary* to prevent that hypothesis from coming to the test.

The fourth possibility, however, is the most frightening, since it's the one by far most likely to take place, the one that most clearly appears already to have taken place. This fourth possibility is that such a leader could be "of the people," *but be a non-empiricist.*

✤ ✤ ✤

But before considering that prospect further—the prospect that we may already have undergone a non-empiricist coup—let me return for a moment to my seemingly benign but in fact equally ruinous non-empiricist academic colleagues.

※ ※ ※

When we left them, these colleagues were faced with the serious problem (once they'd been metamorphosed from predominantly thinking creatures into predominantly feeling ones) of being unable to distinguish their *enemies* from those to whom they were bonded by feelings of human equality—or, perhaps more accurately, by *human-equality-feeling*. In embracing humanity, that is, they ended up embracing *all* humanity, a terrible thing for a liberal, since it means embracing not only the deserving but also the likes of financial titans, corporate leaders, admirals, generals, CEOs, investment bankers, Dick Cheney himself, and so on.

The colleagues, in other words, were in trouble because of their misreading of "all men are created equal" as meaning "all men are equal." Since there was not really any way that that misreading could be corrected in, if you will, a world of consumerist feeling-ism, it was lucky that the colleagues had the aforementioned corollary to fall back on: that all men are equally capable of feeling pleasure and pain.

The use to be made of the corollary required, again, a misreading *and* a misapplication of it, but such can be no deterrent to forward movement in a world of intellectual ruin like the one that has developed around us since the end of World War II, and at a more accelerated pace since the end of the 1960s.

My colleagues, even earlier than 1970, were much more certain of what they were against—always the easier thing—than of what they were for. And, as they became unknowingly more consumerist, and therefore increasingly more feelers than thinkers, it became only the harder for them either to know or express exactly what they were for, yet ever easier to identify what they were against— and what they were against, in a word, was the corporate-military-market state.

As the situation reached this point, two or three tenets were sufficiently evident and clear that even those who did not enter the Age of Simplification until what might be thought of as its very late adolescent or early adult period (the early to mid-1970s) could consider themselves firm and unequivocal about them. In other words, the ideas were very easy. Not necessarily true, but taken by the colleagues as truth, they were these:

1. The corporate-state is oppressive.
2. The corporate-state is oppressive of *minorities*.
3. Those oppressed by the corporate-state suffer pain.
4. Members of the oppressive corporate-state (the "privileged") do *not* suffer pain.

That each of these four assertions is a half-truth[15] doesn't matter right now; what matters is that each was taken as valid and true by my increasingly non-empirical colleagues, who, although they believed the four assertions to be sound because based on empirical evidence, were actually becoming, with each passing semester, increasingly conviction-driven and less empirical, and therefore increasingly less able *or* inclined either to see or be concerned about errors in validity or logic, especially on "their" side of an argument.

They felt strongly, that is to say, about the assertions. One might even say that they felt *more strongly* about them in inverse proportion to the extent that they *thought* about them. In other words, thinking was out and feeling was in, just as observation was out and conviction was in. Any empirical evidence that showed elements of falsehood in each of the assertions as it was stated—any empirical evidence that would save each from the status of a half-truth—was unwelcome. That is, *thinking* about them was unwelcome. Holding the *conviction of their truth* was highly welcome.

This was the period—the early to mid-1980s—when the Age of Simplification first matured in such a way as to fall truly hard upon us, become indisputably visible, and to grow faster than ever before. It was the beginning of what came to be called the "culture wars," the period when the "politicizing" of the college and university curriculum became explicit, heavy-handed, and zealous (particularly in the humanities), the time when—the sickeningly familiar example—the grim family of ghastly attitudes named "political correctness" came calling and showed no sign of retreating back into their cave any time soon.

This ganglion of acts and attitudes that I've just described makes for very familiar territory indeed, and has been written about widely, often, and for a long time. To my way of thinking, nevertheless, the subject is far from depleted, and possibly hardly begun.

Few that I know—certainly not from inside academia—have written convincingly or directly about exactly how ruinous the situation we're in may prove before it changes. If, indeed, it *can* still change, since one of its central elements is the wholesale collapse of empiricism itself, the very bedrock foundation that our nation and attendant freedoms rest on. We may be a *Titanic,* going down, but this time without even lifeboats.

What happened in the humanities during the 1980s and afterward is a microcosm of what happened to liberalism generally during the same period, and consequently also to the Democratic Party. It's a great question whether any of these three sick men of the culture—liberalism, the Democratic Party, and academic humanities—will be able to regain even a semblance of the strength, power, and significance each once had.

Possessing only the last few shreds of empiricism as a method of thinking, my colleagues in the humanities, in need of *some*thing to distinguish the good from the bad, turned to the four half-truths I've cited. With these as their premises, they made a single deductive step that, however worm-eaten and fallacious by merit of itself being built on half-truths, nevertheless changed things forever. They did this by giving to what was in fact a program of intellectual, artistic, and emotional stagnation and simplification the *appearance* of a thing built on a foundation of absolute and irrefutable moral authority.

My colleagues, like almost everyone else, were largely blind to the actual nature, complexity, and origins of the corporate-state's power over them. Like almost everyone else, they were largely blind also to the true nature, complexity, and origins of that state. That is, they were largely blind to the actual nature, complexity, and constitution of *power*. And yet they knew with an absolute certainty that the state and power were *bad*.

And they were right, of course. But they weren't entirely right (both of those last absolutes, about the state and about power, remaining, still, half-truths).

Nevertheless, *believing* themselves right, they looked for evidence of their *being* right. This evidence had to be very plain, very easy to see, and very hard to refute. And so my colleagues turned to the Declaration of Independence. To them, as we've seen, the Declaration meant that all men are equal. My colleagues took this affirmation's corollary—that all men have equal capacity to feel pain or pleasure—and, applying it back to the misunderstood *first* assertion, came up with *this* assertion: that all men have the equal right not to feel pain or to suffer, that is, the equal right, *no matter what, not to be oppressed.*

And there it was, the single moral precept on which everything else was so largely to turn: the few simple words that were to do so much to help bring into being thousands more just like my two talking and non-empirical students; help give the coup de grâce to empiricism in general; help bring down in boisterous ruin the houses of literature and the humanities, first inside academia, then out; and help—above all—smooth the way for the bringing into power of a non-empirical, and therefore a virulent and extraordinarily dangerous, administration like that of George W. Bush.

six

There would be nothing wrong and all would be well if only empirical thinking were to continue *after* the making of the premise. As things are, however, we've let ourselves be formed, misled, and conditioned—or we have failed to prevent ourselves *from* being formed, misled, and conditioned—in such ways and into such situations that we seem now to have outdistanced the life-ropes, leaving us destined to slide gradually into more and more complete loss of those very qualities that once made our national life (albeit not always and not everywhere) noble, energetic, humane, and enviable.

It's obvious, in the spirit of the Enlightenment, of Voltaire, of the American founders themselves, that every man indeed does, should, and must have the right not to be made to suffer, the right not to be oppressed. The Declaration itself is dedicated to the ridding of the colonies from the oppression of the crown, and the Eighth Amendment declares, as all know, that "excessive bail shall not be required, nor excessive fines imposed, nor cruel and unusual punishments inflicted," which, though not identical to the right to freedom from oppression, is very closely related indeed.

And yet, at the same time, none of what's said in the Declaration, or any of the guarantees, rights, and liberties that are enshrined in the Constitution—none of these declare that any man or woman is other than a free agent; nowhere in the founding documents is any sane man and woman excused from responsibility for his or her own actions.

All men are created equal, but *after* the point of creation, not all men are equal by any means, since men become what they are by means of what they *do,* and what they *do* determines what they become. Some do things that make them criminal; others, things that show them to be altruistic; others still, things that show them to be lazy, self-indulgent, sensual, egocentric, shallow, ungifted, nonintellectual, cowardly; while yet other men do things that show them to be tireless, inquiring, stoic, generous, perceptive, coura- geous, dedicated to others and to the good of all.

Put this way, the matter seems perfectly obvious: Beyond the point of being brought, at birth, into a state of living existence, people are the product in greatest part of what they *do* (or, con- versely, of what they *don't* do). And a fact equally obvious is that *there is no way other than through empirical observation that the actual quality, nature, and value of the things people do can be weighed, evalu- ated, or determined.*

At this point in the Age of Simplification, however, crippled as we are by having substituted feeling for thinking, we have found it easier to become *half-blind* empiricists: We observe only half of what's there to *be* observed and then compound the damage by declaring that *half* to be the *entirety* of information that's available. In short, Don Quixote has nothing on us as we declare half-truths to be whole ones or, as the Houyhnhnms put it in *Gulliver's Travels,* as we go about proclaiming "the thing which is not."

My literary colleagues in academia have devolved over the past fifteen or twenty years into one of the clearest examples of a group adhering to this reductive—this *simplifying*—half-thinking and half-seeing way of looking at and responding to the world. Since they serve as a microcosmic version of larger social and intellectual elements—of left-liberalism in general, certainly—much of extraordinarily great negative importance can be learned from them.

Programs and courses in academia began changing most obviously and dramatically at exactly the time when feeling began replacing thought, when "all men are equal" began replacing "all men are created equal," and (empiricism becoming increasingly unfashionable and beginning to atrophy) when the gauge of a person's significance came to be not what that person did or accomplished but either what that person *was* or, in a particularly deft application of half-blindness, what was done *to* that person.

It must be obvious to everyone, on this point, that the great outcry for "multiculturalism" that grew up in the 1980s was in fact rooted *not* in a sense or recognition of accomplishment or merit in any person or group, but in virtually the opposite: It was rooted in a bitter and often solipsistic sense of victimhood and of what had been done *to* people, not what people *had done.*

If only a sturdily empirical intelligentsia had still been in place during the mid-1970s, both inside the colleges and outside of them, how easy and in fact how likely it might have been that academia would survive the Vietnam era, even be strengthened and enriched by it. Instead, though, academia was overwhelmed by the equivalent of simple *shouting* and by forces not of reason but of zeal and conviction. Since academia itself had already begun its own Age of Consumerism descent into half-seeing and half-thinking, it was already almost entirely defenseless against the unnegotiable demands for *rights* being made of it by both the non-empiricists and the half-empiricists (the "activists," they were often called) from 1968 on.

What those angry and righteous undergraduate students, graduate students, and faculty-to-be were demanding, presumably, was the "inclusion in the curriculum" of objects of study (this really meant *groups*) that hadn't been in the curriculum before. But, as was obvious even then to anyone looking at the matter clearly, that wasn't *really* the demand. The groups to be "included" (that is, "studied") were, of course, groups like blacks, gays, Hispanics, and women, with other subdivisions waiting on the flanks to make demands of their own once the ground was softened up. Now, nothing stood in the way of "inclusion" of these and other groups in the curriculum—after all, all of them were *already* studied, and could easily be studied both *more* and more diligently in disciplines ranging from history to anthropology, psychology to literature, art to biology. But inclusion of that kind wasn't good enough—and the claim that the groups wanted *inclusion* was itself a falsehood: What they wanted was not to be included but to be the *center*. What they wanted wasn't to be *in*, but to *outrank* the other parts of the curriculum. And so it came about that disciplines like history, anthropology, literature, sociology, psychology were demoted, or made to step aside, while the various groups themselves became *not only the subject of their own study but the method of it as well*.

How could this be? What did a person *study* when that person studied a black? A woman? A gay? A Hispanic? What did one study, that is to say, if it wasn't in fact art, or literature, or history, or anthropology, or psychology? Indeed, if the continued existence of women's studies, black studies, gay studies, Hispanic studies, and so on, were to be justified, there had to be some element or ingredient, something unique, some method, approach, or *subject* in these "fields" that qualified them to deserve continuation separately and independently from the earlier and still fully functional disciplines.

And that subject was this: It was *oppression*. The content of the fields of study, the subject and source of their significance, was the subject of *suffering*. What made the fields unique, and what justified their existence and support, was *pain*.

❖ ❖ ❖

It isn't very often that developments inside academia, at least not in the humanities, end up having an obvious and major influence on world affairs. In this case, however, that's exactly what happened. In the middle 1970s, when for the first time in history *pain and suffering* were converted into an academic subject *and* converted simultaneously into an academic *discipline*, the implications weren't seen by many, but they were enormous indeed. It was a change quintessentially part and product of the Age of Simplification, if only in its absolute and perfect confusion between thought and feeling. At the moment the change occurred, there came into being the plethora of what some now call "victimology" studies or "victims' studies." Victimology grew like mushrooms, sprang up everywhere, expanded wildly, and had about it the cloak and aura of moral and ethical *good*, making it all the more saleable, imitable, bandwagon-worthy, and adoptable.

But it all was, and is, a fraud, guarantee of enormous damage that was to follow. Nor was that damage to remain confined within the halls of academe alone. What we were really seeing, after all, was the perverting and then the disappearance of nothing less than liberal political thinking itself, the dying of any effectively coherent or muscular or robust or agile intellectual opposition to the right wing.

The liberal intellectuals, in short, were about to do something that couldn't conceivably have made the corporate-state or the far right happier. They were about to lock themselves into position gazing at their navels, all the while *believing* that they were reforming the world.

seven

The direction taken by liberal intellectual life in the aftermath of Vietnam was determined not just by what did happen but by what *failed* to happen. Social and cultural simplification were already well enough advanced by 1975 that the enormous moral and political victory represented by the war's end proved incapable of bringing about any positive or constructive forces to follow it.

Those countless people—most of them young, most of them students—who felt, and rightly, the enormous and exciting surge of moral achievement at having been victorious in influencing the state when it was in error, successful in having been able to help *bring about something good*, were also the children of consumerism. They had been taught all their lives less to think than to feel and had had instilled into them their rights, even their *obligations*, to consumerism, impulsiveness, and gratification; they had been taught, in other words, all the habits and values purveyed by an omnipresent media that functioned in the service of the corporate-consumerist-market-state.

They had been trained into adopting, as if it were normal, a heightened self-consciousness—more accurately, a heightened self-involvement—and a heightened sense of the right to self-indulgence, while at the same time they had been molded and nurtured in such a way, through countless models and influences and prototypes and styles and varied elements of daily life in late-twentieth-century America, to trust, value, and prefer feeling over thinking, emotion over thought.

They were, in other words, normal Americans, or what normal Americans had come to be by this time. In 1975, however, they were also more exercised and more excited than usual, and their sense of justice was aroused to an unprecedentedly high and in fact righteous pitch. This heightening had come about by merit of their having been denounced, denied, thrust down—even shot at and killed—by the inimical and power-driven corporate-military state and then, in an abrupt turnabout, most extraordinarily rewarded by military defeat of the United States and an end to the war.

Just imagine what might have taken place at a historic moment like this. Imagine, that is, what might have happened if it had been a more soundly educated, a more sophisticated, a less *consumerized*, less *simplified* population that had been brought to an equivalent intensity of political and social thinking, industry, and activism. Imagine what might have been accomplished, what kinds of constructive measures might have been taken, what possibilities there might have been for newly engaged politics, for reclamations of the power and role of the *local* not only in the machinery of representative government itself but in commerce, agriculture, distribution, production, markets, and town and city planning, and in communications, media, and the arts—and in *education*. Academia might have become strengthened, enriched, emboldened, enlivened, and made more rigorous through a challenge of this kind: that is, through a reclaiming of and insistence upon *the value and strengths of every individual in relation to the whole,* and perhaps above all a reclaiming of the essential and fundamental importance of free agency, of the accountability of each and every individual for his or her own achievement—and not only accountability for the judgment and justification of that achievement's worth but responsibility for determining in what ways it could be put to uses for the good of the whole, perhaps even serving the whole by *resisting* certain aspects of that whole and seeking to function as a corrective to it.

Ambitious, yes, idealistic, no. In other words, it could have been a moment for the reawakening of the active self and for a reassertion of the extraordinary, the *essential,* importance of the relationship—in every way—between the active self and the cultural, political, economic whole.

❧ ❧ ❧

But it didn't happen. Too much damage had already been done for any newly useful or meaningful *popular* energy to manifest itself. Too great a deterioration in both the concept of and the free agency of the individual self had already taken place, and instead of there being a time of applied and constructive thinking, we got, instead, a time of zealous and highly simplified *reaction*. The moral intensity of the antiwar movement sparked no new awareness of the nature and importance of the self and of its relation to the whole. Instead, that moral power led only to the far simpler, far more obvious, even patently crude idea that moral power and strength, as exemplified during the antiwar effort, lay not with the individual but with the *group*.

This simplification—the simplification of assuming there to be greater significance in the group than in the self—especially when coupled with the generalized substitution of feeling for thinking, has proven utterly disastrous. The social, political, intellectual, artistic, even aesthetic damage caused by it has, furthermore, been all the greater owing to the simplifieds'[16] additional equating, as we have just seen, of *suffering* with *meaning*.

As always, there is *some* truth in such an equation as that between suffering and meaning, but in no way can it constitute a whole truth. And yet, since 1975, it has routinely been taken (and applied) as such inside academia, with the result that humanities studies have been demeaned, debased, and brought to a state of ruin. A thing once of richness, nobility, depth, and strength has been pauperized, defamed, rigidified, misunderstood, sickened, and diminished.

Worse, what began in academia has, like a contagion, spread throughout the nation, enervating and paralyzing all that it touches.

✤ ✤ ✤

The groups that demanded and were given academic "inclusion" after Vietnam are well known to all. In order for the claim for inclusion to be made, it was necessary, originally, that the groups be "minorities," although that word quickly proved inaccurate— as when "women's studies" came into being, for example, women not being a minority. The true criterion for inclusion, clearly, had in fact nothing to do with any numerical value, but instead with the claim of having been oppressed, of having had things *done* to you—of having *suffered.*

One must tread delicately here, for the piety and righteousness surrounding these issues are nothing if not powerful and rigid. Humor, too, is quite, quite absent in and from any and all such considerations. A healthy and useful sense of humor, in fact, was one of the earliest victims of the Age of Simplification, and one of the most deeply to be mourned. Even some small bit of it could be of enormous help in cleaning the intellectual stables and getting rid of confused thinking—which is doubtless the real reason for humor's carefully, even grimly, maintained suppression. Let's allow for a brief digression on the subject. What normal and intelligent person, for example, if still firing on all eight intellectual cylinders, wouldn't laugh at the acronym CLAGS for the Center for Lesbian and Gay Studies in the City University of New York? If "clags" doesn't sound funny—for a number of reasons, which you won't find here—what does? Or, in the same academic center, how about something referred to as LGTBQ needing to be spelled out, I presume, since it *appears* to be unpronounceable, though I suppose it could be pronounced "lightbulb," or perhaps "light-book." What it—obviously?—stands for is Lesbian/Gay/Transgender/Bisexual/ Queer, as in the following passage, itself of interest:

> "LGTBQ Studies has grown tremendously since Martin Duberman hatched the idea for CLAGS," she [Alisa Solomon] adds. "The Center is proud to have been a part of shaping and expanding the field. In today's conservative and economically difficult times, we face tough challenges—which makes our work more important than ever."[17]

The hilarious "words" that are used, the stream of clichés flowing from the lips of the speaker ("hatched the idea," "shaping and expanding the field," "today's conservative and economically difficult times," "tough challenges"), the boilerplate vacuity, the politician's tone and banality—all of these are hilarious indeed, as is also, for example, the idea of "gender studies" being thought of as a "minority" studies field, even though it can and must indeed include every single member of the human race, bar none.

Hilarious, yes. And yet the effect of simplification has been such as to "elevate" the idea of gay studies almost to the point of its being sanctified—so that to laugh at it won't have the desired and at one time inevitable effect of stripping away its cheap silliness and leaving its more durable bones exposed, but will instead, in the eyes of the simplifieds, show cause that the one who *laughs* is the one to be vilified as being not—well, not a believer, or, worse, not being someone who is concerned about other people's *feelings* (and *rights*, of course). That rights and feelings aren't *in the least* what are being laughed at is a fact that the minds of the simplifieds will not and cannot so much as entertain, with the result that not only is it impossible to discuss politics with them on any significant level, but it's virtually impossible any longer even to *laugh* in any significant way.[18] And, then, too, when there's nobody else to laugh *with*, the whole thing can quickly stop being funny anyhow, no matter how deserving of ridicule it really is. This is exactly the feeling I've had in many a faculty meeting, department meeting, curriculum committee meeting—of wanting to laugh, to show where the fallacies are, the strutting banalities, the dread vacuities; of wanting to be constructive, to get at the heart of things, to discuss matters at a *meaningful* level. But it doesn't happen, never did, certainly not after 1980 or so. A person gives up after a while, gets worn down by making so great an effort in regard to a development so paltry, so empty, so ruinous, grim, and calamitous, so anti-intellectual, so compromised, depraved, contrived, misconceived, unappealing, and hollow, so hypocritical, so *silly*, so foolish, so low-level, so unserious, so *unacademic*.

And so well guarded by near-absolute pieties. Not, in a word, open to debate. Not on the table. Just like penetration, consequence, or deep seriousness in American politics, a notion *not even to be entertained.*

\# \# \#

One of the things that's wrong with the "studies" courses and programs, as I've suggested, is that they *really don't exist.* That is, they *exist,* but not for any academically, scholarly, or defensible pedagogic reason. They exist, and can exist, for political reasons only. In this sense, they are lies: They claim to be academic when in fact they are partisan and political—thus my use of the word "hypocritical" a moment ago.

Let me return to the question of what, exactly, it *is* that's to be studied in such programs. If events of the past, then why not do that in a history course? If emergence of human types and cultures, then why not do that in an anthropology course? If music that has been produced, art that has been created, literature that has been written, then why not study those in courses in music, art, or literature? The answer—in every case, whether the "studies" are black, Hispanic, Puerto Rican, women's, gay, gender, or ethnic—is and must be the same: What's studied *is* the black, *is* the Hispanic, *is* the Puerto Rican, *is* the woman, *is* the gay, *is* the gendered (though, again, isn't that everybody?), and so on.

But in each of these cases, what *is* there to study in and of and about woman, Hispanic, Puerto Rican, gay, black, and so on, that isn't properly and appropriately capable of being studied in existing and, if you will, academically pedigreed disciplines like those I've already named, as well as in, say, psychology, biology, neurology, or medicine?

The only cogent and logical response academically is that yes, there's nothing to study in, of, or about any of these groups or types that shouldn't or couldn't be studied rightly and effectively within the already defined, tested, and qualified disciplines. But that cogent and logical response, *being* cogent and logical, is not a response to be heard in a simplified, rights-driven, consumerized, decreasingly intellectual and decreasingly empirical academia. In *that* academia, the heard response begins by sidestepping and evading the true question; then it relies upon an obfuscatory term to hide its real meaning and is, therefore, a response not only not cogent, not logical, but *not honest.*

The response, for example, in simplification-ese, might be that what's being taught is the Hispanic *experience,* or the black *experience,* or the female *experience.*

All right. Let's go ahead and pretend for a moment that we know what "experience" *means* in this context. The logically following question, then, must be this: How is *that* to be studied if not through the books, art, music, movies, literature, history, poetry, journals, speeches, politics, or through the psychology, anthropology, sociology, or biology of, by, or about the persons or groups in question? And why is this "experience," then, not suitable for study within one or more of the already existing disciplines previously named?

And the response now? Well, we have here proceeded to the end of the road of logic, and at the end of that road only one response (as in "Ganges has four legs") is possible—namely, that the existing disciplines are indeed perfectly suited to do the job; the things to be studied are perfectly suited to be studied *in* them; and, therefore, that's where each of them can and should appropriately be studied.

But that logical and cogent thing *must not be said,* just as "clags" and LGTBQ *must not be laughed at* even though they're absurd, parading, and silly. If the logical, cogent, and true statement *were* uttered, after all, and if it *were* to be acted upon (as it should be, since it's valid and true), the resulting consequence would be *the dismantling, the nonexistence, or the discontinued existence* of the black studies program or department, of the women's studies program or department, of the gay studies program or department, and so on.

And, of course, they *must* exist, and must *continue* to exist. Why? Let me come back to that question in a minute. But first, let's have a look at what their backers, advocates, and proponents can do (and have done, and do do) to keep the programs in existence.

The only thing they can do is turn to a defense of their programs that's built on deceit. For these programs to be defended and protected, their backers must assert half-truth as whole truth; follow a path of fallacious deductive logic; use empiricism half-blindly; and, preparatory to all the preceding, substitute feeling for thinking.

An interesting parallel thus emerges between academic intellectuals, on the one hand, and the nation's highest leadership, on the other. For these unseemly and fraudulent defenses necessary for the protection of academic victimology programs reveal themselves as being absolutely identical, as the reader can hardly have helped noticing, to the unseemly and fraudulent devices used by the Bush administration in order to perpetrate and impose its "preemptive" war in Iraq.

The moral, intellectual, and ethical bankruptcy of the Age of Simplification thus reveals itself, like mildew, to have taken hold everywhere, *not* just in the high mansions of military-corporate-government but in the lowly hallways of education also (where, much more likely than not, it *began*), where my own colleagues, ostensibly and self-declared liberal intellectuals, reveal themselves in actuality, in the innermost workings of their minds, to be identical to the ruinous, destructive, deceitful, and blindly opportunistic Bushists. Consider for a moment what this remarkable overlap, this virtual cloning, means. It shows once again how right George Orwell was all the way back in 1948, since here we see, again, that in the American Age of Simplification, lies are truth. Even lies *within* lies are truth. Imagine, for example, the academic intellectual who

professes opposition to Bush's war in Iraq on the grounds of its having been deceitfully and fraudulently achieved, while at the same
time using identical deceitful and fraudulent means for bringing
about and protecting his own academic program. In such a case,
we have only one of two possibilities: Either we're dealing with a
professor who lies when it suits him, and not when it doesn't;
or with a professor who is entirely ignorant of the fact that he's
lying at all. Might as well flip a coin, I think, all the while asking yourself, "How good a professor could *either one* of these guys
possibly be?"

✢ ✢ ✢

Put too strongly? No. Put very strongly? Yes. And really true? Yes.

From their inception in the 1970s, the victimology programs
were hypocritical, destructive, self-deluding, and harmful—to
those within them, to those they purported to celebrate and serve,
to the college curricula that housed them, and, far from least, to
the culture and the nation itself.

Let's analyze. In defending the programs (just as they did, also,
in originating them), their backers will, either first or finally, have
to reveal this as the fundamental, bedrock beginning point of their
argument: The groups being studied are oppressed; these groups
suffer and have suffered; these groups are and have been treated
unjustly; these groups therefore hold a unique significance and
deserve their own unique program.

Earlier, I said that courses and programs like black, gay, or wom-
en's studies, though in truth bred from "stagnation and simplification," nevertheless *appeared* to be "sustained by an absolute and
irrefutable moral authority"—and now we can explore this seeming contradiction.

The old conundrum about wife-beating pertains here. If a man is
asked whether he has stopped beating his wife, he is condemned as
a wife-beater whether he answers yes or no. Even "I don't beat my
wife" or "I've never beaten my wife" are likely to be taken as false

protests, since *of course* a wife beater would deny that he's a wife beater, and the worse wife-beater he is, the more fervently he'll deny it. I'm now in a position myself not far different from that of the man asked that question. If, having said the things I've said so far in this chapter, I were asked whether I approve of black, gay, women's, or Hispanic studies, it's unlikely that any answer I gave would or could clear me from the charge—and presumption—of bigotry. I could say no, I don't approve of them. But that answer would leave out the entire question of what things are studied in the programs and how. The better answer would be in the affirmative but with qualification—"Yes, I approve of them, but not as separate programs housed independently or with academic autonomy." If I were then asked—as certainly I would be—*why* I felt that way, I would respond with the long and careful arguments I've tried to explain in this essay. And then the *real* trouble would begin.

My questioner, that is, would play the pain and oppression card: He or she would explain to me that these are oppressed groups that are treated unjustly, that they suffer pain and are damaged. Therefore, he or she would go on, they deserve their own independent or autonomous academic programs. Don't they?

I would say no, they don't, since the logic is invalid and doesn't follow. You can imagine the trouble I would be in then (and *have* been in for much of the thirty-five or so years of my teaching life). For in the Age of Simplification, it is invariably taken as an inescapable truth that if I'm against such programs, then I must be "against" their subject matter. I must be anti-black, anti-gay, anti-woman. I must be a racist, bigot, and misogynist. And I must be *doubly* against these groups, *doubly* racist, bigoted, and misogynist, if I refuse to accept these groups' suffering, oppression, and pain as reason for their being separated from the rest of the curriculum and studied inside the programs and "disciplines" of black studies, women's studies, gay studies, and so on—all in a virulent and blind circularity.

Now, the objection I anticipate at this point is that I'll be taken as a coldhearted and closed-minded ultraconservative and bigot who looks down with scorn, condescension, and contempt at the liberal left and who *must* therefore side solely with the enemy, making me hopeless, despicable, and beyond redemption.

Not true. I'm in no way "for" pain, injustice, or oppression—after all, the liberal and progressive view that sees the elimination of these as among the first and highest duties of government comes from the same origins as does the Declaration of Independence with its self-evident truths, as we saw earlier, that all men are created equal *and* that all suffer equally upon exposure to pain.

For me, the Declaration is near-sacred, and I dedicate myself *against* the dishonoring of it. And, no, I'm not a right-winger, bigot, misogynist, or racist. I'm a left-leaning liberal, have been so throughout my adulthood, and expect to be until my death.

But that better not mean I can't or mustn't *think*. It better not mean that I can't or mustn't criticize error when I see it and when that error in fact does damage to and dishonors the highest truths of the Declaration *and* the nation, not to mention my own profession. It better not mean that I can't and mustn't attack liberalism when in fact liberalism deteriorates into something other than liberalism, both in a local, academic way and in a universal, national way. When it adulterates, diminishes, misunderstands, distorts, exploits, and makes impotent the very thing—literature specifically, the arts generally—that I myself live for, devote my life to, and now see failing and crumbling everywhere around me under the forces of ignorance, simplification, and do-goodism. Or when liberalism becomes a failed and self-deceptive mental machine that, while still thinking that it's leading the world into the fields of the right and good, in fact, through its own narcissism, loss of imagination, and shamelessly fallacious reasoning, becomes peripheral, withered, neutered, blinded, and made impotent by the same self-administered bad medicine that causes it *not even to see what it's doing*, so that, caught up in its own navel-gazing follies and thinking them worthy of notice by the world, it in effect removes itself from political power altogether, rolls out the carpet, steps aside, and holds the door for George W. Bush—adolescent, liar, thief, non-empiricist—to walk through to the presidency and happily take the opportunity handed over to him to finish the odds and ends of transforming the nation into a one-party state—where lies mean nothing, nor does the self, or equality, or freedom, or *meaning*, because self-interested power alone is what counts for the present leadership in any way at all, and power is a thing, as the reigning Bushcisti are well aware, that the liberal intellectuals have fumbled, tossed away, failed to understand, and lost.

✢ ✢ ✢

Academia in the humanities as we see it now is hardly at the head of anything, but thirty years ago it was indeed the vanguard that led to the suicide of intellectual liberalism. The ruinous tools that were, have been, and continue to be put to use with such astonishing success toward that destructive end aren't admirable, and even just to list them is an unpleasant task: group-think, tribalism, and the abandonment not only of empiricism but of logic itself. And at the root of all three of these failures lies the Age of Simplification's endemic and epidemic disease, the substitution of feeling for thinking.

Let me briefly describe again what took place, then return to analyze certain aspects of it. In a nutshell, beginning in the middle 1970s, victimology studies replaced conventional disciplinary studies in the humanities. The change was in large part prepared for by the hyper "rights" syndrome that bloomed after the Vietnam War; that syndrome itself was fueled by the greatly heightened sense, and understandably so, of evil deeds, misdeeds, and sheer injustice that the years of the Vietnam War had produced and put on view. The rest of the story, though, has nothing salutary about it. When feeling took over for thinking, the first delusion—

which accompanied the takeover—and the most beguiling, was the delusion, as I've said, that pain and suffering *do* have meaning in and of themselves—if, that is, they're caused unjustly. And the second delusion, a good deal more crude, was the two-part delusion that, first, pain and suffering not only could be shared *but could be transferred from one self to another*, and that, second, in and during and through that transfer, *the meaning and significance of the prior suffering* would come along to its new recipient also.

In a moment, I'll turn to Sophocles' *Oedipus the King* to look at the subject of pain and suffering. First, though, it's impossible for me not to put on record how bad, in fact contemptible, I think these ideas really are. Victimology in general claims to revere past suffering, and yet what a disservice it is, and how demeaning of everyone involved, to take the suffering of those in the past who really did undergo it and to claim it now as one's own, even if only claiming a possession of the *significance* of it. It is one thing to study history and gain knowledge, to insist upon the importance of that knowledge and use it in every possible way to preclude the recurrence of suffering, injustice, cruelty, pain—these are not only understandable pursuits but *right* ones. Victimology, though, doesn't do this. Victimology is fatally confused, if only because it argues simultaneously that suffering is bad *and* that suffering has meaning—that it is *meaningful* to suffer and that that meaning can and should be studied. This is an impossible situation, since it argues that suffering must be ended, yet at the same time that suffering must *not* be ended, since then, if it were, there would be nothing to study.

The "victim," in other words, must remain victim in order to remain meaningful. This fact makes it impossible to escape the conclusion that victims' studies programs are based on a deep, even vicious, and certainly corrupting hypocrisy. They advocate reform but resist reform, becoming, in fact or in effect, proud of their suffering and making claims of vindication whenever newfound contemporary examples of abuse, pain, or injustice arise or are identified—whether actually or putatively, often ludicrously, as in the case I alluded to earlier of Cornel West and Harvard. If a syndrome of this kind of dysfunctional contradiction—being denunciatory of something and at the same time wanting and needing that thing—were to manifest itself in a single person, it would be identified as neurotic, paranoid, passive-aggressive, maybe worse. One of the central reasons, though, perhaps *the* reason, why such diagnoses aren't made in the case of victimology studies is this: There *is* no single person, no individual, to hold accountable or to be held accountable. There is only the group—in fact, there is only the ur-group, the heavily-relied-upon group known as the tribe.

Except in the Age of Simplification, I doubt that any of this would or could have come about. As the product of an age, however, that gradually but surely steals away the true self while unremittingly beguiling the mean, willful, voluptuary, righteous self with unending vanities and flattery—as the product of an age of this sort, it becomes understandable. In order to maintain an intellectual position that was untenable and could *not* be maintained, the victimologists weighted things away from thought and toward feeling, a position where logic could not make its customary demands. In order to maintain a moral and ethical position that was untenable and could *not* be maintained, the victimologists gave up the last vestige of the true, authentic, irreducible, free self and replaced it with the *group,* or with the *tribe,* then took refuge in the idea of "the people" who make up that group or tribe. By this time, thinking had ended, since the self was gone, while feeling, instinct, and an un-intellectual sense of the just and righteous gained prestige through being identified, not with a single individual and accountable human mind, but with the democratically enshrined concept of a "people."

Brothers joined brothers, sisters joined sisters, and the programs were here to stay—built on sand, inward-looking, self-involved, not really political, not really intellectual, not really ambitious for reform, not really honest. And so academia began its fiddling—and is fiddling still—while the Age of Simplification helps see to it that America burn.

✤ ✤ ✤

It's nothing if not odd that literature should be filled with warnings against exactly this kind of extreme or imbalance—excess, whether of feeling or of intellect—and yet that my colleagues, defenseless against the Age of Simplification and not well enough read, should have so readily swerved in one direction even so. A high theme in much of great Western literature has to do with the loss and depravity that *necessarily* follow a move to either extreme on this philosophic-emotional spectrum, and yet my literary colleagues, embracing victimization as if victimization and meaning were the same, appear wholly unaware of their own extremism. The situation provides yet another example of something that has the *appearance* of being perfectly regular and familiar and normal, with the result that people don't even see it.

Any attempt to examine the true nature of suffering and pain can benefit by the towering example of Sophocles' *Oedipus the King*, often known as *Oedipus Rex*. In that play, although some might think otherwise, it isn't *pain* that ennobles Oedipus, nor is it suffering. His nobility comes, instead, from two things: The first is his ability—without the aid of gods or anything else beyond his own intelligence and skill—to save Thebes from the plague the *first* time, when he enters the city, and then soon afterward, having saved it, becomes its king. And what ennobles him the second time, even more greatly, is the same thing: his ability, without the aid of gods or anything else beyond his own intelligence, skill, dedication, and courage, to free Thebes from the corrupting plague *again*.

In each of the two instances, as everyone knows, Oedipus must solve a riddle in order to save the city. The riddle is posed, the first time around, by the Sphinx, who brought the plague upon the city but agrees to lift it if any man can answer her famous riddle, which, childlike as it may be,[19] in fact asks the great humanist question, as we saw also with Swift and Voltaire, "What is man?"

No one but Oedipus is able to answer this question, and, in gratitude for his having thus saved them from the Sphinx, the Thebans make him their king—their own ruler, Laïos, having been killed. All seems well, the story goes, at least over a time long enough for Oedipus and Iocasta to bear their four children, Antigone, Ismene, Polyneices, and Eteocles. When the plague then returns, however, the riddle that must be answered in order to get relief is much harder than it was the first time, even though in *essence* it's the same riddle. This time around, however, the great soothsayer Teiresias has told Oedipus that the cause of the plague on Thebes is Oedipus himself: that *he*, the king, is the murderer of the previous Theban ruler, Laïos, and is therefore himself the pollutant, the source of the poison, now destroying the city.

The reader knows—as did the Sophoclean audience—that Teiresias is right and that he's telling the truth about Laïos's killer. Oedipus, on the other hand, who of course *doesn't* know that the charge is true and *doesn't* know what crimes he's committed in killing his father and marrying his mother, goes into a towering rage, denying that he's in any way to blame—yet simultaneously, in his majestic, wondrous, and blood-chillingly ironic proclamation to the Theban people, dedicates himself utterly and wholly to the finding out of Laïos's murderer.

A person reading carefully enough might conclude at this point that Oedipus, in fact, did *not* know the answer to the original riddle, even though he answered it "correctly." He knew what went on four legs, then two, and then three—but he didn't know what a man *was*: He didn't know what a man was *made up of;* he didn't know what a man was *capable of doing;* he didn't know *what was inside a man.*

That is to say, he didn't know *himself,* or what he *himself* was capable of doing, or what the driving forces inside him *were*. And so, this time around, he has to answer not just the question "What is a man?" but the far more difficult question "What am *I?*"

People often think that in answering this more difficult question, Oedipus *becomes* a tragic figure, but they're wrong. Oedipus is *already* a tragic figure—though he doesn't know it—insofar as he's already done what he's done, already *is* what he is. *He* doesn't know, but *we* know. And we know that he is something quite horrible, base, and vile: Like the Sphinx herself, with her lion's body and woman's head, he is partly human and partly beast, a combination of animalistic blood-instinct and rational, humanizing intellectuality.

Oedipus, in short, is a human being; he is, like everyone, imprisoned inside his own state of that human being-ness, imprisoned inside his own individual self, the one and sole thing in the universe that he can use as *eyes* to look out through, or with, into existence and the nature of existence, and the one and sole thing in the universe, also, that he can use to look *inward,* can use in finding out what he is and what he's capable of. Putting the case most simply, you can say that Oedipus uses his intellectual, rational power of mind as a tool that enables him to find and identify the existence of his nonrational, bestial, violent, animalistic self (the id, we might choose to call this, or the subconscious). Looking at him this way, as a man examining himself to find out what the *whole* self is, we can see Oedipus as undergoing, or practicing upon himself, the first psychoanalysis in literature, possibly in history.

And what does the analysis reveal? Although he is the *last person in the world he would suspect of such things,* the analysis reveals that he is putrescent with guilt, a patricide living in incestuous marriage with his own mother, sibling to his own children. Psychologically speaking, he is tragic because of what he *is*—which is to say, again, human. Not everyone, of course, murders his father and marries his mother, but everyone *is* composed of elements, forces, and powers that are both bestial, on the one hand, and rational, on the other, animal on the one hand and intellectual on the other. What traps Oedipus so horribly, then, isn't the cruel curse of Apollo, declaring the baby Oedipus's inescapable destiny to be that he'll grow up an incestuous patricide—that stuff about the Apollonian prophecy is just a *story*, after all, and a story that depends on magic, to boot, which doesn't exist. No, the Apollonian prophecy is a *symbol* of the *real* thing that traps Oedipus. And the real thing that traps Oedipus is the fact of his being *human*. As I said, he is trapped *in* his human-ness.

Indeed, again, Oedipus does things that are more extreme than the things most people do, thank god, yet he symbolizes all humans in that he is *made up of*, like the Sphinx, the rational and the instinctive, the "human" and the bestial, the enlightened and the brute, the godlike and the animal.

The trouble, of course, lies in his *not knowing* that this is true. The trouble lies in Oedipus's *assuming* that the intellectual and rational part of himself is all there was to him—an understandable error, perhaps, especially for unusually brainy people (like Apollo—and like Oedipus) who are good at math, puzzles, and riddles. The pride or *hubris* so often talked about (far too simplistically, as a rule, and relied upon too crudely) in discussions of the classic tragedians can be seen, in the case of Oedipus, as the blindness to the *whole* self that comes about through a prideful overreliance on the "reasoning" part of the self, the Apollonian part, the part associated with light, and above all with the eyes. This "higher" part has difficulty "seeing" the other part (it's in the dark, after all, where even Apollo's eyes don't work), *yet both parts are of equal importance to the whole self and of equal significance, value, meaning, and even danger.* Both parts, the animalistic and the intellectual, are essential to the human, and both are equal—exactly as, twenty-two centuries later, Voltaire was to insist that the "Thunder" and the "Tronckh" aspects of the self were equal *and* equally essential. In our post-Freudian world, this idea of not "seeing" or "acknowledging" both parts of the self is often thought of as "repression," and sexually repressed, neurasthenic, hyperintellectualized characters are common throughout literature—from Agamemnon in *The Oresteia,* Pentheus in *The Bacchae,* and Jason in *Medea* on through Arthur Dimmesdale, Blanche Dubois, Prufrock, and so on.

But our subject was pain and, specifically, this question about it: whether pain *in itself* can have meaning; whether pain *in itself* can or does generate or create meaning.

✤ ✤ ✤

And, from a study of *Oedipus*—or of *The Oresteia,* if we had time for it—it can be learned that the answer is, no, it doesn't, and no, it can't.

If this answer is in fact correct—if pain, oppression, and suffering don't generate or create meaning (we'll look further in a minute)—what academic justification can or could there be for victimized groups being made the *subjects* of independent or autonomous courses, programs, or majors? If suffering has, creates, or generates no meaning, and if the subjects of study are those who *have undergone* suffering, and who were chosen *because* they have undergone suffering, then, the logic dictates clearly, the resultant study would in fact be the study of nothing at all. If this reasoning is correct, we can't avoid the conclusion that victimology studies are not only mistaken but based on lies, claiming to be about something when in fact they're about nothing.

✤ ✤ ✤

One of the most horrible but inescapable truths about existence is the truth that pain can't be shared. Each person's body is the sole and perfect container of his or her own agony, and nothing whatsoever can change or ameliorate the dreadful, awful, absolute isolation brought about by that fact. No one can diminish the pain of another—not even of one's own child—by, say, drawing some aspect or part of it out of the sufferer's body and into one's own. Nor, on the other hand, can a sufferer diminish the intensity of felt pain by pushing, sending, or telegraphing some of it into another's body.

This idea or theme is common throughout literature, from Homer and Sophocles on up, and notably so in literature from the post-Enlightenment, empirical world with its concomitant diminishment of religious literalism and fundamentalism (religious faith having been one of the most common ways of escaping or seeming to escape—through *belief*—the absoluteness of the self's isolation).[20]

The very structure of entire novels can allude to the theme—as, for example, in Joseph Conrad's *Victory* and Virginia Woolf's *To the Lighthouse:* Important scenes in each book have to do with a boat drawing farther and farther away from a place significant to the characters, until any link—even visual contact—between the two becomes attenuated, then broken or lost. In *To the Lighthouse,* as Mr. Ramsay moves farther and farther away from shore, even his book of poems alludes to the theme: Contained in the book is "The Castaway" by William Cowper (1731–1800), and Mr. Ramsay declaims the line aloud, "We perished, each alone."

Earlier in the novel—in the book's chronology, ten *years* before Mr. Ramsay sails to the lighthouse—when the fact of Mrs. Ramsay's death at age fifty is revealed, here is how Woolf reveals it:

[Mr. Ramsay, stumbling along a passage one dark morning, stretched his arms out, but Mrs. Ramsay having died rather suddenly the night before, his arms, though stretched out, remained empty.]

Even the brackets—let alone the emptiness of Mr. Ramsay's arms—suggest the theme of separateness: Not in pain, not even in death, can anything be suffered except by one single, irreducible being at a time, alone. In *Waiting for Godot,* as they wait in vain for their imaginary savior to arrive, even Samuel Beckett's high-philosophic clowns, who've got plenty of time to kill indeed, become another means of alluding to the theme of pain as solitary and incommunicable, a thing unable to cross the barrier between one locked-in self and another:

VLADIMIR: Hand in hand from the top of the Eiffel Tower, among the first. We were respectable in those days. Now it's too late. They wouldn't even let us up. (*Estragon tears at his boot.*) What are you doing?

ESTRAGON: Taking off my boot. Did that never happen to you?

VLADIMIR: Boots must be taken off every day, I'm tired telling you that. Why don't you listen to me?

ESTRAGON: (*feebly*). Help me!

VLADIMIR: It hurts?

ESTRAGON: (*angrily*). Hurts! He wants to know if it hurts!

VLADIMIR: (*angrily*). No one ever suffers but you. I don't count. I'd like to hear what you'd say if you had what I have.

ESTRAGON: It hurts?

VLADIMIR: (*angrily*). Hurts! He wants to know if it hurts!

✦ ✦ ✦

Pain, then, can be suffered only by one, and never in any other way.[21] But what about the *meaning* of pain? Even though we now know for certain that pain can't be shared, there's still the question of what it can *mean*.

I would ask readers, however unfeeling and monstrous the notion may at first seem to them, nevertheless to give serious consideration to the premise that *pain in itself doesn't and can't mean anything.*

It isn't difficult to think of *uses* of pain. In the case of Oedipus, for example, it's extremely important to understand that the reason Oedipus is tragic is not *because* he feels pain. There's also another essential distinction that has to be made, and this may be as good a place as any to make it: and that's the distinction between physical pain and the only other kind, *emotional* pain. As Oedipus begins looking into aspects of himself previously unexamined, he feels increasing anxiety, fear, guilt, disbelief, terror ("Ah, what net has God been weaving for me?").[22] But physical pain is another matter. When physical pain befalls Oedipus, it does so *because he brings it about. He determines, causes, and dispenses it to and upon himself.*

That the physical pain is self-inflicted is tremendously important for at least a couple of reasons. One of the chief uses of pain, after all, is as punishment, or as a tool that produces punishment. That the pain in this case is *self*-inflicted reveals that Oedipus understands the absoluteness of free agency and takes full responsibility for what he has done. It's not that he now *becomes* tragic but that, from this point on, his stature *as* a tragic hero emerges for us into greater and greater visibility. The tragic paradox remains in place just as it has since the opening scenes of the play: that in order for Oedipus to save his city and thus fulfill his highest role as its king, he must simultaneously be *destroyed* as its king by revealing *himself* to be the cause of its pollution.

Equally important, Oedipus at this point in the tragedy is *obeying himself as king*—that is, following the legal dictates of his own royal proclamation, back at the opening of the play, when he said that the offender against Thebes must be discovered. Oedipus, then, is both ruler of Thebes *and* subject of Thebes—and he must, of course, obey.

In his proclamation, though, Oedipus didn't make any precise definition of the penalty that was to be brought upon the killer of Laïos once identified. "As for the criminal," he said only, "I pray to God—/ Whether it be a lurking thief, or one of a number—/ I pray that that man's life be consumed in evil and wretchedness."

And doesn't this mean that Oedipus, in the end, could have chosen another kind of punishment for himself, even one *without* physical pain, or without a type of physical pain as terrifying, repulsive, and horrifying as the stabbing out of one's own eyes? Doesn't this mean he could have chosen something less awful and *still* have shown himself obedient to the terms of his own proclamation?

Of course, we know that Sophocles inherited the Oedipus story from an antiquity deeper to him even than the antiquity, to us, that we now think of Sophocles as having come from—and that the destruction of the eyes was not only a part of the story as passed down to him but also a profoundly symbolic part, *and* something his audience fully expected as an element of any performance.

But those facts simply require us to rephrase the question: Why was the punishment, even when the story first grew up as part of the ancient legend, such a grotesque, ugly, horrifying one?

Part of the answer remains unchanged—the grotesque punishment is there because the symbolism (of the eyes, that is, or the mind, that didn't "see") is both aesthetically eloquent and thematically revealing. But there is another reason, one more closely related to the subject of pain as we're approaching it here. Pain, as we've seen, can't be shared or transferred, but remains isolated and contained inside the self or body of the single one who is suffering it. Therefore, it's impossible for any myth, legend, narrative, story— or drama—to move its audience by causing it to *feel* the pain being felt by a character, whether it be Gloucester or Oedipus, in losing their eyes, or a figure like Ilioneus as he's slain by Peneleos in *The Iliad.*[23] Being unable to *feel* the pain, the audience must be moved through being made to *fear* the pain instead.

The towering authority here, of course, is Aristotle, whose phrase in *The Poetics* is "pity and fear." Some may find it a quibble, but it seems to me that the fear must come first, in order to bring the pity into being: All emotion, after all, *must* have its first origin in the senses, and pity's origin *must* lie in fear of pain. Be that as it may, readers will remember Aristotle's famous contention that the tragedian's *purpose* in causing this feeling of pity and fear is to create in the audience or viewer the *catharsis* of those same feelings, such purgation being the aim of tragic drama.[24]

Whether or not Aristotle is right about catharsis and the way it works in drama is something we can leave aside, at least here. But certainly the philosopher brings us back once again to look, even more closely this time, not at the subject of pain but at the subject of the *uses* of pain.

For isn't it in fact becoming more clear that there isn't any meaning in pain or suffering, but that meaning can reside only in what is done *with* pain and suffering, in response *to* pain and suffering, or as a consequence *of* pain and suffering? Isn't it becoming more clear that in pain and suffering themselves there isn't and can't be any meaning, since, by definition, they consist *only of feeling*, since feeling is what they *are?* And, feeling being what they are, they can hold no *meaning* but can hold only *feeling*. There can be no meaning in suffering or pain; there can be only suffering or pain.

In and of themselves, feeling, suffering, and pain are incommunicable and absolute; they are without language and unable to be discussed; they are mindless and mute, tongueless and blind, imprisoned and isolated absolutely within only the one single organism that is experiencing them.

However horrible, callous, unfeeling, insensitive, and monstrous as all this may sound to certain ears, the sad and awful but all-important truth is nevertheless that meaning comes—*can* come—into existence *only with thought*. And *thought,* unlike feeling, *can* be communicated, shared, weighed, evaluated, refined, accepted, or rejected, *can* be revealed as being meritorious or not being meritorious, as having validity or not having it.

For this central reason—though others are almost as important—it is not merely contemptible but, even worse, ruinous to the maintaining of any aesthetic or intellectual well-being or strength in the humanities for writers, artists, publishers, and "professors" to have taken the easier route, gone the simpler way, and diminished themselves, their prestige, and certainly their political significance and strength as liberal intellectuals, by permitting themselves to abandon thought and, in its place, substitute feeling, and by permitting themselves to believe that meaning is created by what is done *to* people rather than by what people *do*.

✦ ✦ ✦

The corruption and loss of liberal intellectual thinking in America have had overwhelming and ruinous consequences. The absence of reason, logic, and coherence; the factionalizing that has resulted from the rise of me-ism; the erosion of dignity as one group after another has indulged in its own special pleading; the incorrect assumption that suffering in itself causes significance or meaning; the *impossibility* of forging any practical, robust, or energy-filled political-intellectual argument or vision that's based on the passivity and grudge-keeping of victimization rather than on a genuine passion for the commonweal—all of these failures have brought about the collapse of liberal thought that, among other things, has left the door standing wide open, allowing ultrareactionary opportunism to walk in with ease, bringing the republic itself, and certainly many if not most of its humane protections and progressive reforms, to the very brink of survival.

This breakdown on the part of the liberal intellectuals has been almost total, as I have been trying to show, and the resulting powerlessness of the liberal institution, both inside and outside academia, is also very nearly total. Nor will any of its sorely needed power be recoverable until such time as the liberal establishment can learn once again to put *thought* in a place of importance equal to that of feeling or belief.

I'm not optimistic, since for a transformation of such a kind to occur, the liberal intellectuals must first find some means of embattling and defeating the very simplification that is so largely responsible for what they have let themselves become. After all, as I've said, these failed intellectuals, from the very beginning, *believed* themselves to be doing good and believe so still: This is because, by the time the mid-1970s came around and the collapse began accelerating, they had already long been simplified enough to be unable to think through clearly what it was they were doing or not doing, and unable therefore to choose another, harder, better course.

And it was, indeed, simple. They saw suffering, pain, and injustice around them. They wanted to oppose and end such things, and rightly so. But their great, disastrous, ruinous error came about through the prior error of thinking that there was meaning *in* suffering, or that meaning was generated *from* suffering. As a consequence, their focus came to be on the latter, suffering, the thing they thought had meaning and was therefore the thing they must study. In making this error, however, they missed the *real* subject, the one and only subject that has or can have anything whatsoever to do with causing, diminishing, or preventing the particular kinds of pain, suffering, and injustice they saw around them. And that subject is *power*. But they thought power was *bad*, and a great many of them even believed it to be their *enemy*, a thing inferior —to feeling, sympathy, the moral, the good—all these latter things being the benevolent fruits, as they thought, of *pain*. It was inconceivable to them that power could be accompanied—as it was, for example, with Oedipus—by nobility, sympathy, generosity, dignity, or corrective purpose, those virtues that they believed instead were solely the products and results of injustice and *suffering*.

It was true enough that by the mid-1970s they had for years watched the corporate-military-state use enormous power in highly destructive, misinformed, wrong-minded, impolitic, unseeing, inhumane, insensitive, calamitous, and unjust ways, with the effect of producing almost unending pain, suffering, and yet more injustice. And the price to be paid was a high one at that crucially important period in the Age of Simplification. Holding, as a consequence of what they had seen, that power was bad, the liberal intellectuals failed to realize that power was in actuality the one thing that they should, must, and could study in order to understand it, command it, *and put it to use for the good.*[25] But, being progeny of the Age of Simplification, they missed that understanding, turned their backs on it, and even threw away the best aspects of those academic traditions (of literary studies, for example) that *had* lent themselves to the study of power and the understanding of it, to the study of the essential self and the understanding of it, to the study of the relationship between the essential self and the world outside it, and to the understanding of *that* relationship, along with *its* own ability to be productive of—yes—*power.*

But both through the exercise of its own means, methods, and qualities and through the inculcating of those same qualities in its progeny, the Age of Simplification—sentimental, self-referential, unexploratory, anti-intellectual—has so weakened and diminished the worlds of the arts, humanities, and publishing that what was once intellectually vigorous and powerful about those worlds, *including* their capacity for generating political significance and being politically persuasive,[26] is now so sickly and ineffective that even though many in them may still *believe* themselves to be in principled opposition to the corporate-state, they have in fact thrown away the last weaponry that might have given them strength in making the world better and have instead become the tools and pawns of the very powers and forces—those of the corporate-state and its intellectual-control arm, the mass media— that they consider themselves the best and most highly principled bulwark *against.*

✦ ✦ ✦

To explain exactly how this situation has come about, we need to return to *Oedipus* for a moment, since we must clarify further how it can be said that there is no meaning in suffering.

To say that it has no meaning is not to say that suffering has or can have no *purpose*. Nor is it to say that suffering has or can have no *results*. Suffering, after all, can be a weapon, it can be a tool, and, like any weapon or tool, it can be used for good or for ill. In itself, of itself, and by itself, however—suffering *qua* suffering—it has no meaning but simply *is*, something like, say, a bullet. A bullet, after all, may or may not be fired, may or may not result in good or ill, but in itself it can't be said to have any meaning: It, too, simply *is*.

We've seen already that the Oedipus story would remain logically intact even without the gouging of Oedipus's eyes but with only, say, self-imposed poverty and exile. But the greater and more horrifying physical suffering is a tool by which Oedipus, through his own choice, demonstrates not just his acceptance of *guilt* as the polluter of Thebes but, more important, his acceptance of *responsibility* for what he has done. He uses the pain as a means of acknowledging, accepting, and asserting his own free agency, his refusal to allow the blame for his "fate" to be shunted off onto the "gods" or onto anything else outside of himself. And, finally, he uses the agony and pain as an assertion of the existence of justice, as a part of the sentence he imposes upon himself.

Oedipus is tragic because of his being caught in the paradox, as we've seen, that he can fulfill himself *only* through his own ruin.[27] But he is *heroic* for these other reasons: because of his acceptance of demonstrated guilt, because of his acceptance of *responsibility* for that guilt, because of the assertion of his own free agency, because of the assertion of his belief in justice and the appropriateness of justice, and because of the extraordinarily high *value* he places on the self and on what the self both does and *is*, a value—*and* a danger—whose enormity he demonstrates by means of the enormity of the punishment he visits on himself.

Without these extraordinary qualities of character, the great drama would not be much more than a compelling riddle and a teasing paradox, and today it would be studied and read—and treasured—to about the extent, say, that the paradoxes of Zeno are read and treasured. As it is, however, the play holds a place of towering significance in the world's literature, and I myself foresee no probable diminishment in its greatness, which is to say in the greatness of its riddled yet probing and altogether uncompromising commentary on the subject of what it is and what it means, for better and for worse, to be a human being functioning at the fullest extent of the capacities and powers that the individual human self is capable of commanding.

No, the danger and probability of diminishment in the stature and significance of Sophocles' great play lies not in it but in us, who less and less seem to know how to read it, to feel impelled to read it, or to be inclined toward an interest in the truths, dignities, grandeurs, and rigors of its meaning.

Again, I blame the Age of Simplification: It has diminished and perhaps destroyed not only our *understanding* of literature at the level of *Oedipus*'s complexity, depth, and brilliance, but also our *ability* to understand it and therefore, greatest loss of all, the very remnants of our interest *in* it. At the age of sixty-four, and after spending roughly forty-five years of that time in and around academia, I today know *two* people—personally, I mean—who think of *Oedipus* as a living thing, who look upon it clearly and wholly and with an unfading interest, who find in it an artwork of fascinating applicability to all of human life as it is lived daily—rather than, as in the prevailing view, finding in it at best a piece of dusty antiquity, something of little or no "relevance" (remember that word?) to our world or lives today, at worst another "classist" stumbling block that the "elitist" culture long made use of for purposes of maintaining, as long as it could, "exclusiveness."

Elitist culture equals power. Power bad. Therefore elitist culture bad.

Or so it's impossible not to think if one listens to one's colleagues, follows academia at all closely, reads the daily papers, and keeps up with the news. One of the simplest things in the world, god knows, and of late one of the most execrably overused, is to put out the accusatory cry of "elitism" and argue for its presumed and presumably salutary opposite, "inclusion." Like other recent and related buzz-notions—diversity, multiculturalism, and so on—the idea of "elitism" is in reality a false, hollow, empty notion incapable of gaining, having, or holding power of any significant kind (personal, social, intellectual, political) because it is, in a nutshell, a falsehood. It's a falsehood, I hasten to mention, that arose, once again, at least in good part from a desire for *good*. But a falsehood it is, even so, because while it *claims* to be based on powerful precedent and self-evident reasoning, in actuality it's based on no precedent at all but rather on a strong appeal to self-satisfaction, laziness, me-ism, and passivity, and on no reasoning beyond the elementary notion that everyone has the right *not* to have their feelings hurt, not to be made to *feel bad*. In the case of "elitism," the idea is that someone *will* feel bad if their racial, ethnic, gender group, and so on, is excluded and that that person will feel *good* if their group is included, somewhat like being asked or not asked to a party. So, for example, if the new professors put together an anthology of short stories, they'll be sure to tokenize it as thoroughly and widely as possible, sprinkling it with stories written by authors from as many of the pertinent groups—or groups *thought* to be pertinent—as possible, so that the resulting "party" will be as "multicultural" and "diverse" as it can be, all in order that any reader who belongs to one of the groups won't feel excluded and sad but included and happy.

It is, of course, a non-literary and non-aesthetic idea, and to my mind also a non-adult and a pernicious one, one quintessentially of and from the Age of Simplification. The diversity and inclusiveness bandwagon, however, positively groans with riders, and it's little wonder that publishers have applied to general publishing the same sprinkling-of-pieties approach used by the new professors in compiling their anthologies and their course reading lists.

That choosing works in this way erodes and degrades the literary merit and interest of the results has already been argued—as has the idea that the literary merit and interest of writing in *general* is and has been driven down not only by the forces and characteristics of the Age of Simplification itself but also by the tokenism method of selection. That the aim of "inclusion" is *pride* reveals the poverty of thinking behind the project: What it aims to produce, "pride," is itself appropriate to the Age of Simplification, after all, in that it is actually a *feeling* that parades as an *idea*. The project, further, places attention on the *self* and withdraws it from the thing *achieved*; makes the deeply questionable assumption that happiness can be achieved thorough "inclusion" (isn't the more important question, inclusion in *what?*); and is built on the assumption that "inclusion" is properly due those who *have suffered* and therefore *are more meaningful* than those who haven't—thus measuring people, again, by what has been done *to* them rather than by what they have *done*.

If you add all these up, just how many fallacies *are* there in this single example of putatively liberal-intellectual thought or behavior? And this is *without* including the obvious paternalistic element that's inescapable in it, or the false "teaching" of what literature *is*, something we covered in the chapter before this one. In all, it's a threadbare policy with unconstructive results whose weaknesses will become only more pronounced as time goes on— though simultaneously this kind of thinking's penury and thinness will also become less *perceived* as time goes on, since those who go through their anti-educations one generation after another will each have less and less art-experience of the genuine kinds that alone can enable them to become art-judges of and on their own. Very possibly the worst thing of all about these responses to—and supposed corrections of—"elitism" is that they grow out of, encourage, and lead to yet more thinking in terms of *groups* and ever less to thinking in and of and through the individual self. Robert Olen

Butler, in his contribution to the State Department anthology discussed in chapter 1, says something in passing that's relevant here. He writes:

> This nation, built on the preservation of the rights of minorities, has sometimes been slow to apply those rights fully.

But of course he's wrong, and he reveals the underlying presence in his own mind of the "anti-elitism" that's possibly the most damaging of all the handicaps or incapabilities that are woven into the thinking of liberal intellectuals in the Age of Simplification. It's not that Butler misquotes, but that he misremembers—or misconceives, or never knew—the nation's founding documents. The nation was *not* "built on the preservation of the rights of minorities," despite what Butler or others might say or think. It was founded on "self-evident" truths having to do with the rights of man, it's true, but the bedrock of the founders' thinking, the very *starting* point from which they understood that those rights of man could and must be conceived and subsequently defended, was reverence not for any group whatsoever but for *the individual*. If group rights have come to be protected, as indeed they have,[28] that protection hasn't come about through a mode of thinking of any kind that was possessed by the founders themselves. In the founders' view, the protection would *already* have been there, and, insofar as it would have been extended to groups, it would have been extended not *because* there were groups, but because the groups were made up of individuals, and the inalienable rights of each of *those* were what, in their view, must be reverenced, maintained, and protected. The political and cultural damage caused by misunderstanding or misinterpreting this concept, as with Butler, this *mis-seeing*, is simply enormous, and incalculable, when you consider that it's a mis-seeing that has spread throughout and been incorporated into almost all liberal-intellectual thought, both inside the academy and out. The result is that the liberal intellectual movement, no longer rightly named, has done as much as any other force—except for its coworker and abettor, the mass media—to help bring about the erosion, enervation, and ruin of the true, valid, authentic individual self *and the consciousness of and reverence toward that self* that, taken together, constitute the one essential building unit of the nation, *and the only unit that can generate either meaning, on the one hand, or power for purposes of the common good, on the other.*

In the senses that we're dealing with here, the *group* is in fact the enemy of the individual, the enemy of the nation, the enemy of us all. The group could be defined as a self without eyes, a blinded self. And yet, everywhere around us—as we saw so clearly in the first chapter of this book—the group in one sense or another is unvaryingly given primacy, embraced, celebrated, and followed, while the self, by *all* its enemies, both those desiring good and those desiring ill, remains unseen and is left to die. If and when it does in fact die, so will our nation, our culture, and ourselves.

◆ ◆ ◆

There's a great deal to say by way of clarification of what the self, in the way I'm talking about it, both is and isn't. First, although of course it must have will *in* it and couldn't survive without it, this self is nevertheless not so much made *up* of that will or concerned *with* it as it is, instead, more largely made up of consciousness and concerned with that. This is a very important clarification, for the moment someone like me begins talking about the self, declaring that its autonomy *must not* be compromised, what pops into most people's minds is an Ayn Rand kind of self, with its weathered face, clenched jaw, narrowed eye, and dreams of industrial wealth and mastery. Indeed, Rand's concept *is* a kind of self, but it's one made up more greatly of will and less greatly of consciousness— (the latter being something I'll get back to in a minute). But the essential, life-enhancing, invaluable, and inviolable self that I'm talking about is not by any means, neither by nature nor by leaning, a conservative thing, but a liberal one. Consider for a moment the question of the self in relation to the present administration, an administration generally thought of as being politically to the radical right. I suppose it must be called so, though I myself would prefer it be named simply an administration of lies, thievery, hypocrisy, and thuggery, since its actual behavior, thus denoted, seems more important—and dangerous—than any supposed placement on an imaginary political spectrum. But an administration can behave as this one has, and as it continues to do, only if those in its leadership positions (whether this includes Bush or not is of course debatable) are selves in only the most limited sense, consisting hardly of consciousness at all but almost wholly of will. There could be said not even to *be* a self in someone blind to almost anything *but* will: Such a person, in short, is a zealot, blind to all except the willed thing, which in this case is the attaining of profit through and for the American corporate-state.

As will be more clear in a moment, not the self made up of will but only the self made up more greatly of consciousness can be useful in any way *beyond the merely mechanical* to the world around it, or to the nation. The self blinded to all except *one* thing—blinded, that is, to any relationship other than the relationship between its own desire and the satisfaction of that desire—that blinded self can't conceivably be anything other than mechanical in its relationship with the nation. In the case of our present administration, the relationship between leaders and nation is so one-dimensional, so attenuated, and so narrow that some might argue there to be no relationship at all. Take Bush or Cheney, for example. It might be said that neither of these men, given the nature of the self in each, has a relationship with the nation sufficiently entire or complex to allow them to be of, by, or for it, or, through corollary, to be of, by, or for the people. Their consciousness of the nation is the consciousness of it as something to be bled dry, in the interest of their *own* group, as quickly as possible.

If that's conservatism, I myself have long been under a misconception. It sounds more like a junta to me. And that we've gotten such an administration, it must be said, is all our own fault, and especially the fault of the liberal intellectuals, whose job it should have been all along to train, nurture, and protect the authentic self that alone could protect, guide, and nurture the republic. But they too lost sight of that self—inside themselves and out—and now so much time has gone by that in all likelihood it has died.

❋ ❋ ❋

That self, the authentic or true self,[29] because of its consisting predominantly, or even entirely, of *consciousness,* is the self that is capable of becoming not only the most complex but also the most humane of selves, although for this to happen it must be nurtured both through experience and through education. First, however, it *must* consist more greatly of consciousness than of will, or, at the *very* least, of equal parts of the two. The self that consists solely or even predominantly of will is ineducable, as can be seen in the Bush administration and in enormous segments of the American population. And a self that consists solely of consciousness becomes incapable of action or direction—a common, although in my view very greatly mistaken, way of looking, for example, at the ever-postponing Prince Hamlet.

Like Oedipus himself, Hamlet, in fact, offers one of the world's best examples of the kind of self we're now talking about—and are in danger of losing entirely. It's possible that Hamlet possesses the fullest and most fully realized *consciousness* of any character in literature, thus possessing also the most complete *self.*[30] The kind of self we're talking about, after all, *is* largely consciousness, and the more complete this consciousness, the greater, more complex, and more humane will be the self.[31]

Consciousness *is* perception, and *if* the range and quality of things to be perceived, things for the self to become conscious or aware of, aren't bounded or circumscribed by any external authority, and *if* the self gets plenty of practice, through experience, and keeps on with such practice, then the limits of this consciousness will very possibly never be reached. This aspect of the authentic self was well understood in the Renaissance, as can be seen, for example, in the lines that Christopher Marlowe's Faustus speaks on the occasion of his deciding to become a professional black magician—that is, to become a professional user of his mind and imagination, a professional *thinker:*

> His dominion that exceeds in this
> Stretcheth as far as doth the mind of man.[32]

The same idea of the limitlessness of thought or consciousness is suggested in Hamlet's words to the newly arrived Rosencrantz and Guildenstern, even though, partly to keep his mistrusted old classmates off guard, he ends his speech anticlimactically:

> O God, I could be bounded in a nutshell and count myself a king of infinite space, were it not that I have bad dreams.[33]

Hamlet knows perfectly well that every person is trapped inside the self, but that the self's consciousness nevertheless can extend to "infinite space." Earlier I said that the self is an eye we look through into existence, and that's so, but now it's time to drop the metaphor of eyesight, sight being only one single sense, and open up the idea by turning to the metaphor of the true or irreducible self as *thought itself.* That is, the authentic or full self isn't simply an *eye* that we see out through into existence but, instead, an entire *mind* that we think-perceive with, or perceive-think through, in this way gaining consciousness of our own and the world's existence. We're all trapped inside the confines of the self in exactly the way Hamlet is confined inside the nutshell—that is, inside his own head, or skull, or mind. But at the same time the self, *if* it's nurtured and prodded and educated and fed well, will gain awareness— thought-consciousness—not only of its own imprisonment but also of its opposite or alternative: The real self, that is, will gain consciousness of both the inside and the outside, the self and the other, the prison, on the one hand, and the world, on the other. And, even more important, it will never do either of the following two things: It will never make the calamitous error of assuming the inside and the outside, the self and the other, to be the *same*; and it will never make the equally calamitous error of assuming either of them—the inside or the outside, the prison or infinity, the self or the world—to be *any more real, valuable, or meaningful than the other*.

This self, being constituted of perception or thought, if encouraged to do it and left free to do it, can gain consciousness of *all* parts or aspects of existence available to it, so that, for example, not only will it become conscious of the inner world and the outer world, of self and other, but it will *also* become conscious of another thing, namely, the *relationship between the two,* since that relationship itself, which does exist, is therefore also a part of existence.[34] Once we understand that the irreducible self becomes conscious in this way of *three* aspects of existence, we can understand why it is that the self is and must be the foundational unit—though "organism" may be a better word—that "the nation" must be, can be, and *is* built on and of rather than the *group*. No group can *think.* No group can eat, sleep, write, compose, or paint. No group can *perceive.* Certainly, thus, no group can be conscious of the *relationship* between itself and other. It doesn't matter in the least whether the interests that a group—any group—is formed to advance, promote, serve, or quell are *good* ones or *bad* ones. At exactly the instant when *anyone* goes blind to the irreducible self and "sees" instead, or sees in its place, through the *group*, a small death occurs. At that moment— as we saw again and again in the first chapter—clear, honest, true, coherent, organic, energy-driven thinking is paralyzed and dies.

Although there are variants of it, this paralysis, preliminary to death, is what has taken hold with the new professors, progeny of the Age of Simplification, and it is what has taken hold also—the same thing but on a larger scale—of liberal thought in America.

It's not difficult to understand the necessity and practical utility of groups, classes, political parties, associations, and so on, whether they're formed for good or for ill, for purposes one agrees or disagrees with. But groups in this sense aren't the subject here. The subject here is a way of *seeing*, a way of *thinking* or *perceiving*. The irreducible self will always, insofar as it's possible, perceive or think in a direction that moves from the concrete *to* the abstract, in the manner of the empiricist, moving from particular evidence to general conclusion. But the Age of Simplification has worked long and relentlessly to bring about a change in that pattern. It has worked assiduously to bring into being within people a certain quality of passivity, a certain quality of laziness, that leads them to be content with an easier and less demanding standard by which to determine what may or may not, will or won't, be taken for *real*. To ease the standard of the real in this way is not in effect but in actuality to blind people, to make them unable (or unwilling) to "see" at the more demanding—the empirical, perhaps, or the material—level of determination of the real, thus "bumping them up" to accept a level of greater generality as what they'll now "see" as the logical *starting* point for consciousness, perception, or thought. We saw examples of this in the first chapter, in the repeated inability of the writers there to see or think clearly or with an accuracy based on true and individual observation. We can understand now that the reason for their failure was that they routinely accepted as a *starting* point for thinking a level of consciousness that was in fact already a preformed generality, an "idea" not observed but made of buzzword or code. Beneath whatever generality those writers took as true and *started* with lay at least one entire level, if not more, of the *true real* that might or might not (more likely not) have led them, had they begun by observing empirically, to the generality they did in fact choose to begin with though never having seen it. The results of leaving out the empirical first step were, as we saw, disastrous. Certainly without knowing it, what those authors had in fact given up was their own existence in, of, or as irreducible, authentic selves. They had agreed to be blinded, or at the very least they had let themselves *become* blinded, to the true self's freedom, presumably its inalienable freedom, to determine the real and the true in and of and by and through itself and itself alone, beginning at the most basic observable level possible.

In other words, by abdicating—or by abandoning, losing, or permitting to be stolen from them—the authentic, irreducible self, they went blind. They couldn't see anymore. They became useless and powerless. Their words were meaningless and hollow. There was no purpose left for them except to consume.

eight

Now, as I've said, we can see not only why this self alone, only this authentic and irreducible self, is and must be the brick that the entire nation is built on and built of, but also why only this self can nurture and sustain and support the nation—keep it healthy, you might say. The reasons, really, are two. For one thing, this self is the only thing in the universe that *can think,* and, as we've suggested, it may even *be* thought itself. On the other hand, to say it again, a group doesn't think, nor does a *believer,* whether a conventional religious believer or any other kind of zealot, like George W. Bush and most of his advisers, who, like conventional religious believers, are consumed by their desire for a certain thing to the point that they become blind to other things and cease being empirical, losing even any interest *in* empiricism except insofar as it might support their own preexisting opportunism.

To refine the idea of the irreducible self being the only thing that can think: More accurately, it's the only thing in the universe that can think wholly, the only thing in the universe that will insist that half-truths can't be whole steps in thought, that will insist that half-truths (because incomplete) can't even be accepted *as* thought, and that will remind us that half-truths will always come into existence—as with our writers in chapter 1 or the new professors in chapter 2—when a level of generality is taken, mistakenly or deliberately, as constituting a first-level, empirically based starting point for thought.

That the true self always seeks *whole* consciousness in thinking and being, then, brings us to the second reason why it alone can aid and nourish or preserve the democratic republic or nation: In being aware of both the self and the other, of both the inner existence and the existence outside, this irreducible consciousness-self will accept both internal and external, microcosm and macrocosm, as *equal* in value and essential to life. The zealot will necessarily do something dramatically unlike this, giving to one *part* of existence a value hugely in excess of another, as will all those who are blinded—again, like our authors in chapter 1. The real self, on the other hand, since it understands that both parts—inward and outward, internal and external—are essential to the whole and can't be valued one over the other, will serve as a kind of watchdog or monitor, always noticing any imbalance in the well-being or health of the one as opposed to the other and being inclined to bring the weakened part back to the wholeness of the stronger.

Thinking of the nation or state as an organism in this way goes back at least to Plato's *Republic*, where Socrates suggests that, like a person, the state has a mind, a heart, and genitals, the mind being represented by the rulers, the heart by the warriors, guardians, and police, and the genitals by the workers, laborers, producers, and generators of substance. The *Republic*'s strongly antidemocratic and non-egalitarian flavor is understandably distasteful to moderns like us, since Plato so clearly arranges his three classes in a hierarchy of *value*, the few and invaluable rulers at the top and the myriad and more dispensable workers at the bottom. This common objection to the great dialogue, however, should stand for us now as a cautionary note, since what the *Republic* still *does* have, egalitarian or not, is a concept of the nation as organic, not mechanistic,[35] and thereby dependent for its well-being both on thinking *and* on feeling, on the inward *and* the outward. In the Age of

Simplification, our own nation is in ever more serious danger—as the individual grows increasingly incapable of existing as a *whole* that consists of thought and feeling—of becoming purely mechanistic. When the organism does become mechanistic—that is, when its cells atrophy—it will die.

Some of the greatest and most memorable suggestions, expressions, or artistic manifestations of the concept and nature of the organic state come, again, from the literature of the Renaissance, or as some prefer to call it, the Early Modern. *Hamlet* alone offers a well-known and stunning richness of imagery and idea having to do with the microcosm of the bodily king, on the one hand, and the macrocosm of the kingdom (things that we, in language hearkening back to the same idea, still call the head of state and the body politic), on the other, the microcosm of the self or of the human mind, on the one hand, and the macrocosm of the external world and, as we've seen, of "infinite space," on the other. When Claudius pours poison into King Hamlet's ear, he is poisoning not only the king but the kingdom itself, causing the unseen agent of corruption to begin working from within both the body of the king and the body of the state—and making it appropriate for Marcellus, having seen the ghost, to remark famously, "Something is rotten in the state of Denmark," and for Hamlet himself, conversing later with the Norwegian captain, to say, "This is the imposthume of much wealth and peace, / That inward breaks and gives no cause without / Why the man dies." Throughout the play, similar suggestions occur: Small spheres like the nutshell or Yorick's skull (or Hamlet's) parallel large spheres like the cosmos itself, while small decayed places, like the garden, parallel the entire kingdom ("Fie on't! ah fie! 'tis an unweeded garden, / That grows to seed; things rank and gross in nature / possess it merely").[36]

For Hamlet—and, I would argue, for Shakespeare as well—in a world preceding empiricism, the small organism and the great *were* organically one, not merely symbols or representations of one another. For us, in our post-Enlightenment and post-Newtonian world, a *believed* oneness of such a kind as that can no longer exist, since it has no empirical basis—a good part of the reason, indeed, why monarchy is a thing of the past, since it depended upon a belief—the superiority of nobles—that is unsupportable empirically.

It's simply not possible, therefore, that any modern republic can ever be an organic whole on the Platonic or Elizabethan model, where an individual self can *be* the whole and the whole can *be* the individual self. In the case of our own model, then, the question can't be whether the nation is organic or inorganic, but the equivalent question must be this: whether the nation has *intelligence,* on the one hand, or is purely *mechanical,* on the other.

The closest equivalent today of the ancient or the Elizabethan *organic* state, then, is the democratic egalitarian state or republic whose elements influence, affect, and relate to one another with the greatest possible intelligence for the good of the whole. The fundamental unit, as we've seen, must and can be only the irreducible individual self, and that self, as we've also seen, must always be as holistic in its consciousness as possible, must be encouraged in this holism, and must be given practice in it. When these requirements are met and in place, a nation will be intelligent: Its basis will be in the balanced and holistic thought of irreducible individuals, and the thinking of those individuals, thinking that is responsive and whole, will have the effect of *caring for* the state, in this sense making the state a part *of* the individuals and the individuals a part *of* the state as their thought leads them continuously to shape the state into what it should best be for bringing about the good of the whole.[37] Now, on the other hand, if the irreducible self is lost, compromised, or weakened, or if it is blinded even partially to the nature of existence and is therefore no longer capable of *whole* thought—that is, if the autonomous self is no longer individual and real, no longer irreducible—then the self is also no longer *generative* and can no longer *care for* the state, which will cease then being intelligent and will become mechanical instead. Instead of the generative and shaping power rising up from the bottom *into* the concept of the state, the flow of things will be reversed. Instead of the people caring for the state, the state will care for the people. The only two things certain about the state in this latter model are, first, that it will be incomplete, not whole, not generative, and not responsive; and second, that instead of receiving its power from the people, it will now exercise its power *upon* the people, exploiting them for its own ends, whatever and however reductive, destructive, or tyrannical those may be.

This second model has come into existence and has grown well established in America, with all of its potential for loss, diminishment, and ruin, and the question is so far unanswered as to whether we can conceivably ever again return to anything more closely resembling the first model.

❖ ❖ ❖

Just like muscular or aerobic fitness, the authentic self is quickly lost if it isn't exercised and put to use regularly—and with the loss of its fitness, its well-being, or its full-sightedness, there will also be lost its invaluable capacity for thought that is accurate, basic, and whole. Throughout this book, I've argued that in a long history beginning around 1947, the mass media, functioning essentially as an arm of the corporate-state, have had the effect—to what degree intentional and to what degree not makes no difference—of dwindling, shrinking, weakening, simplifying, narrowing, blinding, and making passive the irreducible and authentic self in order to advance the interests not of the people or of the nation, but solely of the corporate-state, which has, like a tumor except that it's more mechanical than organic, continued growing and growing until now it has pushed out, displaced, or suffocated what I call the intelligent—real, living, responsive—state virtually to the point where it no longer exists. The most cataclysmic thing, at least to my own way of looking at the entire dismal picture, isn't that the corporate-state and mass media have *done* this. After all, they've been at it since 1947, always right out in the open. Books upon books have been written about it, and all of us with eyes *saw* it being done. But the worst thing, at least for me, is that I never truly believed it would be done so *well* or so *ruthlessly* or, above all, so *completely*. What I really never believed—naïf that I was and doubtless still am—was that so sweeping an entirety of the *intellectual* classes would prove to be just as vulnerable as any other and would end up just like the rest—narrowed, conditioned, blinded, and simplified in such a way as to have been co-opted, without even *knowing* it, defanged, de-horned, converted wholly unawares into slave-servants of the increasingly mechanical and unloving corporate-state itself.

Some will say that I'm wrong, that I'm being simplistic and alarmist. I wish those people well, and I extend to them all my blessings—may they, please god, find evidence, indications, and examples multitudinous showing that I'm wrong. I said earlier, though, that what I call the new professors, at least in the literary part of the humanities, aren't so much educating their students as doing the equivalent of poking out their eyes, making them passive and mechanical instead of encouraging and strengthening the capacity and talent they have for whole and autonomous intelligence—intelligence of the kind that's needed if there's to be, accordingly, an intelligent state. I would readily, if not happily, change my view if people could show me that I'm wrong. But the kind of evidence that keeps coming to me, instead, looks like this:

Making Talk Work Across Cultures:
Multicultural Awareness Week
In order to embrace the notion of diversity and celebrate our differences, the conscious expressions of racism within our society must first be identified and then intellectually addressed. Dealing with stereotypes, biases and different personal values while constructing a climate that fosters intergroup interaction and understanding, requires sensitivity and empathy. To increase the sense of understanding, educators must initiate and lead

discussions on multi-culturalism in an effort to reshape the minds of young people. Not doing so will continue the pervasiveness of disrespect for individuals who are different.

In an effort to answer this question and to generate respect for diversity among students, faculty, administrators and staff on our campus, the Division of Student Development at ——— is sponsoring a series of activities which will address these issues.

Try as I might, I can't help but find everything wrong here and nothing right. Here we have *groups*, not individuals. Here we have "thought" beginning not at the level of a real thing concretely observed, but at the level of a generalization that's been *received*. Here we have nothing seen by an irreducible individual—or an individual at all—but buzz-notions one after the other, these, to a one, *utterly* empty, being nothing but jargon used to name, again, the received generalities ("diversity," "racism," "stereotypes," "biases," "personal values," "interaction," "multi-culturalism"). Here, worse, we have not the asking of questions that might actually lead to recognition, but, instead, the giving of *commandments*—"embrace," "celebrate," "must . . . be identified and . . . addressed," "must initiate and lead." And from where do these commandments come? Is there *no* room for questioning them? On what authority are they handed down? On *whose* authority? On what basis of prior observation, if any, and, if there is any, observation of *what*? Of "racism"? In whom? When? Where? Or what about a person who is *not* racist? Must that person, too, come to *embrace* and *celebrate* and, since he or she is a part of "our society," have certain things be *identified* in him or her, and *addressed*?

Everyone can see the extraordinary degree of simplification here, the total absence of any *thinking* whatsoever, the utterly willing acceptance of wholly unexamined and hand-me-down generalizations, the *mechanistic* quality both of the project itself and of its expression here.

But what most people might not see immediately is that the whole undertaking, along with the expression of it, is nothing less than intellectual thuggery, nothing less than a *mugging.*

Look back at the memo again. Look closely. What you'll find is something less akin to education than it is to a lobotomizing.

❖ ❖ ❖

By now, I trust, the reader has looked back, reread the passage, and, among other things, found the revealing—incriminating—metaphor. It's impossible to overlook the imperative that precedes it—"must initiate and lead" (from where? says who?)—making this language of tyranny and Big Brotherism all the more unpleasant and sinister: "in an effort to reshape the minds of young people."

And there we are: "an effort to reshape the minds of young people." Not education, but indoctrination; not intelligence, but mechanics; not a leading of the self into or toward a place or condition where it can see for itself, but an inserting of the hands directly into the clay of the brain and molding, molding, molding until the damn thing *is the shape it's supposed to be.*

And *this* atrocity, believe it or not, *this* benighted ruination of all that undergraduate education ought to be, *this* example of simplification and almost perfect failure and of—I'll say it, tyranny—comes about, in large part, *from the desire to do good.*

How intolerably damaging is this simplified desire toward goodness. What more than this, after all, could the corporate-state possibly ask, than that the colleges and universities of America do exactly what this memo suggests is being done: all that *can* be done—whether people know they're doing it or not makes no difference—to thwart, repress, starve, wither up, deaden, limit, narrow, and atrophy the real self, the irreducible self that alone can think in a way that's intelligent by merit of its being self-dependent and its being *whole.* What this self needs is *food and exercise,* not "reshaping." What this self needs—as I said all the way back in chapter 2—is *experience*, not data collection or exposure to "issues," as the memo, with absolute predictability, calls the matters at hand. What this self needs is education—from *e* and *ducere*, that is, a "leading out"—not *in*doctrination, which means little more than the stuffing of dogma *in*.

Granted, the memo comes not from a classroom but from an office, not from a faculty member, that is, but from an administrator—pardon me, from a *division*, which is to say from a *group*. Nevertheless, the approaches and assumptions are little different from those approaches and assumptions held dear by the new professors who, as we were saying in the last chapter, tell their students what to think (though "think" isn't the right word) and reduce literary works to the role of evidence-manuals in courses where students look at "issues" and then choose the "good" side over the "bad." The reader will remember that I suggested, some way back, that "elitism" is a red herring used in good part as a justification for reducing literature to a tool for group therapy, a less than auspicious approach for the exercise or development of the true self. At that time, I said, too, that the cry of "elitism" actually makes a strong appeal to self-satisfaction, laziness, and passivity—a subject it's time to return to now. One of the hardest of all things to do is *think*, as anyone who's ever tried it knows, or as anyone knows who's made a true effort to teach, say, a course in freshman composition. Writing is murderously hard, and thinking is equally so—but how easy it is to *pretend to be thinking*, and I don't mean pretend to *others* but pretend to *yourself*. And isn't this exactly what has happened in the Age of Simplification? It is *so easy* not to think— just as it's *so easy* to be "entertained"—that a patently incredible thing has come about. This is a development that couldn't possibly make the corporate-state happier, since what the corporate-state wants is total control—and exploitation—of everything and everyone, the purpose being to maximize profits. And the *last* thing the corporate-state wants is large numbers of true selves that actually have whole consciousness. The resulting development? The resulting development is that almost everyone—writers, professors, *certainly* deans—has simply stopped thinking, though they have no idea whatsoever that this has happened. They go on *thinking* that they're thinking; they go on *believing* that they're thinking.

And it is *so easy* this way.

How extraordinarily easy it is for the Division of Student Development to turn on the wind machine, blow out a flurry of familiar buzz-notions, and announce that *we must reshape the minds of young people in order to save them and save us all,* we must question nothing whatsoever, *and,* best of all, we must bask in the pleasure of the honor being bestowed upon us *because we are insistent to the death upon doing good.*

Oh, would that it were so. But it's not. In reality, this is all evil, all the sheerest laziness, all the easiest path, the simplest thing, the equivalent to the world of thought that "entertainment" is to the world of art. No irreducible self will find it necessary *here* to think in order to grasp, since there's nothing to grasp, though there may *seem* to be; no irreducible self *here* will have an unpredicated or unpreviewed or unforeseen or unpredictable *experience*—like the experience, let's just happen to say, of reading *Hamlet,* with guidance, yes, but *without* being told beforehand what the play means, what it *is,* what's *wrong* with it, what it's *about,* what you're *supposed* to think of it and about it, or what it's *like.* That kind of experience, in any area of the arts and in most areas of the humanities and in much of life, is what *should* happen in education, in the process of a "leading out." Only through the experience of things that require the mind to be *used,* or that require the mind to *use itself*—only through the experience of things not previously experienced, only through the experience of things whose meaning is *unknown ahead of time*—only in these kinds of experiences can the real self, the irreducible self that's imprisoned in the flesh and mind of its one solitary human host, be stirred, be encouraged to discover its own powers *and* its own solitude, be enabled to achieve by and for itself a consciousness as *whole* as possible, as fully *seeing* as it can be.

In the process of any education, I'm fully aware, there are certain things that simply have to be said, shown, demonstrated, told, memorized—*learned,* you might say. But all of that can be done, even done well, by a person who can still remain effectively uneducated if he or she still doesn't know *what* the irreducible self is, this prison that is also an eye into existence, a doorway to the very consciousness of *other,* therefore also to the very consciousness of *self,* and finally also to a consciousness—as whole a one as possible—of the relation between the two, the inner world and the outer, as well as the indispensability of both to the health of either.

Only the person who does understand the irreducible self in these three ways, and such a person alone, will be able not only to think but to have a desire to do so. Only such a person, therefore, will be able to see through the omnipresent lies, deceit, conditionings, shortcuts, and hypocrisies that constitute *and* perpetuate the Age of Simplification all around us at every moment of the day and night and that nevertheless are unseen and unsensed by most. Only such a person, one who still can see, could make it possible that something, somehow, might still be done to save us all.

And yet where such a person might come from, although I may once have known, I no longer have the least idea.

NOTES

Chapter 1: Watching America Go Blind

1. A number of relevant and interesting essays appear in *Dumbing Down: Essays on the Strip-mining of American Culture,* edited by Katharine Washburn and John Thornton (New York, 1996). Of special note is Cynthia Ozick's wonderful "The Question of Our Speech: The Return to Aural Culture." Anyone interested in American speech as a cultural barometer should look also at John McWhorter's *Doing Our Own Thing: The Degradation of Language and Music and Why We Should, Like, Care* (New York, 2003).

2. This argument goes all the way back, for example, to Marie Winn's *The Plug-in Drug* (New York, 1977).

3. Available at: www.nea.gov/pub/ReadingAtRisk.pdf.

4. That is, emotion that has some degree of complexity and thereby can and may even necessarily lead to thought. "Simplified" emotion (more on this later) can't have the same effect, nor can mere laughter when, that is, it's brought into being or exists as an end in itself.

5. With *very* rare exceptions, this requirement now also applies not just to general programming but to the news.

6. Anyone well read enough will recognize that what I'm saying here about *The Sopranos,* and about television drama in general, is equally applicable to all but an infinitesimal sliver of the trade fiction published in the country today.

7. The discussion of "rights" and what they mean will reappear in chapter 3.

8. The author takes no responsibility for changes to the content of http://usinfo.state.gov/products/pubs/writers/ subsequent to this book's publication.

9. "She currently teaches at Mills College, Oakland, California," according to the download.

10. A person might better say "subtlety or complexity," but I'll stick with only the latter. Subtlety, after all, of the kind I'm talking about, is by its nature complex, as well as being also the product and producer of complexity.

11. William Strunk Jr. and E. B. White, *The Elements of Style* (New York, 1979).

12. And paid for. Each writer received $2,499 from the U.S. government (*New York Times,* December 7, 2002).

13. See George Orwell's once widely read and now apparently widely ignored essay, "Politics and the English Language."

14. Wilfrid Owen, "Futility" (1918).

15. Browning Brooks, www.fsu.edu, September 2001.

16. For an idea of Robinson's more recent thinking, readers should turn to her often explosively brilliant *The Death of Adam: Essays on Modern Thought* (New York, 1998). Much of her own concern in that volume has to do with what I'm calling the Age of Simplification, as when she suggests that "there is no place left for the soul, or even the self" (p. 74), and that the age is one of "our ceasing to value inward experience" (p. 84).

17. Robinson's long-awaited second novel, *Gilead,* was published in November 2004, by Farrar, Straus, & Giroux.

Chapter 2: The Death of Literary Thinking in America

1. I say "seeming" opposites because they're more than just opposites: they're also essential for one another's existence—*greater-than-opposites*, you might say.

2. On April 30, 1956, Eliot spoke on "The Frontiers of Criticism" at the University of Minnesota. I was then fifteen and remember listening to him on the radio in the kitchen of my family's farmhouse. It seems a thousand years ago. Who could imagine such a thing today, a major *literary* address carried live on commercial radio?

3. *The Closing of the American Mind* (New York, 1987).

4. *BAD, or, The Dumbing of America* (New York, 1991).

5. According to whonamedit.com, an online biographical dictionary of medical eponyms: "Hans Zinsser obtained his doctorate from Columbia University in 1903. From 1903 to 1905 he was a bacteriologist at Roosevelt Hospital, 1905–1906 at his alma mater. [From] 1907 [to] 1910 he was assistant pathologist at St. Luke's Hospital, and from 1908 also instructor for bacteriology at the Columbia University. In 1910 he became associate professor at Stanford University, full professor there in 1911, 1913 at Columbia University, 1923 at Harvard University. [He] made major contributions to bacteriology and public health. In 1906 he developed a medium and a simple method to plate anaerobic organisms. He did extensive work on typhus and in 1934 developed a vaccine of killed rickettsias that would protect against typhus. Zinsser was assistant to the bacteriologist Philip Hanson Hiss (1868–1913), and was co-writer with him on a textbook of bacteriology" (http://www.whonamedit.com/doctor.cfm/495.html).

6. See, for example, *Perpetual War for Perpetual Peace: How We Got to Be So Hated* (New York, 2002).

7. Gore Vidal's description of the birth-moment of the "military-industrial complex" is instructive, as is his connecting of it with the mass media: "Fifty years ago, Harry Truman replaced the old republic with a national-security state whose sole purpose is to wage perpetual wars, hot, cold, and tepid. Exact date of replacement? February 27, 1947. Place: White House Cabinet Room. Cast: Truman, Undersecretary of State Dean Acheson, a handful of congressional leaders. Republican senator Arthur Vandenberg told Truman that he could have his militarized economy only *if* he first 'scared the hell out of the American people' that the Russians were coming. Truman obliged. The perpetual war began. Representative government of, by, and for the people is now a faded memory. Only corporate America enjoys representation by the Congresses and presidents that it pays for in an arrangement where no one is entirely accountable because those who have bought the government also own the media" (*Perpetual War for Perpetual Peace*, p. 160).

8. Probably the simplest, best, and also one of the foremost places to find examples of what I mean by this kind of "need" (in prose, that

is) is in the classic American short story. It's very clear, for instance, in Sherwood Anderson, say, in certain works of Willa Cather, and certainly in the earlier short fiction of Hemingway.

9. I should probably say "experiencing" it as a crafted object. But Whittemore was demonstrating not a final achievement but a process toward an end. However imperfect a means it may be, the student's *describing* a poem has as its aim making possible the *experiencing* of it.

10. For a fascinating analysis of how Newton and Descartes may have done more harm than good in perpetuating mechanism and dualism, see Stephen Toulmin's *Cosmopolis: The Hidden Agenda of Modernity* (New York, 1990).

11. *Iowa Writers' Workshop Newsletter,* Fall 2001.

12. I suppose I could have borrowed from Stephen Dedalus and said that the books should be chosen according to whether or not they had wholeness, harmony, and radiance. The occasion occurred, as I said, in 1991, so I couldn't have cited Harold Bloom, who wrote in 2004 that "I have only three criteria for what I go on reading and teaching: aesthetic splendor, intellectual power, wisdom" (*Where Shall Wisdom Be Found?* [New York], p. 1).

13. Not even if the double standard replaces a previous double standard. One may as well treat a cancer patient by infecting him or her with syphilis.

14. For an extraordinarily thorough discussion of them, see Robert D. Putnam's *Bowling Alone: The Collapse and Revival of American Community* (New York, 2000).

15. And on this side of the subject, the *thinning* of our social fabric, *Bowling Alone* is, again, encyclopedic.

16. For a book-length argument that the way Americans have been spoiled and made passive is through "flattery" by the media, see Thomas de Zengotita's often remarkable *Mediated: How the Media Shapes Your World and the Way You Live in It* (New York: Bloomsbury, 2004).

17. For an expression of this absolutist idea, as well as its total confusion with "liberty," see Andrew J. Bacevich, *The New American Militarism: How Americans Are Seduced by War* (New York: Oxford University

Press, 2005). Bacevich writes: "Critics might cavil that the resulting militarization of U.S. policy in the Persian Gulf amounted to a devil's bargain, trading blood for oil. [President] Carter saw things differently. The contract had a third element. On the surface the exchange might entail blood-for-oil, but beneath the surface the aim was to guarantee the ever-increasing affluence that underwrites the modern American conception of liberty. Without exception, every one of President Carter's successors has tacitly endorsed this formula. It is in this sense that World War IV and the new American militarism manifest the American will to be free" (pp. 182–183).

18. "The Storm over the University," *New York Review of Books*, December 6, 1990.

19. www.webdelsol.com/NorthAmReview/NAR/HTMLpages/ NARToday.htm.

Chapter 3: Consumerism, Victimology,
and the Disappearance of the Meaningful Self

1. "Hence, horrible shadow! / Unreal mockery, hence!" *Macbeth*, III, iv, 106–107.

2. There's an obvious parallel between this use of or appeal to absolutism in place of empiricism and my colleague's similar denial of complexity by saying, in our curriculum meeting of 1991, that "everything is political" (see chapter 2).

3. *Candide, Zadig, and Selected Stories*, translated by Donald M. Frame, with a new introduction by John Iverson (New York, 2001), p. 21.

4. "[U]n de ses frères, un être à deux pieds sans plumes, qui avait une âme."

5. Jacques' own word is "être," or "being." "Creature" is used by Donald M. Frame in his translation.

6. And with a belief in the corrupting influence of *all* authority—a position held by many in the oppositionist movements of the 1960s.

7. The same goes for his incorrigible and loathsome son, the Jesuit, who, because he remains a blind, non-empirical adherent to the institution of nobility by birth, is *the only one* to be ejected from the little garden of Eden ("this little society") at the close of *Candide*. The

little garden, of course, can emblemize postrevolutionary France-to-be or the United States-to-be. The nobleman-Jesuit is Satan, ironically expunged from the garden instead of Adam, Eve, and its other tenants.

8. "Certainly, this [why General Mahmoud, while visiting Washington, DC, sent Mohammed Atta $100,000] is one of those questions that will be asked during the coming impeachment trial of George W. Bush" (Gore Vidal, *Dreaming War* [New York, 2002], p. 56).

9. IV, iv, 35–41: "What is a man, / If his chief good and market of his time / Be but to sleep and feed? A beast, no more. / Sure, He that made us with such large discourse, / Looking before and after, gave us not / That capability and god-like reason / To fust in us unus'd."

10. See Vidal, *Dreaming War,* especially pp. 23–37.

11. Eve's musing, before eating the apple, is apropos (*Paradise Lost*, IX, 756–757): "For good unknown sure is not had, or, had / And yet unknown, is as not had at all.

12. Wendell Berry, *In the Presence of Fear: Three Essays for a Changed World* (Great Barrington, MA, 2001), pp. 25–33.

13. Or, currently, "the oil-and-gas Cheney-Bush junta" (Vidal, *Dreaming War,* p. 12).

14. As described, in part, in chapter 2. See also Vidal (*Dreaming War,* p. 58) on "a public education system that no longer teaches geography in primary schools, much less comparative history or even relevant American history."

15. My students seldom know that a half-truth remains a half-truth even if more than half of it is true, even as much, say, as 75 percent, or even 99 percent. The point is that all four assertions require qualification in order to become valid, or at the very least each requires more exact definition of terms.

16. The pattern is that once a "consumer" is simplified, he or she *continues* to simplify things in his or her own thinking and views. Thus, a typical "liberal" academic today is both a simplifier and a simplified—as are, in fact, all consumers, and therefore virtually all of the population. This fact has an enormous bearing on the impossibility of discussing politics on any significant level in the United

States, as mentioned at the start of this chapter. On July 23, 2003, came news of the U.S. military having killed Qusay and Uday, the two elder sons of Saddam Hussein. But why? Through what authority? According to what legality? By what right? Under the imprimatur of what legislative or interpretive body? Vile as the brothers were, they were nevertheless, it seems to me, murdered. It is impossible among simplifieds, however, even to broach, let alone discuss, such an idea. Furthermore, the killing "looked like" battle and didn't "look like" murder, just as a junta is not a junta if it doesn't "look like" one.

17. *CUNY Matters*, Summer 2003, p. 11. *CUNY Matters* is published by the Office of University Relations, The City University of New York, 535 East 80th St., New York, NY 10021.

18. Vide our discussion of "entertainment" in chapter 1.

19. What animal goes on four legs in the morning, two legs at noon, and three legs in the evening?

20. Though fundamentalism, as all know only too well, has experienced an enormous resurgence in—and as another product of—the Age of Simplification.

21. For another example, and a great one, see the William Butler Yeats poem "Lapis Lazuli."

22. *Sophocles: The Oedipus Cycle*, translated by Dudley Fitts and Robert Fitzgerald (San Diego: Harcourt Brace, 1949), p. 38.

23. *The Iliad of Homer*, translated by Richmond Lattimore (Chicago: University of Chicago Press, 1951), p. 307. "He then stabbed with the spear Ilioneus / the son of Phorbas the rich in sheepflocks, whom beyond all men / of the Trojans Hermes loved, and gave him possessions. / Ilioneus was the only child his mother had borne him. / This man Peneleos caught underneath the brow, at the bases / of the eye, and pushed the eyeball out, and the spear went clean through / the eye-socket and tendon of the neck, so that he went down / backward, reaching out both hands, but Peneleos drawing / his sharp sword hewed at the neck in the middle, and so dashed downward / the head, with helm upon it, while still on the point of the big spear / the eyeball stuck. He, lifting it high like the head of a poppy, / displayed it to the Trojans and spoke vaunting over it" (book 14, ll. 489–500).

24. "Tragedy, then, is an imitation of an action that is serious, complete, and of a certain magnitude; in language embellished with each kind of artistic ornament, the several kinds being found in separate parts of the play; in the form of action, not of narrative; through pity and fear effecting the proper purgation of these emotions." *The Great Critics: An Anthology of Literary Criticism,* compiled and edited by James Harry Smith and Edd Winfield Parks (New York: W. W. Norton, 1951), p. 34.

25. The dangerously already simplified minds of the 1970s liberal intellectuals could be seen in their early fondness for the simple and reductive. All who remember those years will remember the popularity of Mao's "thought" that "power comes out of the muzzle of a gun." A classic half-truth if ever there was one, on a par with the equally anti-analytic "all actions are political," the latter a "thought" that, as I've mentioned, was still popular even in the 1990s.

26. In great part by bringing into existence, or awakening and nurturing, the true relationship between every individual self and the whole.

27. "TEIRESIAS: This day will show your birth and will destroy you." *Greek Tragedies,* translated by David Grene, vol. I (Chicago: University of Chicago Press, 1960), p. 129.

28. "In 2003, however, giving unprecedented approval to racial preferences in university admissions in *Grutter v. Bollinger,* the unelected justices of the United States Supreme Court changed America into a society constitutionally committed to group rights, a.k.a. 'diversity'" (Carol Iannone, "What's Happened to Liberal Education?" *Academic Questions,* Winter 2003–2004, p. 60).

29. At one time it could have been called the "liberal self," with "liberal" carrying the same sense it does—or one hopes it does—in the phrase "liberal arts."

30. See Harold Bloom's short and wonderful *Hamlet: Poem Unlimited* (New York: Riverhead, 2003).

31. "Humane," of course, not in the sense of "kind," but in the sense of broadly, thoroughly, complexly, and deeply human, as in another jeopardized word, "humanities."

32. *Doctor Faustus,* I, i, 60–61.

33. *Hamlet*, II, ii, 260–262.

34. Clearly, self-realization of the kind we're talking about necessitates an ability to be conscious of and able to do more than one thing at a time—an ability substantially missing in the simplifieds of chapter 1. Readers may remember the elementary but charming example of Robert Creeley's saying there that "clear and very simple answers" are available in regard to certain questions about poetry, "but they will not be found here." In order to "get" the whole of what Creeley was saying (and not saying), I commented that "a reader must be not only willing but easily able to keep at least three things in mind simultaneously: one being the significance of what Creeley *is* saying, another being the significance of what he is *not* saying, while yet another is the significance of the irony created by the tension between the two." The same idea applies here in the relation between the self and the world it's inside.

35. And closer, at least in this sense, to the post-Enlightenment democratic republic than to the pre-Enlightenment monarchy.

36. *Hamlet*, I, iv, 90; IV, iv, 27–29; I, ii, 35–37.

37. Readers of Jane Jacobs's famous *The Death and Life of Great American Cities* (New York, 1961) will understand this idea easily: neighborhoods, for example, that do or don't nurture their residents *and* vice versa.